Für Wilma und Georg
mit Dank für alles
Rudolf und Artur
New York, d. 9. September 2013

TRIEGLAFF

Rudolf von Thadden

Trieglaff

Balancing Church and Politics in a Pomeranian World,
1807–1948

Translated by
Stephen Barlau

berghahn
NEW YORK · OXFORD
www.berghahnbooks.com

Published in 2013 by
Berghahn Books
www.berghahnbooks.com

English-language edition
©2013 Berghahn Books

German-language edition
©2010 Wallstein Verlag, Göttingen
Trieglaff: Eine pommersche Lebenswelt zwischen Kirche und Politik 1807–1948
By Rudolf von Thadden

Library of Congress Cataloging-in-Publication Data

Thadden, Rudolf von.
[Trieglaff. English]
Trieglaff : balancing church and politics in a Pomeranian world, 1807–1948 /
Rudolf von Thadden ; translated by Stephen Barlau.
pages cm
Includes bibliographical references and indexes.
ISBN 978-0-85745-927-5 (hardback : acid-free paper) —
ISBN 978-0-85745-928-2 (institutional ebook)
1. Trzygłów (Poland)—History—19th century. 2. Trzygłów (Poland)—
History—20th century. 3. Thadden, Rudolf von—Family. 4. Trzygłów
(Poland)—Biography. 5. Germans—Poland—Trzygłów—History. 6. Christianity
and politics—Poland—Trzygłów—History. 7. Trzygłów (Poland)—Church
history. I. Title.
DK4800.T87T4313 2013
943.8'16—dc23

2013005539

British Library Cataloguing in Publication Data

A catalogue record for this book is available from the British Library

Printed in the United States on acid-free paper

ISBN: 978-0-85745-927-5 hardback ISBN: 978-0-85745-928-2 institutional ebook

Contents

Contents

Illustrations

All figures are courtesy of the von Thadden family's private archives.
Thanks to Wallstein Verlag publishers for use of their files in production
of this edition.

Preface to the English Edition

The final impetus to writing this book was lent by a 100-year-old American from Wisconsin whose ancestors emigrated from Trieglaff 150 years ago. During my visit with her in a nursing home in West Bend, she presented me with a small chest containing letters, stretching over half a century, from her relatives in Pomerania. She handed me the box with the words, "You'll still be able to read the old German handwriting. Nobody here can anymore."

Already before that, Polish friends from today's Trzygłów had requested of me that I should write up something about the history of this Pomeranian place. After the war, they came to the area lacking acquaintance with the former German world and were for that reason interested in learning more about the people who had lived there before. It did not seem adequate just to pay attention to some memorial stones as testimony to a German past.

Lastly, my German relatives and friends put pressure on me following my retirement as emeritus professor of history at Göttingen to get at the partially rescued archives of the family and to evaluate the testimony they offered to the Trieglaff of former times. Given the terrific losses that also — and not least — private archives from the earlier eastern regions suffered at the end of World War II, it devolved upon me as historian to exploit the remnants still at hand.

This book deals with the history, over five generations, of the Pomeranian village of Trieglaff in what is now western Poland. It is about the people that lived and toiled in this village in good times and bad. Architecturally, the place was dominated by the mansion of the von Thadden family, which is at the center of the following analysis of Trieglaff's society, economy, politics, and culture. While the book is largely based on the family archive with its many documents, it also relies on a variety of other testimonies, including a set given to me by several families in Wisconsin, in the United States, whose forebears had emigrated from Trieglaff some 150 years ago. Their correspondence with those who stayed behind in Pomerania suggests an intriguing transatlantic link between Trieglaff and the Midwestern United States.

All this has enabled me to write a book that examines the lives of individuals, the socioeconomic and cultural structures, and the dynamic changes in the village throughout some 150 years of German and European history. The Thaddens lived in Trieglaff from the Napoleonic age to 1945. They were involved in Prussian politics during the Bismarckian period. Later in the twentieth century, several of its members joined the resistance against the Nazis and Hitler's church policies. Reinold von Thadden played a prominent role in the anti-Nazi Protestant "Confessing Church," and his sister Elisabeth was arrested by the Gestapo for her activities and executed in September 1944 at Plötzensee prison in the suburbs of Berlin.

The changes in the social and economic structures analyzed in this book primarily concern the gradual dissolution of the lingering feudalism that had been undermined in the wake of the French Revolution. But these changes also affected the Protestant churches of Prussia, shaking the traditional foundations of state and church and initiating a process of secularization that spread to the rural parts of the country.

Readers of this book will expect an explanation of these processes. Especially in the United States, it is not easy to understand why the so-called defeudalization created so many problems in German and European history. The peoples of the New World, having escaped life in feudal conditions under an ancien régime, did not have to grapple with the transformation of societies shaped by structures of domination, where social and economic stratification was defined by estates, a landed nobility, and an autocratic king.

Readers of this book will also be curious why discussions over the relationship between church and state played such an important role in Europe and in Prussia in particular. This relationship—a part of the Old World since the Middle Ages—had produced ties between the two institutions that time and again were threatened by an overly rigid alliance between "Throne and Altar." Thus it was hardly a matter of course that a place like Trieglaff and people like the von Thadden family would enter into conflict with the ruling "Landeskirche" and ultimately even break almost entirely away from it. This break would prove consequential for the Thaddens' later confrontations with the Nazi regime. Having already opposed an earlier, strongly state-dominated church, it was easier for them to join the resistance against Hitler's church policies in 1933 and to create Free Church structures under the Nazi dictatorship.

The book ends with two chapters on the period after World War II, during which Trieglaff was first subjugated by the Red Army and then incorporated into Poland. Events in those regions that had been allocated to Poland were frequently overlooked during the years of the Cold War between East and West. Many years passed before the two sides resumed contact, whereupon even most of the Germans expelled from the territories east of the Oder-Neisse Line began to work for peaceful reconciliation. Trieglaff was to play an important role in this respect, too.

On one especially memorable occasion, descendents of Trieglaff natives who had emigrated from Pomerania to Wisconsin participated in a reunion that transcended a once impregnable border. It is highly gratifying that the translator of this volume, Stephen Barlau, hails from these U.S. families. He deserves special thanks for taking on this translation. I am also grateful to Georg and Wilma Iggers, who were driven from their Central European homes by the Nazis; they have involved themselves with sensitivity and great sympathy in the publication of this study. I also owe a debt of gratitude to Barbara Fox, née von Thadden, who built her own life and work in England. Following the writing of this book with the eyes of a loyal kinswoman, she offered most helpful advice.

This Preface concludes with two further words of thanks due to Berghahn Books for agreeing to publish *Trieglaff* in English and to the Thyssen Foundation for supporting the translation. And finally, I acknowledge that I would not have had the strength to write this book if I had not always had my wife Wiebke at my side and our children prodding me to complete the project.

Rudolf von Thadden
Göttingen, Easter 2013

Translator's Remarks

"I could be in the cemetery at Trieglaff," Rudolf von Thadden observed as he surveyed the cemetery at Zion Lutheran Church at Wayside, Wisconsin, on a visit in September 2008. German naming has regional and local qualities, and the names on the gravestones spoke Pomeranian to him.

Trieglaff in the U.S. Evidence, etched in granite. Add the vibrancy of a Pomeranian heritage that is still celebrated and the Lutheranism that is so prominent in the area, and Trieglaff can be said to be still with us—probably truer to its native stock than is contemporary Polish Trzygłów. The heritage lives on, here as in other places, of course amalgamated into contemporary culture. Rudolf von Thadden's *Trieglaff* in English translation will be welcomed by not only those who count themselves within this community, but also all to whom such a history as this, of a given time and place, appeals. It is intended for them.

For scholars, the book's value lies in documentation of a place and a period in history, approached from the vantage point of the von Thadden family. The family archives are exploited extensively for original material. Yet given the breadth of the family's involvement in both political and religious affairs, there is no lack of integration into history on the large scale. Footnotes and bibliography range far beyond the archival material. The work knows its place as contribution to the writing of social history. Researchers will welcome this translation of an "inside" view—of resistance to feudalism's decline and banishment, of Bismarck's formative background, of one influential individual's unflagging opposition to Nazism, and of inter-nation territorial transfer, among many other topics. May it serve them well.

Indeed, I hope all of its readers, whatever their motivation for taking it up, will find this edition of von Thadden's work to their satisfaction.

Wilma Iggers played a critical role in the translation, bringing her European and German background to bear at the cost of many hours of editing. I owe a great deal to the profuse corrections and improvements she made to the work. Royal Natzke read and commented on the entire manuscript, furnishing important guidance that proved highly beneficial. Markus Ciupke and Hajo Gevers of Wallstein Verlag, publisher of the original German edition, provided unqualified support and assistance. For Berghahn Books, Jaime Taber carried out the essential service of putting my style and syntax in order, a monumental task. Thank you, Jaime. Others offered valuable criticism of a more general nature, especially at early stages of the undertaking—perhaps Jennifer Stewart should be mentioned. I am indebted to them. Faults and shortcomings are my own.

Sincere thanks go to Rudolf von Thadden for extending to me the opportunity to translate *Trieglaff* into English, and to Georg and Wilma Iggers and Royal Natzke for their instrumental roles. It was an experience, a privilege, and a pleasure. My wife Anita (Natzke) has, as always, stood by most helpfully.

Stephen Barlau
Merrill, Wisconsin, April 2013

Genealogical Diagram of the von Thadden Family

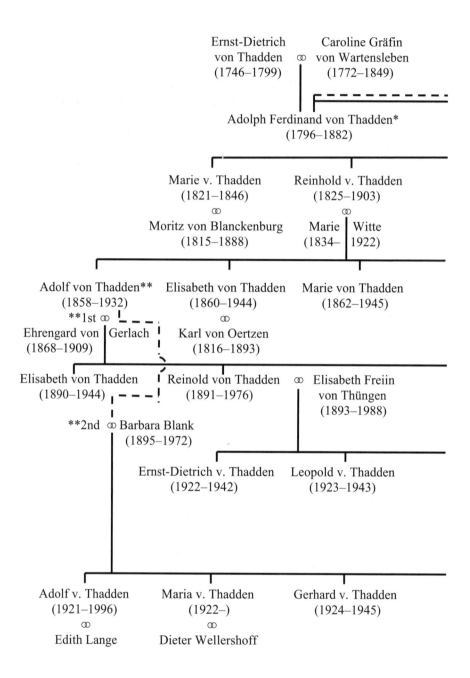

Ernst-Dietrich von Thadden (1746–1799) ⚭ Caroline Gräfin von Wartensleben (1772–1849)

Adolph Ferdinand von Thadden* (1796–1882)

Marie v. Thadden (1821–1846) ⚭ Moritz von Blanckenburg (1815–1888)

Reinhold v. Thadden (1825–1903) ⚭ Marie Witte (1834–1922)

Adolf von Thadden** (1858–1932) **1st ⚭ Ehrengard von Gerlach (1868–1909)

Elisabeth von Thadden (1860–1944) ⚭ Karl von Oertzen (1816–1893)

Marie von Thadden (1862–1945)

Elisabeth von Thadden (1890–1944)

Reinold von Thadden (1891–1976) ⚭ Elisabeth Freiin von Thüngen (1893–1988)

**2nd ⚭ Barbara Blank (1895–1972)

Ernst-Dietrich v. Thadden (1922–1942)

Leopold v. Thadden (1923–1943)

Adolf v. Thadden (1921–1996) ⚭ Edith Lange

Maria v. Thadden (1922–) ⚭ Dieter Wellershoff

Gerhard v. Thadden (1924–1945)

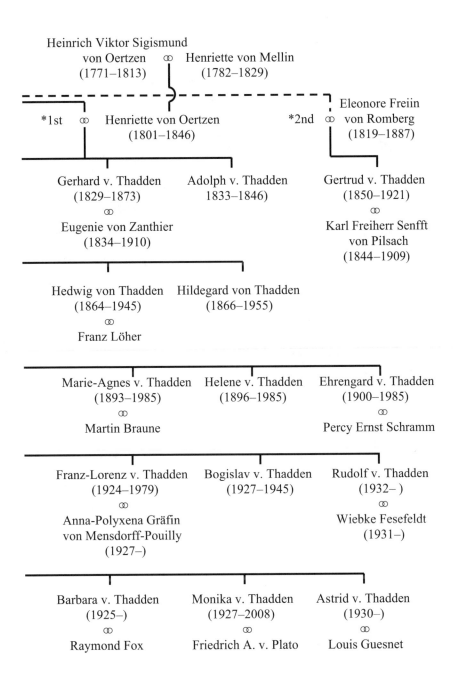

Heinrich Viktor Sigismund
von Oertzen ∞ Henriette von Mellin
(1771–1813) (1782–1829)

*1st ∞ Henriette von Oertzen (1801–1846)

*2nd ∞ Eleonore Freiin von Romberg (1819–1887)

Gerhard v. Thadden
(1829–1873)
∞
Eugenie von Zanthier
(1834–1910)

Adolph v. Thadden
1833–1846)

Gertrud v. Thadden
(1850–1921)
∞
Karl Freiherr Senfft
von Pilsach
(1844–1909)

Hedwig von Thadden
(1864–1945)
∞
Franz Löher

Hildegard von Thadden
(1866–1955)

Marie-Agnes v. Thadden
(1893–1985)
∞
Martin Braune

Helene v. Thadden
(1896–1985)

Ehrengard v. Thadden
(1900–1985)
∞
Percy Ernst Schramm

Franz-Lorenz v. Thadden
(1924–1979)
∞
Anna-Polyxena Gräfin
von Mensdorff-Pouilly
(1927–)

Bogislav v. Thadden
(1927–1945)

Rudolf v. Thadden
(1932–)
∞
Wiebke Fesefeldt
(1931–)

Barbara v. Thadden
(1925–)
∞
Raymond Fox

Monika v. Thadden
(1927–2008)
∞
Friedrich A. v. Plato

Astrid v. Thadden
(1930–)
∞
Louis Guesnet

Map of Pommern

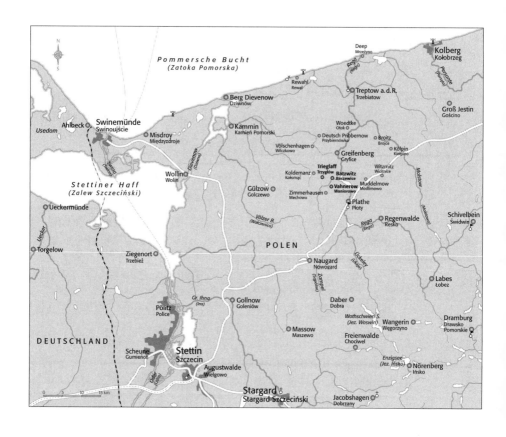

Map of Trieglaff

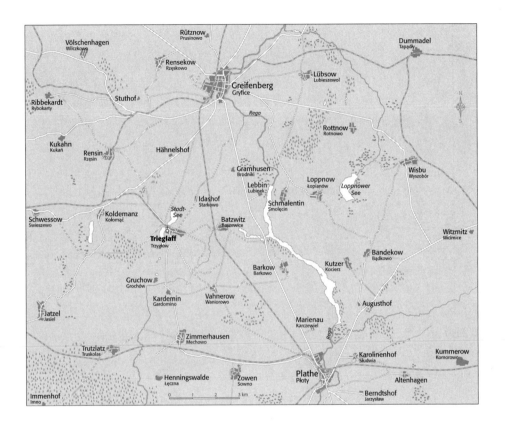

Introduction

The history of Trieglaff presented here is laid out generation by generation. At its center is the von Thadden family. This arrangement aims to
develop a historical continuity that will be unique to it without necessarily
coinciding with the continuities commonly exhibited in historical writing. Generations acquire life and vitality through their connections with
each other, and are characterized also by reciprocal influences upon and
from the political and social worlds around them. Hence they neither exist exclusively as independent successive stages, nor are they ever strictly
confined solely to their respective eras.[1]

A history structured generationally does assign a special measure of
significance to biographical context. This significance arises because issues of property and inheritance are in the balance, but it is owing also to
people's intellectual and political orientations, which undergo development over the course of a lifetime rather than simply reflecting the governing political circumstances.

In any case, it is certain that memory plays a meaningful part in a history laid out by generations. Because generations gain legitimacy through
respect for their interconnectedness and their cohesion, they cultivate
their own culture of memories, a culture that at times can gain autonomy.
Generations live with a historical memory that itself has the substance of a
reality. We are required to come to terms with this reality.[2]

But what meaning does that have for Trieglaff? A generational history
requires that the deepest components of the history are brought into the
light and examined. This initially pertains to the family history of the titled landholders, the von Thaddens, who took up residence in Trieglaff at
the time of the Napoleonic wars and there developed a unique tradition of
piety. Then there is the history of the place itself, bound to a unique world
and way of life. Its understanding makes an evaluation of historical social

and economic conditions essential. Lastly, there is the general history of the province of Pomerania, of Prussia, and of Germany, which left its imprint upon Trieglaff and framed conditions for pivotal developments. All these components are interwoven with each other.

The family history of the Thaddens is closely tied to trends in church history. These introduced a dynamic of their own, for in their wake religious and political developments proceeded under great tension, by no means embodying the harmony that characterizes the conventional image of the throne-and-altar alliance.[3] The forces of resistance spawned in Trieglaff in the nineteenth century in opposition to the demands of the official state church would bear fruit in the twentieth century, in the battle against the ecclesiastical politics of Nazism.

Local history, for its part, is bound in the first place to geographical givens. How could it be otherwise? Trieglaff and its neighboring villages lay (and lie) apart from any major long-distance transportation routes or rail lines. It is only half as far to the Baltic Sea as to the Oder River. To compensate, it has two large lakes rich in fish, which, while certainly less entwined in legend than Fontane's setting of Stechlin, nevertheless lent and still lend to Trieglaff a charm of its own. What nourished legend rather were the primeval oaks in the churchyard. There, according to *Pomerania*, Bugenhagen's famous chronicle published in 1517, an image of the three-headed heathen idol Triglav was supposed to have been hidden. Its priests had saved it from the Christian missionaries of Bishop Otto of Bamberg and brought it to a widow in Trieglaff.[4]

Thus Trieglaff exemplifies how situation, though it has meaning for the everyday, is not the most prominent element. In contrast to neighboring Vahnerow, the village's social distinctiveness derived from a layout that had a section for farming people at one end and centered upon a traditional manorial estate at the other (Figure 2). The village accordingly featured not only the juxtaposition of an agrarian workforce alongside a feudal propertied gentry still associating itself with a waning knighthood-based social status, but also a triangular relationship among estate proprietors, workers, and farmers (*Bauern*). The last were for the most part scarcely emancipated from serfdom during the initial years, with consequences for the configuration of later conflicts.[5]

General political history unquestionably holds a significant place in the history of the development of Trieglaff and its neighboring villages. There have existed a pre-Prussian, a Prussian, and a German Trieglaff, and since 1945 also a Polish Trzygłów. The Trieglaff of the Thaddens (see Figure 1)—from 1820 to 1945—extends from the Prussian to the German period. The time stands out because the estate household had immediate and particularly intense experience of the conflict and accommodation

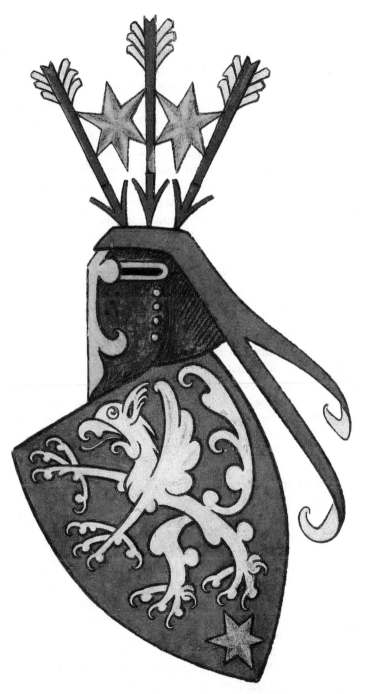

Figure 1. Coat of arms of the von Thadden family, Nesnachow branch

that attended relations between erstwhile Prussia and the new German Empire (das Deutsche Reich, 1871–1918). This developed out of the estate family's close, even intimate acquaintance with Otto von Bismarck.[6]

With respect to the history of society, the demise of feudalism runs like a red thread through Trieglaff's Thadden era. Politically, it began with the Stein-Hardenberg Reforms of 1807 and ended for all practical purposes when manorial estates were dissolved as autonomous civil jurisdictions in 1927. Under way in the generation prior to the 1848 Revolution, although relatively slowly and ponderously, it then accelerated during the unification of the empire even as conservative forces mounted forceful resistance to the breakup of feudal structures, especially at Trieglaff itself. The Pomeranian estates continued to be a vital part of an ancien régime—an old order—up to the end of the Weimar Republic in 1933.[7]

Noteworthy here, with respect to social history, is that the processes of defeudalization and acquisition of middle-class or burgher rights follow separate timelines.[8] The Thaddens in Trieglaff began entering into marriages with non-aristocratic individuals in 1855, but did not for that reason cease to think in terms of a stratified society. And families of commoners who acquired the traditional manorial estates did everything they could to preserve relics of the tradition and assume its manners of living. Within their circles, political liberalism made no gains at all.[9]

Here arises the unavoidable question why class order and feudal ways of life were able to persist so stubbornly, even though the processes of economic and technological modernization were making rapid progress. The transformation from class-defined "lord of a manor" to modern commercial agriculturalist was, after all, in full swing even in Pomerania in the nineteenth century. But advances in democracy did not, as adherents of the 1848 Revolution hoped, mend the gap that defeudalization tore open. There developed instead a nationalistic flood that in many respects overflowed its banks. The generation of the Wilhelminian Era held thinking on a national scale to be modern, and feudal thinking to be old-fashioned—though granted, also *schön*, nice.[10]

At the time, not even the "Trieglaffers" had yet grasped that, in the absence of reconciliation with the world of democracy, there was no escape from the dead end of nationalism. Critical thinking brought forth in the village metamorphosed rather more toward religious initiatives. Hence the ecumenical movement, with its international clubs and organizations, assumed an appeal for the younger generation of the Thaddens: it set the parameters within which they sought out new paths.[11]

Consistent with this, the Trieglaff manor's resistance to the Nazi regime initially concentrated on the struggle with its church policy. The "Confessing Church" (Bekennende Kirche) was the field upon which confrontation with the nationalistic and racist German Christians (Deutsche Christen) took place. The hard path trodden by the family's eldest daughter, Elisabeth von Thadden, to Ravensbrück and a bitter end in Plötzensee, would similarly have been inconceivable absent the background of the Kirchenkampf, the established church's struggle against Nazism.[12]

The generational history of the Thaddens in Trieglaff and Vahnerow does not end with the Red Army's entrance in March of 1945. Quite the contrary, it continues there until December 1948, when local headquarters of the Soviet military in Trieglaff were withdrawn and the last German residents had to leave their homes. In these three and a half postwar years, old class-based relationships still cast their shadow on affairs as core members of the manorial proprietary families stayed behind, thereby exhibiting solidarity with families of workers on the land.

Upon conclusion of the Prussian-German phase of Trieglaff's history, many questions persisted. One had to do with relating to the new Trieglaffers—the Polish people who settled in the villages and tended the fields. Were there still lines of continuity, and if so, was it still possible to transmit experiences of the former German generations to the contemporary Polish ones?

But the questions do not confine themselves to the German-Polish relationship. They pertain as much to the discussion amongst Germans themselves about what the history of the region east of the Elbe River, including Pomerania—"East Elbian" history—means for them today. What influences can such a premodern world exert to keep bonds of human solidarity from dissipating even more swiftly in industrial societies, for example? Can life experiences from a time predating the rise of civil society shield against the narrow-mindedness of the middle-class way of life? And do memories of social ordering that antedate nation-states guard people against nationalistic paths of error?[13] Those are questions for the next generation as it seeks the road toward a European Community that sees itself as more than an economic alliance.

The state of research into the history of Eastern Pomeranian localities, now Polish, is not very satisfactory. Polish historians must conduct their initial research in the history of the region using German sources. And their German colleagues in the discipline are more likely to specialize in the history of Western Pomerania, which remained German after 1945.[14] Nevertheless a bilingual (German and Polish) inventory of the holdings of the Stettin state archives is now available, providing a view of archival materials that have been preserved.[15] Beyond that, the few family archives still at hand must assist to fill gaps.

A productive source on the economic situation of the manorial properties and larger independent farm operations in Pomerania is the agricultural directory of properties (*Landwirtschaftliches Güter-Adreßbuch*) dating from 1939.[16] Not only are holdings in livestock and acreage set forth in it, but names of owners are given along with those of managerial heads or supervisors (the *Inspektoren*), who oversaw and directed estate operations (known as bailiffs on English estates). Only business results are absent from the tallies making up its contents.

According to these records, Trieglaff and both of the adjacent associated places, Vahnerow and Batzwitz, were among the numerous estate-centered settlements in the District of Greifenberg. Management of Trieglaff extended also to two outlying agricultural entities, Gruchow and Idashof. The estate had 2,834 acres (1,147 ha) of land, of which 2,078.2 acres were arable, 182.9 meadow, 180.4 pasture, 224.9 wooded, 81.5 lake-covered, and 210 non-arable. Holdings in livestock comprised 80 horses, 270 head of cattle, 180 swine, and 1,500 sheep. Alongside ten medium and smaller independent farmers, there was also one large farm on 61.8 acres (25 ha), of which 49.4 were arable, 7.4 meadow, 2.5 pasture, and 2.5 unfit for farming. He owned 2 horses, 15 cows, and 15 hogs.

In Vahnerow there were no independent farmers, only the estate property. It was listed as having 1067.5 acres (432 ha), of which 741.3 acres were arable, 84 meadow, 37.1 pasture, 185.3 wooded, and 19.8 unfit for farming. Livestock holdings encompassed 32 horses, 100 head of cattle, 180 hogs, and 170 sheep. Trieglaff, in comparison, was nearly three times as large.

Figure 2. Aerial view of the village of Trieglaff, 1934; foreground "Bauernende" (farmers' end), background the estate

In Batzwitz, which for 18 years in the nineteenth century belonged to the Thaddens and then to the related family Senfft von Pilsach, the estate occupied 1114.45 acres (451 ha), of which 714.1 acres were arable, 64.3 meadow, 59.3 pasture, 237.2 wooded, and 42 non-arable. Making up holdings in livestock were 36 horses, 140 head of cattle, 200 hogs, and 450 sheep. Alongside the estate, eight independent farmers operated on a total of 729 acres (295 ha) of land, including 565.9 acres that were arable, 76.6 meadow, 45.7 pasture, 12.4 wooded, and 28.4 unfit for farming. They owned 27 horses, 152 head of cattle, and 140 swine in total.

In the matter of churches, too, the places were distinct from each other. In Trieglaff there were two churches from 1855 on, in Batzwitz one, and none at all in Vahnerow. As one of the oldest village churches in Pomerania, the medieval Trieglaff house of worship was the most impressive historically: St. Elisabeth's (*die Elisabethkirche*) was first mentioned in a document in 1297, one hundred years after Christianization of the land by Bishop Otto of Bamberg. The Batzwitz church was smaller and was not dedicated until some 150 years later, in 1440. Vahnerow belonged to the Batzwitz parish.[17]

That church affiliation occupied a place in people's memories here is attributable to a split that had a host of consequences for historical accounts. In 1847, large segments of the local communities, identified as Old Lutherans (*Altlutheraner*), separated from congregations of the established Church of the Prussian Union. This left traces in the generational history of the von Thadden family, but its effects carried as far as the United States. The families of émigrés from Trieglaff cultivated and are still cultivating their Old Lutheran traditions, even to the present day.

Notes

1. For comparison see Ulrike Jureit, *Generationenforschung* (Göttingen, 2006), 7ff., 62f. In addition, two volumes have in the meantime appeared under the rubric *Göttinger Studien zur Generationsforschung*, edited, with somewhat differing emphases, by Bernd Weisbrod: vol. 1, *Generation als Erzählung* (Göttingen, 2009), and vol. 2, *Historische Beiträge zur Generationsforschung* (Göttingen, 2009).

2. Cf. Rudolf von Thadden, "Umstrittene Erinnerung," in *Der Streit um Erinnerung*, ed. Martin Sabrow (Leipzig, 2008), 119ff. Further, Jacque Le Goff, *Histoire et Mémoire* (Paris, 1988), 10: "La mémoire est la matière première de l'histoire" [Memory is the first material of history].

3. Cf. Rudolf von Thadden, "Die Geschichte der Kirchen und Konfessionen," in *Handbuch der Preußischen Geschichte*, ed. Wolfgang Neugebauer (Berlin, 2001), 3: 592ff., 626ff., 654ff.

4. Johannes Bugenhagen, *Pomerania,* reproduction and translation of 1517–1518 manuscript [Latin/German], ed. Norbert Buske (Schwerin, 2008), 156.

5. Cf. Albert Ulrich, *Chronik des Kreises Greifenberg in Hinterpommern* (Dithmarschen: private printing, 1990), 351ff. For a concise glossary of terms that, like *Bauer,* have to do with estates and estate life, see Royal Natzke, ed., *The Nobleman Among the Brothers* (Bloomington, IN, 2006), 71, trans. Alma Ihlenfeldt. [In German, Wolfgang Marzahn, *Der Edelmann unter den Brüdern* (Lahr-Dinglingen), 1978.]

6. Cf. Rudolf von Thadden, *Prussia: The History of a Lost State,* trans. Angi Rutter (Cambridge, 1987), 57ff.

7. Cf. Patrick Wagner, *Bauern, Junker und Beamte* (Göttingen, 2005), 592.

8. Regarding the problem of the middle class in the nineteenth century cf. Jürgen Kocka, ed., *Verbürgerlichung, Recht und Politik* (Göttingen, 1995), 3: 7f.

9. Cf. Monika Wienfort, *Patrimonialgerichte in Preußen* (Göttingen, 2001), 22.

10. Wolfgang J. Mommsen, *Bürgerstolz und Weltmachtstreben* (Berlin, 1995), 7/2: 198ff.

11. Reinold von Thadden, *Auf verlorenem Posten?* [A lost cause?] (Tübingen, 1948), 63ff.

12. Cf. Jörg Thierfelder, "Von der Kooperation zur inneren Distanzierung," in *Elisabeth von Thadden,* ed. Matthias Riemenschneider and Jörg Thierfelder (Karlsruhe, 2002), 107f.

13. On the subject of nationalism cf. Norbert Elias, *Studien über die Deutschen. Machtkämpfe und Habitusentwicklung im 19. und 20. Jahrhundert,* ed. Michael Schröter (Frankfurt am Main, 1989), 193ff.

14. This is shown by a look through *Baltische Studien, Pommersche Jahrbücher für Landesgeschichte* 76 (1990) to 96 (2010).

15. State archives of Stettin (Staatsarchiv Stettin), directory of holdings up to 1945, prepared by Radoslaw Gazinski et al. (Munich, 2004), Rep. 66, Greifenberg.

16. *Niekammers Landwirtschaftliche Güter-Adreßbücher,* vol. 1, *Pommern* (Leipzig, 1939), 192. (Cited areal measurements have been converted to units familiar to Americans. One hectare is 2.471 acres, and one acre 0.405 hectares, so 40 acres equals approximately 16 hectares. Discrepancies between some of the totals given and totaled itemized entries are present in the source figures.)

17. Cf. Ulrich, *Chronik,* 403f., 383f.

Chapter 1

The Founding Generation

Preservation of Feudal Structures?

Trieglaff lies, as it always has, out of the way in eastern provincial Pomerania. Notwithstanding, it has a dynamic history. In the past two hundred years it has twice been occupied by foreign troops. Twice the village itself has experienced warfare. The lives of the five generations that molded Thadden-era Trieglaff played themselves out between these two events. The first occupation was by troops of the French emperor Napoleon's victorious army, who in the spring of 1807 took up quarters in its homes and demanded tribute. The second time, units of the no less victorious Red Army, during their advance to the Oder in March 1945, made Trieglaff a regional base for their army and set up a local headquarters (*Militärkommandantur*) in the castle. Each of these occupations triggered grave consequences that affected both the people and the land.[1]

The events of the wars left quite varied impressions on people's memories. The one persistent memory from the French occupation following the defeat of Prussia was the onerous tribute that long continued to burden the land. By contrast, the wounds inflicted by the Russian occupation five generations later have not entirely healed, even to the present day, for this domination brought not just passing distress and difficulties, but also, and above all, a wholesale replacement of the population that marks a breach in the history of the region. The Polish people moving into Trieglaff after it ended were at a loss for local traditions to which they could attach.[2]

But what did remain in remembrance of this 200-year past that was worth preserving? In the manor house in Trieglaff, an author who described the milieu of Prussia east of the Elbe like no other retained a privileged place in the library until 1945. This was Theodor Fontane, a writer of Huguenot ancestry who hailed from the March (Electorate) of Brandenburg. In his first novel *Vor dem Sturm* (*Before the Storm*), set in the time of the decampment of Napoleon's *grande armée* for Russia, he depicts the two faces of the French adversary people were then encountering as it overran Prussia. One was that of a great nation, "whose courage, spirit and capacity for sacrifice" warranted high praise; the other, that of "a tyrant who has murdered liberty," whose war of conquest left "property depreciated, harvests pillaged, the farm half burned down by brigands."[3]

The estate-holders of Trieglaff experienced the "time of the Frenchmen," as it was called, with like sentiments toward France.[4] The owner at the time, Heinrich Victor Sigismund von Oertzen, who had been selected as district administrator (*Landrat*) of the District of Greifenberg following the French invasion, wrote to his brother full of concern that the quartering was "burdensome" and official business "sad," and that "Lessening of might has to be replaced by growth of virtue." A few months later he averred that things were better with his wife again, since "the last Frenchman passing by here whacked away a couple of dozen young trees out of my Reinigungs-Allee."[5] Five years later, in the European wars of liberation from Napoleonic domination, he himself would fall at Leipzig. Through his daughter Henriette, Trieglaff then made its way into the possession of the von Thadden family.[6]

But there were also other memories of the Napoleonic era. It was regarded—not without cause—as the epoch of transition from the feudal ancien régime to modern egalitarian society. Such memories originated in realities that remained quite potent in their impact. Thus each and every Pomeranian was affected by the so-called Stein-Hardenberg Reforms, introduced during precisely this period in answer to the challenges of the French Revolution of 1789. They affected the living conditions of farmers and farm workers as well as estate holders, because they engendered a process of dissolution of the feudal order and, at least with respect to legal rights, created the conditions for acquisition of private property. This was a step on the way to making landholders out of serfs and peasants.[7]

Yet it is necessary to draw some distinctions. The historical memory of the aristocracy rested upon developed traditions. It stored up the experiences of past generations and was also capable of resisting new historical realities. The memories of the agrarian and sub-agrarian strata, by comparison, reached as a rule only as far back as to the generation of their grandparents and were unconnected with titular rights, unlike the memories of the landed aristocracy. Underclasses did, however, form attachments to other elements within the world familiar to them, and frequently made use of other courses of action to gain their ends.[8]

Stored still differently were the memories of those who in the course of the nineteenth century decided to emigrate from Pomerania and settle in the United States. They soon freed themselves from the realities of their old homeland, becoming independent in the new world beyond the Atlantic. At center for them has always stood the pious Trieglaff estate holder Adolph von Thadden (Figure 3), who took care of "his people" and intervened for them when there were conflicts with officialdom, for he assisted their ancestors on their way to a "new world," going so far as to see them off in their ship at the Hamburg harbor.[9]

Lastly, even the Polish people living in Trzygłów today honor the memory of the Trieglaff life and world of this venerable Thadden. A flyer for visitors that appeared in two languages, German and Polish, explains what Trieglaff had that is worth knowing:

> In the history of this village each century has been rich in important events. In the 19th century it was the strong center of a German religious movement, that of the Lutheran Pietists. In the year 1820 the first conference of pastors and followers of Pietism in Prussia took place there.[10]

Hence there is no road that bypasses that first Thadden on the Trieglaff manorial estate, who has impressed himself upon the memories of a great variety of individuals associated with the place. Who was this Adolph von Thadden, who after the Napoleonic wars married into the von Oertzen family, owners until that time, and became, according to unanimous testimony, hub of an extraordinary pietistic culture?

In the *Allgemeine Deutsche Biographie* (general biography, *ADB*), he found a place as a unique, self-willed, charismatic personality, aiding the spirit of Pietism to far-reaching effects in Pomerania in an "awakening movement." Later his pietism even influenced Otto von Bismarck. And through it he acquired importance in Prussian conservative circles.[11]

But this judgment expresses little concerning his immediate life and world, which, after all, was first and foremost agriculture. Adolph von Thadden had to gain an initial foothold in the world of Eastern Pomeranian agricultural estates, literally to "get his feet on the ground," if he wanted eventually to be influential in religion and politics as well. Without a grounding in estate business this was not possible.

We possess a richly revealing source about this side of Adolph von Thadden, one that survived the chaos of World War II somewhat adventurously.[12] It is a manuscript inventory of the estate that he compiled in 1820, shortly after his marriage to Henriette von Oertzen. Subsequently, he

Figure 3. Adolph Ferdinand von Thadden (1796–1882), leader of the awakening movement in Pomerania

first managed, and then rented, the estates Trieglaff and Vahnerow, the former with its outlying farmstead of Gruchow.

According to this document, both of these properties were in bad condition. There had been negligence under the preceding management during a custodial period established upon the death of the prior owner. Their condition was also a consequence of uncertainties caused by problems putting into effect the so-called regulatory edicts (*Regulierungsedikte*) of the Stein-Hardenberg Reforms.[13] On the one hand these caused many farm people to lose land to estate owners in exchange for acquisition of greater rights of ownership and immunity from feudal services and levies; on the other, however, they gave farm people the possibility of acquiring private property after traditional use of common pasturage (*Almendewirtschaft*) was suspended.

So the Thaddens took over Trieglaff and Vahnerow during a phase of intensive change on the way from the old feudal order—known to the French as the ancien régime—to the world of a modern entrepreneurial society in which private property without associated social obligations constitutes the basis of economic, social, and political life. In everyday rural life, the core of this drawn-out process consisted in the liberation of farmers from feudal bonds of serfdom or "hereditary subjection," as people in Prussia preferred to say,[14] under which land had belonged hereditarily to the nobility and people hereditarily to their allotted parcels of estate lands. But what was the cost of this liberation?

Adolph von Thadden had thought about this question. He had set his mind upon life on the land early on, studying "rational agriculture" with Albrecht Thaer, the leading agricultural economist of the time.[15] Having learned from Thaer that up-to-date estate management was a business in which interest in profit plays a role, he held to that notwithstanding all his openness to the spirit of romanticism.

So disposed, the young estate owner prepared a carefully articulated, detailed business inventory presenting the holdings in farmland, livestock, and barns in exact figures and values. A very thorough section on "field management" assesses the consequences of the regulatory edicts using a concrete example. In it he voices the criticism that the old apportionment of clover fields was "in complete disorder," and suspects that this "came about because people had expected the regulations to be enacted earlier for farmers." And further:

> 2 of the best fields which are to go to the liberated peasants (*Bauern*) in the future had manure spread on them; they consequently cannot be sown to clover then either, therefore this year there is not only no clover hay at all, but we also have on our hands the worst clover pasture.[16]

Uncertainties about rearranged ownership statuses were leading to fields not always being managed in the customary way. It is possible to interpret the presentation in this way. There follow, however, no complaints about the end of the good old days, but only thoroughly modern profit calculations:

> On the main Trieglaff property this year 8 loads first crop and at most 12 loads of second crop clover hay will be harvested, when we might instead have harvested nearly 100 loads of clover hay; this loss is the more meaningful as the property only has very little meadow hay.

These profit-and-loss calculations appear also in the other sections of the inventory, above all that on livestock holdings. Here he makes a critical assessment that of twenty-six plow horses at Trieglaff: "7 head don't need to be wintered through at all"; "if 6 teams are to be kept continuously, then at least 3 horses must be purchased and an entire team completed from the young stock." Holdings in cows looked no better: here, at least ten to twelve head had "to be culled on account of age." For that reason, "a purchase would be necessary, and as one likely won't get more than one decent cow for 2 old ones," it would be "necessary to throw in some cash." And the sheep appear to get his particular attention:

> The flocks of sheep are overfull, with about 600 head for sale. Regardless of this, 162 ewes at some 10 Thaler per head and 30 wethers at 4 Thaler were purchased last summer that are not in the least better than the sheep at Gruchow, of which at least 100 head could be sold. And because at this time there's no market for them at all, it's to be asked whether these don't have to be sold at 5 Thaler per ewe.

The purchase of sheep from Saxony was in his opinion "entirely unnecessary." Besides, here "a lot of oats had been fed away just in order not to let animals in the flock starve. Where's the advantage in that?"[17]

The man who compiled this sober picture of the condition of the Trieglaff and Vahnerow properties, acquired through marriage and purchase, would nonetheless warn often in the next decades that, in showing concern for "four-legged things," one cannot forget to show the "two-legged" some. He gave a much-noted lecture on 21 April 1837 about the obligations the landholding estate owners had to the former peasants and farm workers who were bound to them in a lingering feudalism. Entitled "Über Menschenschau unter Landwirthen" (Human concern for people by landholders), it was presented in the Regenwalde branch of the Pomeranian Economic Society. In it he spoke almost programmatically about the social duties of estate holders.[18] It would prove true, as he said, "that the business of an estate can be managed not only by and for stomachs, but with a soul and with the heart as well." Concerned care for the workers on the estate merited a place — not the last either: "It is not good if the day laborers and servants are positioned so that they have only one foot in the country and the other on the border." They have to "rightfully receive" their well-earned pay, "their bread earned in the sweat of their brow."

In a second speech, which Adolph von Thadden gave five years later on 10 May 1842 before the general assembly of the Pomeranian Economic Society in Köslin, he set out in even sharper contours his social-ethical and class-political position. Under the heading "Der Schacher mit den Rittergütern" (Exploitation of manorial estates)[19] he spoke forcefully against what we today would call industrial agriculture or agrarian capitalism:

> He who ... regards his estate solely as a source of income, who, for example, visits his yearling barn daily, his village school never, the cattle market always, the district council meeting never, ... whoever readily sacks a loyal worker because he turns fifty, ... he would do well to sell his estate to one who is an estate owner of genuine knightly virtue.

But who, according to Thadden's conceptualizations, was such a "genuine estate owner"? By no means only an aristocrat:

> People would understand me ... very wrongly if they thought that I wanted to claim estates only for one privileged caste.... No, every true man of honor, willing and able to grasp the meaning of that class into which he enters shall be welcomed by us from the heart.[20]

He addressed therewith the delicate theme of the relationship between aristocracy and commoners. In contrast to most of the members of his class, he called for flexible treatment of class membership, spoke of "so-called commoners" and "so-called aristocratic estate owners," and castigated those "*von So-and-So*-tails" who "don't show it." "At that empty 'squirarchy' without substance" — he lectured pointedly — "at the conservatives, who want to conserve only themselves, we laugh rightly. Instead of that, we look for purebred only amongst the four-legged creatures."[21]

Thadden's class-critical attitude was not expressed in words alone. In the life of his own family, he affirmed marriage with non-aristocratic women and welcomed wholeheartedly the union of his oldest son, Reinhold, with a person descended from academic commoners, namely, Marie Witte from Halle, daughter of the famous Dante scholar Karl Witte.[22] She would later be a pillar of the family and, not unimportantly, also of the Trieglaff property.

Also remarkable is that, and how, Adolph von Thadden came to talk about the place of Jews in this connection. He disapproved of the sale of manorial estates to them so long as they were not Christian, but he accepted their freedom, guaranteed by the state, to buy estates for themselves. His justification differed much from later anti-Semitic argumentation: "Far be it from me to revile this unfortunate people. Instead is it greatly to be regretted that this once most highly-regarded of peoples, from whom all salvation has come (John 4:22), and before whose credentials of nobility all others must give ground, is not treated with the respect owed its misfortune." But they continued to be shut out from the dominant associations, "even if it is not to be denied, that nonparticipation of the Jewish people in the riches of salvation and its earthly blessings given to us is and remains a painful and shameful guilt belonging to an in part vicious, though in large part lukewarm, in any case too indifferent, Christianity."[23] These unconventional words concerning Jews, critical of the church, probably irritated many of those present at the gathering.

And how did it assume its shape, this attitude of Adolph von Thadden's, so characterized by elements of nonconformity? What was its background in his family history? It is striking that relatively little is reported about his ancestors in the oft-quoted biographies of him. Certain pieces of information are indeed to be found about his father Ernst-Dietrich, who was aide-de-camp to the Prussian kings Frederick the Great and Frederick William II, and about his mother Caroline, who came from the well-regarded family of the counts von Wartensleben. But details do not reach further back than this.[24]

Yet the Thaddens had a thoroughly interesting family history. They held property in the eastern boundary region next to Poland, where the population was in part Kashubian and displayed many another regional peculiarity as well. The region belonged to Stettin's part of Pomerania, so the people living in the districts Lauenburg and Bütow became Lutheran (*evangelisch*), whereas those in Danzig's part remained Catholic, as a rule because of their adherence to the Polish crown. Consistent with this, the

Thaddens, too, were Lutheran in the Lauenburg District, but some family members living east of there were, as Polish nationals, Catholic.[25]

What endured as worth telling from this German-Polish history[26] was that one Stephan Thadden, a Lauenburger, was at first a Catholic priest, but then adopted the Lutheran confession of the Reformation and in 1548 became a clergyman in Leba. In the memory of the family, the question alone remains why no Thadden ever again entered the clergy. Did the Lutheran Church perhaps offer too few attractive positions for a member of the landed aristocracy? No longer was it possible to become abbot of a monastery or be seated on the clergy's bench in the district council (*Kreistag*), for in the Protestant world there were no monasteries, and quickly enough no clerical classes either.[27]

Once Lauenburg and Bütow were merged into Brandenburg soon after the Peace of Westphalia, the Lutheran Thaddens took root in the Hohenzollern state. From the eighteenth century on we find them in military positions, and under Frederick the Great two even rose to the rank of general. The older of them, Georg Reinhold, governor of the fortress and earldom of Glatz in Silesia, was rewarded with an entailed estate in Groß-Babenz in East Prussia. This estranged him from his more modest East Pomeranian homeland, as the property would be passed along successively to (usually eldest) sons. The younger of them, Johann Leopold, became governor of Spandau and lived his waning years in Halle an der Saale.[28]

In Trieglaff during Adolph von Thadden's time, there was scarcely mention any longer of all these originally Kashubian, then later Prussian, tales about the family. Some memories of the era of Frederick the Great had indeed survived, but those most recent experiences from the Napoleonic wars had a far greater effect. His father having died early, young Adolph, following a childhood in the militarily structured life and schooling of a cadet house, lived out the French occupation at his mother's home in Berlin. In 1813, at seventeen years old, he marched off with patriotic zeal to the "wars of liberation" (*Befreiungskriege*). They took him as far as Paris by their close. Upon the return of Napoleon from Elba in 1815, he participated again in the battles that led to the French emperor's ultimate defeat at Waterloo.[29]

These experiences from the Napoleonic era would continue to shape Adolph von Thadden and his generation into advanced age. They were reflected in numerous stories and anecdotes, e.g., when, having suffered defeats followed by hoped-for "victories," he addressed them by commenting, "That was Ligny, Waterloo is going to follow now." In political disputes he used to portray his "Waterloo" with pride, having been the first Prussian to join up with the British: "I found myself on the right wing of the 1st corps, the 1st division, the 1st brigade, the 1st regiment, the 1st company, the 1st platoon, and we marched right."[30]

Yet in no way was his image of France exclusively adversarial. Whoever reads his writings and speeches will conclude that he frequently quoted not only Goethe, Schiller, Kleist, and Claudius, but also the French royalists Chateaubriand, de Maistre, and Bonald, and indeed knew even the social critic Saint-Simon. The Trieglaff library, which was lost when the Red Army took control in March 1945, held numerous works by French authors.[31]

The path to such a career would have stood directly open to the young officer, but for Adolph von Thadden, redirecting away from the military was more important than getting things settled with France. In a letter to his mother, written while he was still in the field, he stressed emphatically:

> The life of a soldier during peacetime is loathsome to me.... We're living now with no connection to the church, without involvement with art or science, without company of the feminine disposition which is so attractive to me, without an enduring home.

And further:

> Having contact with nature, agricultural life, is what appeals to me the most. How splendid a landed aristocrat seems to me to be. He is a little king of his village, during peacetime a father, during war the one who leads the charge, in distress the truest friend to his small citizenry, on top of it a dear wife, queen and mother to the village.[32]

Reminiscent of Max Piccolomini's yearnings for peace—for Thadden did after all have Schiller's *Wallenstein* in his backpack—these statements prepared the ground for the intellectual and spiritual experiences that characterize his years in Berlin following his return from the Napoleonic wars. Not only was he notably inspired by the sermons of Schleiermacher, Hermes, and Jänicke there, but he also found the circle of friends to which he remained bound his whole life long: the Gerlach brothers, who would later play a decisive role in a falling-out with Bismarck, and Ernst Senfft von Pilsach, who became a close companion in his Pomeranian world.[33]

It was certainly no accident that two of the friends soon also became brothers-in-law. Three unmarried sisters from the home of the von Oertzen family in possession of the Trieglaff estate at the time moved within the pietistic circles of Berlin society. In the years that followed, a three-way bond came about: Ida, the eldest, married Ernst Senfft; the second, Henriette, made her life together with Adolph Thadden; and the third, Auguste, married Ernst-Ludwig Gerlach. The women's younger brothers Hermann and Viktor both dropped out of the line of succession to inheritance quite soon, through death and by settlement respectively, while their father, Heinrich von Oertzen, had fallen in 1813 in the Battle of Leipzig.[34]

After that Trieglaff was under custodial administration by guardianship, which made it possible for Adolph von Thadden first to lease the property and later, by settlement with his brother-in-law, to take over completely. The money required for the acquisition came from a legacy he had received from his heirless grand-uncle, General Georg Reinhold von Thadden.[35] He had these means at his disposal because, as the youngest of four siblings, he had survived both his brothers.

In the year 1820, then, Adolph and Henriette were able to marry and move to Trieglaff. There they transposed their spiritual experiences from Berlin into a new way of life. From this there very quickly developed a center of the "awakening movement" that became so well-known in German pietistic history. The name Thadden would be associated with that of Trieglaff from this time on.[36]

The pietistic spirit of the awakening movement expanded rapidly through all of Germany in the years following the Napoleonic wars. In Eastern Prussia it was concentrated in Silesia and Pomerania. But it took root also in the Lower Rhine and Westphalia, regions that then belonged to Prussia. Its unique tone derived from its step-by-step association with rejection of the Lutheran-Reformed denominational union enacted by Prussian King Frederick William III in 1817, the so-called Prussian Union setting up a single united church. Intensification of confessional thinking was the result.[37]

In Trieglaff the awakening movement aroused heightened attention for two reasons. For one, it found an unusually vital home on the estate of the new Adolph and Henriette von Thadden family. Second, for various reasons, the independent farmers and farm workers of the area had a strong need for spiritual experience and personal piety. So the movement transcended social divisions.[38]

To that was added an unhappy local constellation. The village pastor of many years, dutifully devoted to his office, was an adherent of the rationalistic theology of the eighteenth century and thus critically opposed pietistic conventicles of every kind. In his view worship services belonged in church, not in private dwellings in the form of household devotional assemblies. This veteran clergyman, Winkelsesser by name, gave expression to his irritation with the new mode of spirituality in a personal notation:

> Tranquilly, quietly, and peacefully I lived with the departed Captain von Mellin, the grandfather, and the departed district administrator Herr von Oertzen, father of Frau von Thadden residing here now, as well as with

the local inhabitants during the 35-year conduct of my office, until the Festival of St. John of 1820, when a certain Herr von Thadden, who identifies and signs himself as administrator of the estates, moved here. Hardly had the man arrived than he began to assert his manner of living, with so-called prayer times and gatherings in his house.[39]

That was just too much for Winkelsesser. A genuine conflict of generations ensued and became acute when Thadden not only hosted household devotional services with an outside "pious" clergyman, but also applied for exceptional permission, a *dimissoriale*, for the baptism of his first child, his daughter Marie. Winkelsesser replied:

> If Your Highborn Personage has confidence in the Lutheran preacher Palis in Zettin, that he will baptize your child better and in a more Christian way than I, then I have nothing against it, and that ought to be waiver enough.[40]

But it was obviously not enough for him, for Winkelsesser filed a complaint with the consistory in Stettin. It, in turn, sent Pastor Palis a warning, calling attention to the pertinent paragraphs of the Prussian laws (*Allgemeines Landrecht*), according to which parish jurisdictions were to be respected.[41]

Yet it was not to rest with this single occurrence. Much farther-reaching in its consequences was a conflict with the Trieglaff shepherd Friedrich Wangerin, who likewise petitioned that his first child might not be baptized by an "unbelieving preacher." In a respectful letter he requested the master of the estate Adolph von Thadden to "intercede" with the consistory, as Pastor Winkelsesser had "not only refused him" a waiver, but had "also shown him the door."[42] This instance did more than create a sensation in the village. It belongs to the anterior history of a process that reached far beyond Trieglaff and Pomerania, into the history of the emigration of families of Trieglaff farm workers to the United States.[43] The incident is so noteworthy that it must be related in detail according to sources.

The Wangerin letter quoted experienced an uncommon fate. It came back to Germany via a roundabout path—from Wisconsin in the United States. The descendants of Adolph von Thadden learned in 2004 that a copy existed in Wisconsin, where it was found reproduced and translated in a chronicle of the Wangerin family. The knowledge followed from contact by correspondence a number of times with Rev. Royal Natzke, a descendant of one of the families that had emigrated from Trieglaff. The original likely was lost in Pomerania at the end of the war.[44]

In this family history, the letter of the Trieglaff shepherd is of quite extraordinary value. It is presumed to be "a turning point in our history

Figure 4. The old village church of 1297

and perhaps a reason for our being in this country today," along with the child's baptism and the later alliance with Adolph von Thadden in their firm stand regarding their beliefs.[45] It very plainly carries greater weight in the memories of the immigrants to the United States than in the historical memory of the Trieglaffers who stayed in Europe.

There is good reason for this, for forty-two years later the baptized infant, Johann by name, emigrated to the United States and joined the Trieglaffers who had crossed the Atlantic in a first wave at the end of the 1830s.[46] It was his great-grandson who strove, in his family history of 1972, to document the spiritual legacy of old Adolph von Thadden, emphasizing how contemporary Trieglaff was a "seat of resistance" to regimentation of the church by a "misguided" King Frederick William III: "The church was under the domination of the State.... Rationalism prevailed, almost covering Christianity with its philosophy of common sense, basing morality on self interest."[47]

On the European side of the Atlantic, the history looked somewhat different. Firstly the letter, for whatever reason, did not reach the family archives. Then too, a line critical of the church wove through its assertions about the conflict with the Prussian state, emphasizing the weaknesses of German Lutheranism in resisting sovereign political presumptions. Adolph von Thadden's great-grandson Reinold von Thadden, the later founder of the German Protestant Kirchentag (Deutscher Evangelischer Kirchentag)—a lay rally—asks in his critical review of the years of church struggles during Hitler's Third Reich whether it was not "the fault of Lutheranism" that "congregation-mindedness could assert itself only much more weakly in the east than in the Reformed west."[48] He then directly compares the Nazism-opposing Confessing Church (Bekennende Kirche) of the 1930s with the congregation of awakened Christians in the first half of the nineteenth century. Boldly, he sees in the conflict between the old Prussian state and the Pomeranian awakening movement a "historical precursor" of the later Kirchenkampf church struggles for survival.[49] Thus can streams of remembered history differ from one another.

But how did history as it actually took place—that is, history as distinguished from such memories—unfold? Strikingly, a long neglected component of the conflict played a considerable role, namely, the social element of the disputes. As early as the first year of Adolph and Henriette von Thadden's occupancy of Trieglaff in 1821, there was an exchange of letters between the youthful aristocrat administering the estate and the older Landrat (district administrator) in their District of Greifenberg, Heinrich von der Marwitz auf Rütznow. In this exchange, the latter warns expressly against the social consequences of Thadden's communal devotional activity, breaching class barriers and overstepping parish confines. He admonishes:

> Firstly, because through the presence of your family and your wife's family those home gatherings attain in the eyes of the common man too great an importance, and the notion can easily be engendered thereby that such devotional services are more important and more sacred than the public

ones, and secondly, because in the eyes of the villagers I come to be seen ineluctably in an ambiguous light. For by the standard of the above remarks, the utility of diminishing social distance by you and your family, such as people have become accustomed to, does not seem plausible to me with respect to my spiritual welfare.[50]

Thadden, who had attended the devotional times for workers at Rütznow with his household a number of times, responded to these scarcely injudicious reservations fourteen days later already in a letter that is instructive even as it sues for understanding.[51] He first laid out, citing numerous instances from the Bible and the Lutheran confessions, what "the Christian Church, the Communion of Saints" was. "This communion of saints through belief must evidence itself also externally," and so much the more as Christianity since Constantine had also become "a matter of taste and fashion," and Christianity in name and name alone had grown mightily.

Then, after delimitation vis-à-vis the Roman Catholic Church, Thadden emphasized that it was impermissible that the Lutheran Church should have no more than its name from the church that was familiar from the New Testament. For that reason one must exhibit understanding "when the few believers find little or no comfort at all in public services, whereby the gatherings at issue do indeed acquire a meaning greater than they possess as mere household devotions."[52]

Thadden would hardly have been a Pietist had he not appended a personalized note. He asks:

> You fear also a detrimental influence upon the relationship of your Christian subjects to you? Surely it is quite painful to these, the best part of your villagers, to know you to be taking another path contrary to your own spiritual welfare, yes, to be in fact an adversary upon another path, and it would be for them the greatest joy if the highly respected person having dominion upon their estate lands would unite with them in the Lutheran faith too—not that they would by any means then demand that you participate in their gatherings. Accordingly you will under all circumstances have in these Christians the truest of subjects.[53]

Thadden ends the letter with sentences that outline the dangers in the gap between political fraternity (*Brüderlichkeit*) and Christian brotherhood (*Bruderschaft*) and that express the *nevertheless* of faith:

> While every kind of Jacobin intermixing of classes is a horror to me, I cannot and may not, by the power of divine command, surrender community with other Lutheran Christians, however insignificant, simple, low and despised they might be…, but will, according to grace and strength given by God, seek to maintain and promote such community.[54]

So the slogans of the French Revolution and the message of the New Testament did not mesh.

Of course, by taking this position Thadden landed in a veritable thicket separating the social classes. On the one hand he found himself opposite a majority of peers, for whom preservation of their feudal rights was more important than strengthening a community of awakened Christians. On the other he lived in a rural milieu that within portions of its population of farm people was increasingly characterized by the spirit of a movement demanding a living piety. In this, Eastern Pomerania distinguished itself clearly from Western Pomerania, the latter a part of Prussia only from 1815 on.[55]

Reservations about Thadden's attitude could be asserted not only from a social viewpoint but in a legal view as well, however. Thus, following his first visit to Trieglaff in 1821, the later president (chief justice) of the highest provincial court (*Oberlandesgerichtspräsident*) Ernst-Ludwig von Gerlach—close to the family as a friend—thoroughly understood the legal problems arising from preference for "converted" pastors by someone who could, as master of a manorial estate, offer the pastoral office at "his" church to a person of his choice. Certainly he left the estate by himself on Sunday to attend worship services at St. Elisabeth's (Figure 4), affiliated with the established church in Prussia, the Church of the Prussian Union.[56]

The conflict was exacerbated when it became necessary to select a successor to the local "rationalistic" clergyman, Winkelsesser, upon his death in 1825. Thadden now claimed his patronage rights and sought, with all the energy unique to his nature, to push through the appointment of a clergyman who was known for his antirationalistic attitude. This was Archdeacon Johann Heinrich Dummert at the Kammin cathedral. A case was being prosecuted against him for withholding communion from adherents of Union practice.[57]

But the established church, with backing from the government, now showed itself unwilling to go along with this. It dragged the decision out, tolerating a three-year vacancy in the hope that Thadden would yield. Beyond that, the government minister Altenstein intervened, greatly concerned about the general development of things in the districts of Greifenberg and Kammin. He informed the king, who then wrote to the provincial president, Sack, in Stettin, to express to him his "earnest displeasure" about the disturbance of church peace brought about by pietistic excesses. Thereupon the provincial government at Stettin notified the consistory that henceforth all gatherings for worship in homes were forbidden.[58]

Could resistance fail to stiffen in Trieglaff? In the matter of calling the archdeacon, the church officials did concede, so that Dummert was able to assume his office in 1828. But with respect to home devotions and assemblages of Christians in the Trieglaff manor, pressure intensified to the point that penalties were imposed, if, for example, prayer sessions overran curfew. Thadden reacted to this derisively. To the police station in Greifenberg he delivered, instead of the assessed five-Taler fine, a wether—a neutered ram.[59]

During the years when this "pietistic" Pastor Dummert discharged his office, then, the landed family's conflicts with the established church ceased, as the pastor himself frequently took part in the home worship gatherings. A new confrontation with the church developed, though, because Adolph von Thadden also began, as of 1829, to invite clergymen from the entire province to meetings that ran for several days. These earned a reputation under the name "Trieglaff Conferences" (Trieglaffer Konferenzen). Gradually pastors from the other provinces of Prussia began to attend these affairs too. They deliberated far-reaching questions about church life in the land. During the 1830s the participants often numbered more than 100 persons, so that it became necessary to erect a hall, as an addition, on the lake side of the manor house (Figure 5).[60]

At this point Trieglaff was no longer only a place of private family devotions, but also a place of quasi-public gatherings of people who were in large part also officeholders in the established church. So it is no wonder that the ecclesiastical bureaucracy took an interest in the meetings too, with the aim of gathering additional information. It was in Thadden's nature to seize the initiative in this situation, addressing himself to Ritschl,

Figure 5. The old manor house with the hall addition, from a drawing by Hildegard von Thadden

the Pomeranian bishop and general superintendent in Stettin, to lay out for him the purposes of his invitations to religious conferences.[61]

Following a thoroughgoing description of the items of deliberation, Thadden addressed the primary concerns of the conference participants, directly and without digressions. The issues were the problem of the amalgamated Church of the Prussian Union and the associated danger of persuaded Lutherans splitting from it. He laid out examples of persecution of dissenting pastors and laymen in Silesia, emphasizing that this increasingly disturbed Trieglaff's villagers as well:

> I am especially interested in the matter, since several of those who are tenants upon my estate are as of now still dissenters. Their withdrawal has grieved me, and I would regret it more painfully still if I were able to see in it actual and lasting separation.[62]

Here Thadden was also speaking as a patron exercising aristocratic privileges in his local church, someone who might see himself constrained "to give closer consideration to the legal basis." For him it was a question of principle with respect to "dealing with dissidents," and the use of discretionary judgment in the exercise of tolerance. Until that was clarified, "I hold it to be the duty of a loyal subject not to offer my hand in any way for carrying out clearly unjust orders."[63]

The Prussian conservative was thereby asserting for himself grounds of a right to resist. Such a claim was exceptional in the waning absolutistic state of Frederick William III.[64] So it was plausible for Bishop Ritschl to react with little sympathy, calling attention to the limits of what was tolerable in his letter of response.[65] After words of appreciation concerning the "good intentions" of the Trieglaff Conferences, he condemned their effects and said he must "rate gains for individuals far below losses experienced by the whole from it." The danger existed that

> the assembled do not content themselves with a simple exchange of opinions and ideas, but regard themselves as a sort of council, deliberate general church matters according to a specific order of business, passing resolutions by majority which often lie completely outside the domain of a gathering that has not been appointed, but has assembled casually.

Little more, he continued, and, "the proclamation to the Silesian Lutherans, with its reprimand from a royal councillor of the consistory, would have been carried out similarly in Trieglaff."[66]

Consistently, the letter closes with an explicit summons: "I therefore direct to Your Highborn Personage an earnest solicitation to give up these invitations on your own in future ... for the sake of church order and of brotherly concord." Thadden's answer was not in writing but expressed through action: he carried on with the conferences—on the correct assumption that nothing would come of it.

Something did come of it, however, but in a place that a reader of the exchanged letters would not have expected. Anxiety about "separation" had a very real background. For some years a mood to emigrate had arisen among unpropertied farm workers in the districts of Kammin and Greifenberg, people in whom hopes of free land in the United States had been aroused.[67] By no means last among these were those disappointed Lutherans of "true faith" who, not wishing to reconcile with the denominational union, were inclined toward a split with—"separation from"—the established church. These included some of the most loyal farm workers in Trieglaff, ones whom estate operations could scarcely dispense with. And where did this lead?

Here the U.S. sources reveal more than the German. That same Pastor Royal Natzke who facilitated contact with the family of the shepherd Wangerin has compiled a genealogically arranged family history. It clearly indicates that religious reasons were not insignificant in prompting his ancestors to emigrate from Pomerania to the United States. "They came," it states, "with other Lutherans who were fleeing their homeland to get away from the Prussian Union of 1817 which was forcing Lutheran and Reformed Christians to worship together." These Lutherans came to be called "Old Lutherans" (*Altlutheraner*) because they wanted to practice their faith as of old.[68]

In the text accompanying a viewing of "Pomeranian" graves in Wayside, Wisconsin, he brings this state of affairs, still alive in the memories of the family, explicitly to expression. He remarks with some pride that his ancestors were among the first Trieglaff families (four in total) to depart their old homeland in 1839. His great-great-grandfather, Johann Georg, had been a lead worker, a foreman (*Vorarbeiter*), on the estate in Trieglaff and earned his living with the Thaddens.[69]

But Royal Natzke did not restrict his studies to his own family history. He also took up a work that had to do with the former manorial master, publishing an English translation of a little volume about Adolph von Thadden,[70] in whose preface he went into greater detail concerning the background of the events of 1839. There he expressly mentioned the Trieglaff Conferences, where people at odds with the Prussian Union had found a hearing.[71] But for modern readers of the book, who might be amazed by the separation of the two social classes in Pomerania at the time, it was necessary to append an explanation:

> The owners and the workers ... lived in their own parts of town, ... married partners from their own class.... They did, however, worship in the

same church, and the von Thaddens are credited with looking after the welfare of their workers more than many of the other estate owners.[72]

Here the problem that taxed Adolph von Thadden so—of the two types of brotherhood, political and Christian—crops up again. In the memory of the American Trieglaffers, this problem is comprehensible, for the contradictions were set aside by the United States Constitution. But for those who remained behind in the homeland, resolving it seemed more and more urgent. A way had to be discovered in coming years.

Domestic problems at Trieglaff needed to be ironed out prior to that, however. Upon the death in 1829 of Adolph von Thadden's mother-in-law—the matron Henriette von Oertzen—the question of inheritance had to be taken up and decided. How would co-heirs be compensated? A solution was found that established that Adolph would remain in Trieglaff, while it was made possible for his younger brother-in-law, Viktor, to claim his inheritance as a neighbor on the adjacent estate of Ernst Senfft von Pilsach in Rottnow. Therewith, prerequisites for further development of the estate's operations were put in place, allowing sheep breeding to be expanded, among other things. Thadden would not be deterred from traveling as far as to Estonia to select rams, or from forming business contacts beyond the borders of the province.[73]

But how did this benefit the workers? They perhaps received somewhat higher pay now; emigration to the United States of those who were able to do so testifies to that. Yet they had scarcely any chance for upward movement or, above all, any possibility of acquiring land for themselves. This reinforced feelings of dependency among them, even if personally they were dealt with well. Hopes of making better progress and having land of their own beyond the ocean became fixed in their thinking.[74]

Adolph von Thadden sensed this growing unrest. In the end he saw no solution but to avoid hindering those with a will to emigrate, especially families with many children. When the Natzkes and Pritzlaffs set off in a large convoy in May 1839 to undertake a long, well-organized journey to Milwaukee via Hamburg, Liverpool, and New York, lasting an arduous four and one-half months, he accompanied them to the harbor on the Elbe River and wished them God's blessings.[75]

In Trieglaff too something came to an end in the next years. First came the happy marriage in 1844 of his oldest daughter, Marie, to the owner of the neighboring estate, Moritz von Blanckenburg in Kardemin, near Zimmerhausen. But wedding festivities in Trieglaff went awry, and the marriage entered history as "the fire-wedding" because a highly destructive fire was ignited by a fireworks display.[76] Then in 1846 the family was visited by a series of tragic deaths. First the thirteen-year-old youngest son,

Adolph, died of a pernicious fever, having infected his mother, Henriette, who died shortly thereafter. Lastly, death stole Marie away too. She had become the mother of a little daughter herself at Kardemin, but she cared for her own mother in Trieglaff. Suddenly the house was empty.[77]

Just how empty it was is better understood as one comes to know more about the women around Thadden. First, there was the mother, Henriette, who, true to the understanding of that role at the time, held the large family together as the affectionate wife of the father Adolph and at the same time a partner whose knowledge extended even to matters of business and finance. An empathetic and provident mother to her children, she was alert to their spiritual and intellectual upbringing. Lastly, as the mistress of the manor and the estate she concerned herself with the well-being of the people of the village.

It is evident from her letters that she counterbalanced the generous nature of her husband. Thus, regarding the ill-fated conflagration, her focus was the economic consequences for the family, whereas for him its consequences for day laborers and farmers were the primary concern.[78] The family sustained damages totaling 30,000 Taler and carried the debt to the end of the century. Looking back upon her life, the judgment of her brother-in-law Ernst-Ludwig von Gerlach surely applies. In her obituary he lauds "the bright, energetic incisiveness of her character."[79]

Unlike her, and more similar to her father than to her mother, was Marie von Thadden (Figure 6), married to Moritz von Blanckenburg. Marie was, according to every report and testimony, a woman of pervasive vitality and sensitive spirit. Her personality, rooted in Christian faith, also experienced the forces of doubt and inner onslaught. She was exceptionally sociable, read lofty literature, and wrote letters abounding in empathy and intellectual richness. In keeping with this, she shared these moving words with her brother Reinhold a few months before her unforeseen death:

> The bright spring sun ... awakens my oldest, most yearning thoughts and dreams about journeys and beautiful lands, about beauty, riches, perfection—in nature or in human spirit, anywhere—to find them just anywhere! ... Yes, Reinhold, back then I read Jean Paul's *Titan* and fell into such a swoon that lasted several years and caused me to be so readily wounded by every touch of ordinary life that I could have just crawled off by myself. The night hours in my drafty little green room were just my favorites, when I could have cried a lakeful about all those ideal heroes who in fact don't have enough vital force in them to survive reality.[80]

Somewhere between that small drafty room and Jean Paul's *Titan*, Marie lived with her sentiment-based thoughts and imaginings. She required the wide world of literature to get out of the cramped world of Trieglaff.

As she wrote to a friend in Stettin in the year of her marriage: "I feel what is lacking oppressively after a person has been cooped up like this in Pomerania, toasting behind the stove. The horizon closes in—you bump into something everywhere then eventually, when you ought to be replanted elsewhere."[81] And a year later she wrote, to her friend Johanna von Puttkamer, "I find that one becomes unnoticeably so narrow in one's regular homebound cycle of ideas that she should be heartily happy to become acquainted with exotic rarities and points of view."[82]

This interest in other worlds reached far. With an openness to non-conservative-leaning literature that was exceptional for the circumstances

Figure 6. Marie von Blanckenburg, née von Thadden (1821–1846), friend of Otto von Bismarck

of the Pomeranian landed nobility, she directed her attention to the early French socialist Louis Blanc, who had excited notice with his *The Organization of Labor* (*L'organisation du travail*) because he wanted to eliminate the defects of capitalistic social organization through government-assisted formation of worker production units.[83] In the quoted letter to her brother Reinhold, she wrote:

> Louis Blanc has penetrated this far. If only we could get him in French; it is truly an enchanting language. Isn't Mr. Bodinus[84] just totally carried away with delight about it now, for him liberal sentiments have to be arising from within his soul as well?[85]

Against this backdrop it is not astonishing that Marie, in another letter, this time to her fiancé Moritz von Blanckenburg, evinces a tendency capable of leading into areas of complexity. Several months before her marriage, she wrote in sheer innocence: "I don't know what's going on with me. Interesting people attract me violently, so that I can't help myself, yet my whole heart holds back from loving them, yes, even from getting closer to them."[86] Not least of these "interesting people" was Otto von Bismarck, whose whole future still beckoned. A neighboring estate owner at Kniephof, 10 km distant from Trieglaff, he sought an opportunity to learn to know this charming young woman. And he found one, although Marie was already committed.[87]

The story of the reciprocal fascination between Marie von Thadden and Otto von Bismarck has been told many times; it is to be found in every biography of Bismarck.[88] Most interesting within the context of this history of Trieglaff is the place it held in the everyday world and the memories of the von Thadden family. But this belongs as much to the story of the second generation as to that of the patriarch of Pomeranian Pietism, now advancing in years.

Notes

1. Cf. on this Werner Buchholz, ed., *Pommern* (Berlin, 1999), 365–522, in the series *Deutsche Geschichte im Osten Europas*.

2. Ibid., 360. Further, Rudolf von Thadden, "Aus der Wirklichkeit gefallen. Der 8. Mai 1945 jenseits von Oder und Neiße," in *Erinnerung und Geschichte. 60 Jahre nach dem 8. Mai 1945*, ed. Rudolf von Thadden and Steffen Kaudelka (Göttingen, 2006), 72ff.

3. Theodor Fontane, *Before the Storm*, trans. R. J. Hollingdale (Oxford, 1985), 25. To make tensions even more vivid, Fontane personifies aggressive Jacobin France in the figure of a captain "with an olive complexion and a thin, pointed beard" who behaves indecently toward the "lady of the house," a beauty of Huguenot extraction who cannot endure the conflict and succumbs to nervous excitement, ibid., 24.

4. See Reinold von Thadden-Trieglaff, *Heinrich v. Oertzen auf Trieglaff* (Greifenberg, 1932), 23f.

5. Ibid., 25, 26, letters of 3 February 1808 and 10 December 1808.

6. Ibid., 46f., last letter of Heinrich preceding his death on 18 October 1813.

7. Cf. Ernst R. Huber, *Deutsche Verfassungsgeschichte seit 1789*, 2nd ed. (Stuttgart, 1967), 1: 183ff. and 193ff. Further, R. Koselleck, *Preußen zwischen Reform und Revolution* (Stuttgart, 1967), 487ff.

8. Cf. Patrick Wagner, *Bauern, Junker und Beamte* (Göttingen, 2005), 49f., 55, 546.

9. Cf. the foreword by Natzke to Wolfgang Marzahn, *The Nobleman Among the Brothers*, ed. Royal Natzke, trans. Alma Ihlenfeldt (Bloomington, IN, 2006), vff. (In German, *Der Edelmann unter den Brüdern* [Lahr-Dinglingen, 1978].) There too, a glossary of the most important sociological concepts.

10. Polish pamphlet on Trzygłów/Trieglaff from the year 2004, in the carton *Nachkriegszeit* [postwar period], family archives (hereafter FA).

11. Berner, "Thadden-Trieglaff (Adolf)," in *Allgemeine deutsche Biographie* (hereafter *ADB*) 37: 634f. (He himself spelled his name with *ph*). Available online at http://www.deutsche-biographie.de/pnd131898973.html.

12. Report on how business at Trieglaff stood on 1 July 1820. This manuscript account found its way circuitously after the war from Vahnerow, turned Polish, to Göttingen in Germany, FA.

13. Cf. Huber, *Verfassungsgeschichte*, 1:194ff.

14. Wilhelm Treue, "Wirtschafts- und Sozialgeschichte Deutschlands im 19. Jahrhundert," in Bruno Gebhardt, *Handbuch der deutschen Geschichte*, 8th ed., ed. Herbert Grundmann (Stuttgart, 1960), 3: 320f., 325f. [Search *Gebhardt Handbuch der deutschen Geschichte*.]

15. Carl Leisewitz, "Thaer (Albrecht Daniel)," in *ADB*, 37: 636ff.

16. Adolph von Thadden, "Bericht über die Trieglaffesche Wirthschaft" [Report on Trieglaff business], p. 4, FA. Cultivation of clover ranks among the most important innovations in German agriculture from the time of Albrecht Thaer. Subsequently, fallowing and pasturing of cows were pushed out, and the latter was replaced by bunk feeding during the summer. Within the framework of three-crop rotation, now also improved, production of good feed increased manure quantity, allowing the farmer to plant more grain. Cf. on this Heinz Haushofer, *Die deutsche Landwirtschaft im technischen Zeitalter*, vol. 5 of *Die Deutsche Agrargeschichte*, 44f.

17. Von Thadden, "Bericht," 1f. In the ensuing years, Thadden would found his success in agriculture upon sheep raising.

18. Adolph von Thadden, "Über Menschenschau unter Landwirthen," reprinted in Elonore Fürstin Reuß, *Adolf von Thadden-Trieglaff. Ein Lebensbild*, 2nd ed. (Berlin, 1894), 220ff.

19. Adolph von Thadden, "Schacher mit Rittergütern," in Reuß, *Adolf von Thadden*, 246ff.

20. Ibid., 253.

21. Ibid., 253f.

22. Leopold Witte, "Karl Witte," *ADB*, 43: 595ff. Available online at http://www.deutsche-biographie.de/pnd118769596.html.

23. A. von Thadden, "Schacher mit Rittergütern," 248f.

24. Ibid., 3.

25. Still pertinent, Reinhold Cramer, *Geschichte der Lande Lauenburg und Bütow* (Königsberg, 1858) 1: 163ff., 246ff. Further, Friedrich Lorentz, *Geschichte der Kaschuben* (Berlin, 1926), 92ff.

26. Wojciech Kostus, *Wladztwo Polski nad Leborkiem i Bytowem* [Polish rule in Lauenburg and Bütow] (Wrocław, 1954), 100ff.

27. Cf. Rudolf v. Thadden, "Die Geschichte der Kirchen und Konfessionen," in *Handbuch der preußischen Geschichte*, ed. Wolfgang Neugebauer (Berlin, 2001), 3: 564.

28. See Hans Friedrich von Ehrenkrook, "Die Familie von Thadden," in *Genealogisches Handbuch des Adels*, vol. 11, *Adlige Häuser*, A II, 401ff.

29. Cf. Reuß, *Adolf von Thadden*, 8.

30. Ibid., 12f.

31. Personal recollection of the author and remarks in Reuß, *Adolf von Thadden*, 12f.

32. In the carton for Adolph v. Thadden, FA. Additionally, excerpts in Hermann Petrich, *Adolf und Henriette von Thadden und ihr Trieglaffer Kreis* (Stettin, 1931), 18f.

33. Cf. Petrich, *Adolf und Henriette,* 16. On the brothers Leopold and Ernst-Ludwig von Gerlach see articles by Julius Hartmann (Leopold) and Karl Wippermann (Ernst-Ludwig) in *ADB* 9: 16ff., 9ff., and those by Hans-Joachim Schoeps in *Neue Deutsche Biographie (NDB)* 6: 294f., 296ff., www.deutsche-biographie.de/pnd.

34. On kinship relationships see "Reinhold v. Thadden-Trieglaff, Ihr Leben [Henriette], ein Erinnerungsblatt," reprinted in the appendix to Petrich, *Adolf und Henriette,* 3ff.

35. Ibid., 7, n. 1.

36. Marriage on 30 September 1820 by Pastor Johann Jänicke in the Bohemian Bethlehemskirche in Berlin, ibid., 22 and appendix, 6, n. 3.

37. Cf. Erich Beyreuther, "Die Erweckungsbewegung," in *Die Kirche in ihrer Geschichte* (Göttingen, 1972), 4, ser. 1: 33ff.

38. Cf. Hermann Theodor Wangemann, *Sieben Bücher preußischer Kirchengeschichte* (Berlin, 1860), 3: 66ff., 96ff.

39. Cited in Petrich, *Adolf und Henriette,* 3.

40. Ibid., 36.

41. §§ 418 and 419 regulated pastoral jurisdiction (Pfarrzwang). Accordingly, "Those belonging to a [parish with its] pastor could not have their marriages, baptisms and funerals conducted by any other than the pastor assigned to the parish," in Ernst R. and Wolfgang Huber, *Staat und Kirche im 19. und 20. Jahrhundert,* vol. 1, *Staat und Kirche vom Ausgang des alten Reichs bis zum Vorabend der bürgerlichen Revolution,* 2nd ed. (Berlin, 1990), 10.

42. Rudolf A. Wangerin, *The Family Wangerin* (private printing, 1975), 30f., FA.

43. Cf. Lieselotte Clemens, *Die Auswanderung der pommerschen Altlutheraner* (Hamburg, 1976), 33ff.

44. Obviously the writer of the family history, R. A. Wangerin, found and made a photo of the letter in the state archives of Stettin on his journey to Pomerania in the year 1938—with assistance, perhaps, from H. Petrich. There is hardly another way to understand how a copy of the handwritten original of it exists in Wisconsin.

45. Wangerin, *Family Wangerin,* 29.

46. Cf. on this Clemens, *Auswanderung,* 50ff.

47. Wangerin, *Family Wangerin,* 2f.

48. Reinhold v. Thadden, *Auf verlorenem Posten?* (Tübingen, 1948), 34.

49. Ibid., 99.

50. Letter of 9 March 1821 by H. v. d. Marwitz, cited from Petrich, *Adolf und Henriette,* 47f.

51. Letter by Thadden, 23 March 1821, cited from Petrich, *Adolf und Henriette,* 48f.

52. Ibid., 49.

53. Ibid.

54. Ibid., 49f. Cf also Hellmuth Heyden, *Kirchengeschichte Pommerns,* 2nd ed. (Cologne, 1957), 2: 184.

55. Petrich calls attention also to the sociocultural distinctions between Eastern Pomerania and Mecklenburg, *Adolf und Henriette,* 50ff.

56. See Jakob v. Gerlach, ed., *E.-L. v. Gerlach. Aufzeichnungen* (Schwerin, 1903), 1: 131.

57. Petrich, *Adolf und Henriette*, 37f.

58. Ibid., 41. Cf. Also Ernst Engelberg, *Bismarck* (Berlin, 1985), 187ff.

59. Petrich, *Adolf und Henriette*, 42; Reuß, *Adolf von Thadden*, 41.

60. See Petrich, *Adolf und Henriette*, 57ff. Further, E. Engelberg, *Bismarck*, 189f.

61. Letter of 22 November 1838 to Bishop Ritschl, reprinted in Reuß, *Adolf von Thadden*, 169ff.

62. Ibid., 174.

63. Ibid., 174f.

64. Cf. Rudolf v. Thadden, "Geschichte der Kirchen," 584f.

65. Ritschl's letter of 2 February 1839, reprinted in Reuß, *Adolf von Thadden*, 177ff.

66. Ibid., 179.

67. Cf. Clemens, *Auswanderung*, 75ff.

68. Royal Natzke, *The John George Natzke Family* (private printing, 1979), 4, FA. An important collection of sources on the German emigration is found in Wolfgang Helbich et al., eds., *Briefe aus Amerika. Deutsche Auswanderer schreiben aus der neuen Welt. 1830–1930* (Munich, 1988), 11 ff.; for an expanded Eng. trans., *News from the Land of Freedom: German Immigrants Write Home*, ed. Walter D. Kamphoefner et al, trans. Susan Carter Vogel (Ithaca, 1991).

69. "Trieglaffer Family Cemetery Walk," (Wayside, WI: private printing, 2008), FA.

70. Marzahn, *The Nobleman Among the Brothers*, v.

71. Ibid., v.

72. Ibid., vii.

73. Reuß, *Adolf von Thadden*, 42. The matron Frau von Oertzen was born von Mellin.

74. Arthur L. Rabenhorst, *Family Lines*, Part 1: "Our German Roots" (Private printing, 2008), 19.

75. Ibid., 22ff.

76. It is reported about the "fire wedding" that the shepherd Friedrich Wangerin replied, to a question concerning his personal losses, "Everything burned up, not a sheep lost though." Adolph von Thadden thereupon presented him with an engraved golden watch. See Reuß, *Adolf von Thadden*, 69.

77. See Petrich, *Adolf und Henriette*, 67ff. Further, Reuß, *Adolf von Thadden*, 68ff., 80ff.

78. Letters of Henriette von Thadden, as well as "Erinnerungsblatt" [memorial page] by her son Reinhold von Thadden, in the carton for Adolph von Thadden, FA.

79. Obituary by Ernst-Ludwig von Gerlach for Henriette von Thadden née von Oertzen, in the carton for Adolph von Thadden, FA. Reprinted also in Petrich, *Adolf und Henriette*, appendix, 10ff.

80. Undated letter by Marie to her brother Reinhold from spring 1846, in the carton for Adolph von Thadden, FA. Excerpted also in Petrich, *Adolf und Henriette*, appendix, 29.

81. In the carton for Adolph von Thadden, FA. Excerpts also in Reuß, *Adolf von Thadden*, 62f.

82. Letter of July 1845, by Marie, excerpted in E. Engelberg, *Bismarck*, 201.

83. Louis Blanc, *L'organisation du travail* (Paris, 1839).

84. This obviously refers to a fellow student of Reinhold's.

85. Letter from Marie to her brother Reinhold, spring 1846, in the carton for Adolph von Thadden, FA.

86. Letter of 23 February 1844 from Marie to Moritz von Blanckenburg, excerpts in Petrich, *Adolf und Henriette*, 32.

87. See Waltraut Engelberg, *Otto und Johanna von Bismarck* (Berlin, 1990), 16ff.

88. On this see especially the exposition by E. Engelberg, *Bismarck*, 192ff., and the more recent and very worthwhile Eberhard Kolb, *Bismarck* (Munich, 2009), above all 15ff.

Chapter 2

Bismarck's Generation

Prussia Becomes Germany

Invariably present already, hidden within the old, are the roots of the new. As able and industrious farm workers from Trieglaff set out toward the United States and many of the lights in the manor house went out, a new age was dawning in Prussia: the age of industrialization and technological progress. Pomeranian industrial development was lackluster compared to that in Silesia or the western regions of Prussia, but this agrarian province on the Baltic nevertheless felt the impact of the numerous varieties of modernization. The invention of telegraphy, the steam engine, and finally the railroad changed everyday life, even here.[1]

Given the great distances in the Prussian east, the modernization of the prevailing systems of travel and transportation attracted significant attention. Whereas postal coach was arguably the region's most important means of transportation until the mid-nineteenth century, railroads were now making progress as well. And mail service expanded considerably, with added letter and package delivery. In 1849 it cost no more than three Silbergroschen (one-thirtieth of a Taler, some two and one-half cents) to send a letter to any destination in Prussia. The first Prussian stamps appeared in 1850.[2]

It is revealing that in the Trieglaff library there was to be found a work, published in 1859, that set standards in the history of mail service. It is a history of the Prussian mails from their origins up to that time, authored by Heinrich Stephan, later the general director of mails.[3] This talented, creative organizer—originally from East Pomeranian Stolp, we may note—who would invent the postcard and inaugurate the Universal Postal Union, based his interest in the topic on far-reaching thinking:

> Powered movement is effecting an all-encompassing transformation of world transportation. Our steamships carry the products of all the five parts of the world across oceans which appeared to those of long ago so measureless and impassable that they took them to be the limits of the universe.... A single one of our locomotives can transport entire burdens of Levantine caravans to their destination with ease and the speed of flight.

Then follows the philosophy that gives the author wings:

> What timesaving, and what a wealth of exchange of goods and ideas, what a vital element of broadened education and peaceful rapprochement between nations!... No longer does distance hinder instantaneous transmission of thought, for electric current carries it through the expanses of the deserts and the depths of the sea.[4]

Effects of these ideas that were revolutionizing the world reached Trieglaff as well. But their impact is measurable in its entirety only when the ideas are transposed to the actual conditions of life in the little village. As late as the early 1840s, a trip to Stettin or to Berlin, 220 km distant, was still burdensome and time-consuming. The only means of long-distance transportation was the mail coach with its repeated exchange of horses, and roads were generally in bad condition. Since the days of the Great Elector Frederick William of Brandenburg (1620–1688), the extensive province of Pomerania had basically only one route plus half of another:

> Whereas the Brandenburg mounted mail still always made its way via Stargard, Cörlin, Cöslin, Stolp, Wutzkow to Danzig, wheeled delivery was rerouted from Stargard through Greifenberg and Colberg in order to promote travel to these places. At the same time many delays took place along this route on account of the poor roads.[5]

In any case, then, a postal station lay seven kilometers from Trieglaff in the district seat of Greifenberg. From there one could travel twice per week to the provincial capital Stettin. A trip to Berlin required at least two overnights. But all that changed with the laying of railroad tracks. After the first Prussian stretch of railroad was opened in 1838 from Potsdam to Berlin, completion of the leg from Berlin to Stettin followed in 1843. This was extended in 1846 to Stargard. Greifenberg was not connected by rail until 1882.[6]

Under these circumstances, if Trieglaffers wanted to travel to Berlin in the event-filled years before and during the 1848 Revolution, it was necessary for them to go to Stettin by mail coach, or else in their own horse-drawn wagon. From Stettin they took one of the trains drawn by steam locomotive into the Prussian capital, saving themselves one day of travel time.

Skeptical and disapproving statements about the development of railroads have come down to us from many conservatives of the time, yet none from Adolph von Thadden, who readily employed modern means of transportation. He had good cause to do so, as he frequently had to make his way to important meetings within and outside the province.

In 1846, Thadden was appointed to the newly formed Generalsynode church convention, an institution of the Landeskirche (formally established church of Prussia). It regularly demanded his presence in Berlin and was of some importance, for King Frederick William IV personally wanted it. What distinguished this institution above all was that it embraced all Prussia, being made up of seventy-five members from all provinces, from Königsberg to Aachen. In that year it brought together recognized personalities from the church life of the entire Prussian state for a period of three months.[7]

Apart from the convention's meaning for church politics, its organization was a respectable achievement. How could the general synod have come into being without the technological potential offered by rail travel? How would the deliberations have proceeded without the improved communications of a postal system? For Prussia, a state covering quite a large area, these were not insignificant questions.

For Thadden, however, other, more important things played a role. For the first time in Prussian history, a synod was taking in lay members of the church. The seventy-five attendees were to be half clergy and church officials, and half laymen, and hence would represent more than the customary august delegation from church government. This innovation was not something Pomeranians were looking for.[8]

At this general synod, which itself was out of the ordinary in Lutheran terms, Thadden criticized the church in a speech that resonated vibrantly in the press. He not only attacked the clerical ambitions of many clergymen, but also denounced the system of a state church: "The hierarchy can assert itself because clerics, as clerics, serve the state, and thereby rule in the parish. Merely by virtue of their being servants of the state they must rule, whether or not they might wish to."[9]

The speech amplified his critique with a sentence that was beyond belief for a Pomeranian landed aristocrat: "There is nothing in this wide world more hideous than an imperious priestly caste." And further: "A hierarchy is rising on the church horizon that wants to rule without serving." That was not just pietistic congregation-theology, but a step along the road to separation of church and state.[10]

As though he had foreknowledge of Thadden's confrontation of the official state church (Staatskirche) and the bureaucracy of the institutional church (Amtskirche), Thadden's brother-in-law Ernst-Ludwig von Gerlach, one of his oldest friends from their time in Berlin following the wars of liberation, wrote him in a worried tone in advance of the convening of the synod:

> You understand better than I what the position that you have held till now entails and permits. It's tinged with Pietism, separatism, of the best sort. I am your pupil in that. Now, I regard the position itself as inadequate for a representative member. I miss in it progress toward evangelical churchdom.... What it comes down to for me ... is that the synod not cover up the true condition of the church with its division and disorder, but bring that into clearest evidence.[11]

With these words an episcopal-minded "high church" person has addressed a nonconformist "low church" Christian whose priority is congregational worship. The spirit of the awakening movement inspires both. Indifferent to this distinction, however, the synod took a course no one had foreseen by making demands consistent with the synod's liberal tendencies and pushing for reform of the church constitution by way of: introduction of the principle of elections throughout, stepwise from the presbyteries through to the general synod; recognition of periodicity for all synodal meetings; pervasive expansion of synodal jurisdiction vis-à-vis the consistories; and establishment of a high consistory as an ecclesiastical counterpoise to the government's Ministry of Culture. It reeked of parliamentarianism.[13]

The results were unsurprising. The vacillating king ultimately thought it best to dispense with the resolutions of the conference, disappointing eager expectations and thereby contributing in addition to political destabilization in advance of the convocation of a far more important assembly slated for the year 1847, namely, the Vereinigter Landtag (unified parliament) of all the Prussian provinces.[14]

Adolph von Thadden was summoned to membership in this assembly as well, what is more together with a total of ten lay members from the general synod, so that a bridge was established between the two bodies. At this point there entered a personality who contributed a political weight unique in its character—Otto von Bismarck, from Schönhausen (Figure 7).[15]

Regarding the beginnings of Bismarck's political career, it should not be forgotten that only a short time before he had taken a step that was to have significant meaning for his whole future. He became engaged to, and then married, Johanna von Puttkamer, whose roots were in the world

Figure 7. Otto von Bismarck (1815–1898) in early Pomeranian years

of Pomeranian Pietism. Bismarck had met the person who would be his companion through life at the "fire wedding" of Marie von Thadden and Moritz von Blanckenburg, and chosen her as his partner after the death of Marie, whom he had regarded so highly. With that, a portion of the pietistic world of Pomerania became part of the reality of Bismarck's existence.[16]

In a letter that has since become quite well known, he vividly described how deeply the spirit that lived in this Trieglaff home had stirred him at the time. The letter was written to ask Heinrich von Puttkamer, Bismarck's future father-in-law, for the hand of his daughter. Bismarck had found people there, the letter reads, whose profound faith caused him to feel shame for "the meager light of my reason." In Marie, "who became precious to me as ever a sister was to her brother, I had a feeling of well-being such as had, until then, been unfamiliar to me, a family life that took me in, nearly a home."[17]

Marie's untimely death was a crucial experience for Bismarck:

> The stirrings within me came to life when, at the news of the fatal illness of our late friend, the first spontaneous prayer, without dwelling upon its good sense, burst forth from my heart, entwined with cutting hurt over my own unworthiness to pray, and with tears such as were unknown to me since the days of my childhood. God did not hear my prayer at that time, but he did not repudiate it either, for I never again lost the capacity to plead with Him.[18]

These lines have found a permanent place in memory, that of the von Thadden family as well as of pietistic circles in Pomerania. For anyone who found it important to demonstrate that the later imperial chancellor had Christian orientations, these confession-like statements served as reference, and it was claimed that they were anchored in faith-oriented traditions.[19]

It is cause for reflection too that current writings in the Marxist tradition are taking up the matter of Bismarck's faith and finding words that acknowledge it, to a degree. Thus Waltraut Engelberg calls the suitor's letter "a masterpiece" and emphasizes that everything is "written in canny anticipation that he did wish to associate himself with pietistic circles for the time being, but did not want to tie himself to them in principle."[20]

Given these judgments, one might ask how Bismarck's relationship to the Christian faith was seen by the "pietistic folks" themselves in his Trieglaff circle of friends. In this, Marie's judgment ought not rank last in meriting attention. As late as 1845, she had lamented in a letter:

> To see a human who suffers so beneath the chill of unbelief as Otto von Bismarck elicits a kind of melancholy, in the face of which hours and days long one might speak about all the sacred, great truths and still not possibly be able to impart to a pitiable, hardened heart even a drop of the peace that comes from faith; that is deeply painful. He has complaints in plenty, anguish over his own and the world's misery, longing for peace, but yet he cannot and will not believe.[21]

So Bismarck's confession of faith in his letter requesting Johanna von Puttkamer's hand cannot be read altogether impartially. Perhaps it must have met with reservations in the house of his future parents-in-law.

But how was Bismarck's relationship with the Christian faith articulated at the Vereinigter Landtag? Opportunity arose in the debate about emancipation of Jews that flared between liberals and conservatives, excited by a royal decree.[22] Whereas Thadden again advanced theological reasoning and set conversion of the Jews to Christianity as precondition for emancipation,[23] Bismarck argued politically, invoking the Christian foundations of the European states. He no longer expressed himself—as he had done a year earlier—as favoring separation of state and church, but he defended the historically developed structures in concrete terms, noting that in larger cities, the Jewish component consisted "almost entirely of respectable people." In the country too they had a place as "more than just the exception." There, though, acceptance of Jews had not yet reached the point where regulation of equality by law could soon be undertaken. That is, no dogmatism, please—and certainly not on the basis of liberal ideas of equality.[24]

Bismarck's future "realpolitik" manifested itself even more incisively in the debate over a loan for railroads to the East. At issue here was approval of funds to finance the urgently needed rail connection to East Prussia, a great distance from Berlin. Without national support it was not to be realized. In characteristic manner, he argued in the direction of state interests, against the liberals, who disapproved of the loan for the eastern line as a matter of principle on constitutional grounds. Bismarck found himself in harmony with the demands of historical developments and settled for a defeat in the Vereinigter Landtag.[25]

About Adolph von Thadden, we know only that he admired Bismarck for his rhetorical facility. He wrote candidly to Ernst-Ludwig Gerlach: "I'm not going to put myself up against Bismarck, who said really superb things again in the recent sessions."[26] Adolph took no position substantively, though. Much rather, one senses that big-time politics was not for him. He felt more at home in the Generalsynode than in the Vereinigter Landtag.

After the close of deliberations at the end of June he returned to his solitary Trieglaff. There he encountered a well-functioning agricultural concern, to be sure, but now there were also distinctly articulated wants being experienced by workers on the land, and farmers who were suffering the consequences of poor harvests and inflation. These were prompting intensified demands for abolition of remaining feudal obligations in fee and in kind, and in services rendered to the "lord" of the estate, to the degree that these were still in force after the Stein-Hardenberg Reforms. Meanwhile, landless farm workers were for the first time voicing demands for participation in land ownership.[27]

In spring 1847 Bismarck reported on outright disturbances in Pomerania. In a letter to his fiancée, he wrote from Kniephof of alarming happenings he had experienced on his trip:

> In Cöslin there was rioting, still after 12 its streets so packed full that we passed with difficulty and only under the protection of a detachment of the local militia (*Landwehr*) that was ordered in. Bakers and butchers were plundered, 3 houses of grain dealers ruined, clinking of glass, etc. I wish I could have stayed.[28]

There was no comparable unrest in Trieglaff. It was the case, however, that interest in emigration to the United States was once again on the rise, especially because noteworthy population growth after the 1820s sharpened desires for ownership of land and higher wages. Reports received from U.S. émigré families attest that these motives now played a greater role than religious distress had for the first generation of emigrants.[29]

Notwithstanding these storm clouds on the horizon of political and social change, no one in Trieglaff had any premonition that Prussia verged on a European revolution. The one domain where a certain danger was sensed was estate holders' patrimonial jurisdiction, which could become unsustainable without reform. At the time, a landed aristocrat still had police powers and was patrimonial juridical master throughout his estate, even though economic developments had begun to dissolve feudal structures.[30]

Since Trieglaff was a manorial estate, its owner presided as magistrate over not only civil matters but also lesser criminal cases. Hence the Thaddens were judicially responsible for documentation of contracts, recording of testaments, and matters of guardianship, as well as for misdemeanors. Capital crimes had been handled by royal courts since the early eighteenth century.[31]

Such legal questions thus were not immaterial to Adolph von Thadden. Back in 1837 he had complained, in the address at Regenwalde entitled "Human Concern for People by Landholders," of "how frivolously many estate owners think about their modest sovereign rights as masters over inheritance, legalities, and policing," and "how they misjudge their positions of authority for administering law and justice upon their subjects." In good feudal tradition, then, any state intervention in lower levels of social life was suspect.[32]

A number of estate owners certainly recognized the need for correction of the old order. Bismarck himself was one of the none too numerous conservatives who participated in the reform discussion. But ultimately it was the revolutionary movement of 1848 that led to change and suspended the archaic patrimonial jurisdiction exercised by estate masters.[33]

The Revolution of 1848—"*die 48er-Revolution,*" as it was soon generally called—did not merely suspend feudal order in rural justice but shook the foundations of feudalism as a whole.[34] Beyond that, it had a thoroughly European character and altered political and social conditions in every country on the continent.[35] City and country were affected in equal measure.

The Revolution reached Trieglaff in late March, when the king decided to summon the Vereinigter Landtag once again. He needed this body, structured thoroughly on the basis of class, to initiate an election law for the elections he had mandated for a Prussian National Assembly (Preußische Nationalversammlung), which was to produce a constitution. He did not wish to impose the law himself.[36]

Adolph von Thadden participated once again in this Vereinigter Landtag, which convened on 2 April in Berlin. But this time he came forward with a position that resonated vigorously across the country. Specifically, he cast an isolated vote, without regard to circumstances, against a declaration by parliament in which it acknowledged itself "thankful" for the assurances that the king gave to accompany the announcement that he was changing Prussia from monarchy to constitutional monarchy. Thadden's reasoning went:

> I must declare myself opposed to the law pertaining to elections, because it suspends and completely overturns the basic principle of our constitution. I protest against any new election law that departs from the principle of our two church curiae and division into three classes, albeit truly, I am not closed to further organic development of our constitution.[37]

So Thadden regarded it as appropriate, unlike an almost unanimous majority of the members of the parliament and of his class peers above all, to swim against the current of the time and hold fast to a position that really could no longer prevail. When even the king, no less, was prepared to face the facts of the revolutionary realities, Thadden rejected every compromise with the new law, thereby distinguishing himself also from Bismarck, who did accept the program contained in the king's "announcement"—though granted, "not voluntarily, but driven by the pressure of circumstances."[38]

Bismarck defended his position of the time retrospectively by going back to a newspaper article he had published following the second Vereinigter Landtag. Titled "From the Altmark," it emphasized that "the landed aristocrats, like all other reasonable people, tell themselves that it would be senseless and impossible to want to hold back or dam up the flow of time." And, he added, "No less than the ultraconservative Herr von Thadden compared the kind of person who battles for the past with the knight errant who duels windmills and whose bones are broken by its vanes."[39]

How, then, should Adolph von Thadden be judged at this time? Placing him historically in the spring of 1848, with his uncompromising attitude, requires more than labeling him a notorious loner or an anachronistic dissenter. Much better would be to aim to distinguish the character of a revolution from that of a reform, and feel an obligation to ask to what extent revolutionary events necessarily elicit reactions that differ from those of reform movements. If it is true that revolutions of necessity polarize, then this has consequences for parties on both sides of the barricades. In such situations, pragmatic attitudes have a harder time of it than such as are guided by principle.

Nevertheless, this insight is inadequate by itself to explain Thadden's attitude definitively. As a conservative Christian by conviction, he doubtless had principles. That by no means made him a slave to principle. Such a characterization fit a third conservative in the fellowship to a significantly greater degree, one of the individuals who had been among the first to belong to the Trieglaff circle of friends, namely, Ernst-Ludwig von Gerlach, president of the highest provincial court (*Oberlandesgerichtspräsident*). He was an opponent of the revolution and of the introduction of a constitutional monarchy associated with it. He had, in addition, firm ideas about Christian states that left little room for divergent opinion. For him, the state had an irrevocable relationship with the Biblical Kingdom of God.[40]

So it is no wonder that Gerlach already took offense at Thadden's speeches at this Vereinigter Landtag, but above all at Bismarck's, and demanded greater adherence to principle. In a personal letter to Thadden he wrote, schoolmaster-like:

> With your comments you chill the thousands and thousands of hearts that look to you. … Do not think … about the mood of the meeting, but confess simply and emphatically (yes, yes! no, no!) those great truths entrusted to you.[41]

Apparent here is a position going far beyond the class-bound reactions of Thadden and Bismarck. It disregards the altered nature of the times politically and as an outcome ultimately demands ushering in of a counterrevolution. This was not to consist merely of action to restrain the revolution, however; it was also to establish the state of affairs characterized, in the then oft-quoted words of the great French traditionalist Joseph de Maistre, as "the opposite of revolution." "Le rétablissement de la monarchie, qu'on appelle contre-révolution," as it is worded in de Maistre's *Considérations sur la France*, "ne sera point une révolution contraire, mais le contraire de la revolution."[42] (Reestablishment of the monarchy, termed a counterrevolution, would not have been a matter of a countering revolution, but the converse of the revolution.)

A telling absence in the debate among conservative spokesmen was the voice of a significant political thinker from the homeland of revolution, Count Alexis de Tocqueville.[43] For his epochal work *Democracy in America* alone he deserved some attention in Trieglaff, occupied with issues of emigration as it was. Within it is to be read perhaps the most profound analysis there is of the motives for change in the world—not just in Europe—since the onset of the modern era.

A passage in the introduction to this work, which appeared in 1835, reads:

> A great democratic revolution is taking place in the midst of us, everyone sees it; but all do not judge it in the same way. Some hold it to be something new, and seeing it as accidental, they have hopes of still being able to thwart it. To others by contrast it appears irresistible, because they take it to be the most constant, oldest and most enduring feature of history.[44]

This analysis, then, is not primarily concerned with the historical phenomenon of revolution associated with acts of violence, but with the historical process of long-term change in living conditions and development of the world toward egalitarian democracy. A horizon that distant eluded the Prussian conservatives confronted by the revolutionary movement in their own land. It was probably beyond them even to be able to envision it, for the still largely provincial circumstances, in Pomerania and Brandenburg particularly, would not allow it.

Another thought in Tocqueville's work might have caught their attention, however, because it was addressed to the Christian world:

> It appears to me that the Christian peoples of our time present a spectacle that strikes fear. The movement that has them in its grip is already powerful enough that it cannot be halted, yet it is not rapid enough that they might despair of directing it. Their fate lies in their hands, but it is about to be wrested from them.[45]

Though it may not have been fate that was wrested from Thadden and his friends, their capacity to manage events was, at least for a time. Returning to Trieglaff from Berlin, he had to endure the experience that the majority of the villagers denied him their vote in elections to the new Prussian National Assembly, set for the beginning of May, to be formed in accordance with the rules of a general and equal right to vote. Deeply hurt, he recognized that it would be a simple peasant (Bauer) who would represent the interests of the place.[46]

Why, though, was Adolph von Thadden, who after all was generally well liked, not elected? No documents testifying against him as a person are known. However, numerous documents from throughout the land arrayed themselves against the largely still-extant feudal structure, reform initiatives notwithstanding. One generation after enactment of the Stein-Hardenberg Reform edicts, the abundant disappointment that had accumulated regarding their inadequate results could be summarized in one sentence: The winners were the estate holders; the losers, the small farmers and, above all, the stratum beneath the farmers, the day laborers.[47]

Prior to the Revolution essentially two developments had manifested themselves. On the one hand, 84 percent of all feudally obligated farmers had broken free from their duties of service to estate holders in Prussia, who lost service valued at a total of nearly six million days. On the other, this same development had brought about a considerable shortage of labor, while expansion of land utilization augmented it further. What resulted was the formation of a new class of agricultural laborers: farm workers who had no prospect of acquiring property of their own.[48]

It is hardly astonishing, then, that reports from the United States resonated profoundly in Trieglaff, as did one letter especially from an emigrant in the first wave that was passed around in many families. Written by Johann Carl Wilhelm Pritzlaff from the neighboring village of Trutzlatz, it spoke to the sentiments of many people,[49] presenting the state of affairs quite tangibly:

> America is a good country, it blossoms under God's blessing, but it bears thorns and thistles as well. For a man who works, it is much better here

than over there; you can earn your daily bread better than in Germany, one doesn't live so restrictedly and in such servitude as you do under the great estate-owners, you don't have to put your hat under your arm or leave it at the door when you want to have the money you've earned. There is quite a fair amount of equality among men here in America. The high and wealthy are not ashamed to associate with the poor and lowly. If one man works for another, he is not tied to any particular time, rather he leaves when he wants to; everyone is his own master.[50]

The letter made its way to Trieglaff, in accordance with the wishes of its writer. But it was taken up later in a history of the Rabenhorst family, which emigrated in 1852 and is related to the Natzkes. It identifies the yearning to own land as an important root of the desire to migrate: "Opportunity for land ownership distinguishes peasant from serf." But it emphasizes as well that the Trieglaff estate holder Adolph von Thadden was "compassionate" with his farm workers. "He apparently compensated his workers better than did most of the nobles in the region."[51]

The emphasis is somewhat different in the chronicle of the Kiekhaefer family, which goes more deeply into the conditions determining emigration. "Agricultural reform, industrialization, the rise of capitalism, a rise in the birth rate, a potato blight and other crop failures in Germany in 1846–1853 made the United States seem the land of hope and promise." Subsequently, however, the failure of the Revolution of 1848 is expressly identified as a reason for this family's migration. It too, incidentally, originated in the farming class of the Bauern: "There was also a revolution in Germany in 1848 in an effort for a united and democratized Germany which failed. Many came to America then."[52]

The Kiekhaefers departed Pomerania in 1850, soon after the end of the revolutionary movement in Prussia and Germany. They journeyed with incomparably greater ease than the emigrants of the first wave, as their history reports. Steamships and sailing ships now offered regular shipping-line service, and improved mail traffic brought "glowing letters" about the United States from friends and relatives who already lived beyond the ocean. And by this time much information useful to emigrants was provided in German newspapers, travel books, and travel guides.[53]

Of course, the various reports and writings were predominantly focused on the economic advantages of that land of promise, the United States of America. But the letter from Johann Pritzlaff shows plainly that other news about the social conditions governing there, along with its "equality among people," garnered interest in old Europe. This is, in any case, the thought that Alexis de Tocqueville placed at the center of his work *Democracy in America*:

The emigrants who settled in America at the beginning of the seventeenth century in a way disengaged the principle of democracy from all those others against which it struggled within the matrix of the old societies of Europe, and they transplanted it, cleansed, upon the shores of the New World.[54]

In Trieglaff, the "old societies of Europe" did remain behind—with wounds. Patrimonial jurisdiction of estate holders was irreversibly eliminated; the right of people to vote was established constitutionally, even if nothing developed other than suffrage for the three social classes; and the transformation of the aristocratic estate holders into a class of agriculturists by trade set in. Even Adolph von Thadden could not shut his eyes to the changes.[55]

It counts among the peculiarities of this self-willed man, forever declining to conform, that he reacted to the challenges of the Revolution of 1848 less in terms of politics than of church affiliation. As liberals pressed for a modern constitutional state and many conservatives considered launching a counterrevolution, Thadden decided to withdraw from the Landeskirche, the established church in the Prussian territories. He took that step in September 1848.[56]

It was an unusual act for a Pomeranian estate holder. To understand it, one must recall events of the foregoing twenty-five years, which had been marked by incessant disputes about the union of the Lutheran and Reformed churches that underlay the Prussian Landeskirche. What began as rejection of rationalistic theology and the spirit of the Enlightenment in the church soon became a struggle against governmental regulations in the life of faith. In the end it resulted in strong demand for greater independence of the church from the state.[57]

In Pomerania the conflict had come to a head at the end of the 1840s. Increasingly more Lutherans of a strictly confessional bent "separated"— to use their word—from the united church and held their own worship services. In just three parishes in the vicinity of Stettin and Kammin, 2,255 persons scattered throughout 164 localities were known to have turned their backs on the established church.[58]

In Trieglaff the movement gained strength when the pious and much beloved Pastor Nagel broke with the Landeskirche in 1847.[59] He had met with failure in addressing a petition to the king, signed by three of his colleagues as well. It called for doing away with the consolidated administration and the signed declarations of allegiance demanded by Landeskirche pastors. So Nagel resigned his office as the duly installed parish pastor and joined the Lutherans separated from the established church, the so-called Old Lutherans.[60]

An avalanche was triggered. It went further than Pastor Nagel's withdrawal, for the great majority of Trieglaff farm people and day laborers followed him. Only seven families remained loyal to the Church of the Prussian Union. Even those Trieglaffers who had migrated to the United States took an interest in how things were going with their former fellow citizens who were their kinsmen in faith. A picture of Pastor Nagel is said to be in place on many a wall of theirs, right up to the present day.[61]

Such an event, causing a stir within the whole region, had to have legal consequences too. When the occupant of the publicly financed local parish office and practically the whole congregation walked out of the established church, there at once arose the question of what was to happen with the church building, the parsonage, and the parish properties. Who should be permitted to use the house of worship now, the "separated" Old Lutherans or the "united" people holding to the Prussian Landeskirche? And did a second pastor now have to be called to Trieglaff so that the Landeskirche members would have a shepherd too?[62]

The church conflict assumed such robust proportions then that it could hardly leave untouched the man who, according to his prevailing right, was patron of "his" church. Thus Adolph von Thadden saw himself faced inescapably with the question whether he should support the "separated ones" allowing them to share the use of the Landeskirche's church, or whether other modes of religious coexistence ought to be considered. A solution had to be found in any case.[63]

Thadden would not have been Thadden if he had not sought modes of reconciliation. He decided first that the hall he had added to the manor house for the Trieglaff Conferences in 1843[64] would be placed at the disposal of the "separated ones" for their worship services. After that he advocated that both parties be permitted to use the only village church available, each at different hours of the day. Lastly, he built a parsonage for the use of the Old Lutheran pastor, lest the newly called minister of the established church be barred from the old parsonage. Such was Christian brotherhood in Trieglaff.[65]

But the conflict was not to be resolved as easily as the elderly Thadden envisioned it. A few years later, several farmers aligned with the Landeskirche proposed to withdraw right of co-use of the church building from the "separatists." Agreement was reached once more on a form of shared use, but for "renting it, on condition of annual revocation."[66] In the end people decided to build a house of worship for the growing Old Lutheran congregation itself. This was completed in 1855, with substantial help from the estate master (Figure 8).[67]

Trieglaff thenceforth had two Protestant congregations with two pastors: one affiliated with the established church of the Prussian territories,

Figure 8. The Old Lutheran church in Trieglaff, built in 1855

and the other a Freikirche, an independent "free church." What could not be anticipated at the time was how enduring the separation would be. It would continue into the years after the end of World War II, when the last German residents departed the village. Even under the Soviet occupation and initial government by the Poles, the Old Lutheran pastor, who also stayed behind, had a hard time bringing himself to offer the Lord's Supper to the united church's orphaned congregational members.[68]

What course did things take in everyday life, following construction of the church for the Old Lutherans? Here, an informative intergenerational dialogue supplies us with knowledge of dealings pertaining to the church conflict.[69] After the death of old Adolph von Thadden in 1882, Reinhold, his eldest son and heir to Trieglaff, felt it appropriate to compose a handwritten "Meditation" of eight pages having to do with the happenings of the time, discussing in it several family conversations.

According to this document, his father had long hesitated to take the step of leaving the established church, as fraught with consequences as that was. He had for years been, "with his soft heart indignant about the harsh treatment of his persecuted fellow believers," but had not felt constrained "to drop out of the church he had worked so zealously to help to flourish." Only after the death of his wife Henriette in October 1846 did a "transformation" begin to take place when an Old Lutheran congregation formed under the influence of the rigidly Lutheran Pastor Nagel. Father Thadden placed the hall add-on at its disposal for worship services.[70]

In the "Meditation," the elderly Thadden's crossover to the "Old Lutherans" took place in fall 1848. Around the time of his engagement to his second spouse, Baroness Eleonore von Romberg, "he announced to us that he was not disinclined to switch over to the Old Lutherans, who had obtained a secure position by the General Concession in 1845."[71] To be sure, he had been deeply conscious "that his move could appear in the eyes of others to have some connection with his engagement to an unattached Old Lutheran."

Without doubt, the elderly Thadden found it "impossible, spiritually, to live" in a "mixed marriage." But another argument ranged foremost: "It was for my father unbearable to be separated from his people by church divisions." For that reason he would probably gladly have seen his elder son and heir to Trieglaff also convert, becoming Old Lutheran. But he left him alone and did not meddle in his decision. "My father never made serious efforts to draw me over to the other side."[72]

It was not Reinhold, but another member of the family from the younger generation, the second son Gerhard, who converted to the Old Lutheran Freikirche. Heir to the adjacent estate Vahnerow, he became "Old Lutheran at the time of his engagement in 1853" to Eugenie von Zanthier, who was also from Pomerania. Simultaneously, Hermann Wangerin, a son of the Trieglaff shepherd Friedrich Wangerin, became chief shepherd at Vahnerow. He too was a faithful Old Lutheran, of course. It had been Friedrich Wangerin who first triggered the clash with the established church in 1824 with his contentious affair concerning the baptism in true faith of his oldest son.[73] The elder brother Johann Friedrich, mentioned previously, emigrated to Wisconsin in 1865 with his cousin Albert and Albert's father, Martin, and established connections with the American Old Lutherans. In this milieu the united Landeskirche stood little chance.

And what became of Reinhold von Thadden, who alone in the family remained affiliated with the established church? He wrote that he "did not have to suffer personally from the division"; rather, "I felt satisfaction in my independence and was too universally oriented to experience my exceptional status painfully." Too, his father Adolph had been anything but intolerant: "With respect to my posture within the remnant Prussian Union congregation here I had been given a free hand to attend worship services there."[74]

The tale of the Trieglaff churches still is not fully told, however. For one thing, soon after his brother's conversion Reinhold made a match likely to have pleased the Old Lutherans. In 1855 he married Marie Witte, a daughter of the Dante scholar Karl Witte from Halle. She liked Pastor Nagel, who had left the Landeskirche, and she attended the Old Lutheran services occasionally, too.[75] For another, Reinhold lived through the vacillations of his father, who began quite plainly at this time to have negative experiences with his "separatist" fellow believers in the small free church. He noted that his father sought him out at Leipzig in 1866, during the Seven Weeks' War between Prussia and Austria, to "earnestly dissuade me from transferring to the Old Lutherans. He'd experienced genuine fear I might take such a step; but I was to handle his dissuasion confidentially."[76]

This left Reinhold in a serious spot. On the one hand, the Old Lutherans around him dominated, even as the queues of emigrating people lengthened again. On the other, the Trieglaff "patriarch" was increasingly skeptical and observed the development of the free church with sadness. What to do then, if in addition, and hardly least, responsibility for the people in the village was taken seriously? Once more the social argument weighed:

> As father was in the process of handing Trieglaff over to me in 1874 so as to retire to the neighboring property in Batzwitz, and was having a hard time parting with the old home turf, he pointed out to me the difficulties that my association with the established church would cause me in a village that was almost wholly Old Lutheran.[77]

There it was once again—the social dimension, always on the mind of the master of the estate, in thoughts of his attachment to "his people." An estate was simply not just a large agricultural enterprise functioning exclusively in categories of earnings and returns. It was a realm of existence as well, one in which a community of humans had a part. That applied all the more as ways of thinking grew ever more economically oriented through the decades. What place should the Christian Church hold in this rapidly shifting world?

In pursuing the question why Reinhold von Thadden clung so stubbornly to the Landeskirche, one soon encounters someone who had figured in his early years—Oberlandesgerichtspräsident Ernst-Ludwig von Gerlach. As a student, Reinhold had lived for a time in his house in Frankfurt an der Oder. He had completed his internship as law clerk in proximity to Gerlach in Magdeburg as well. Reinhold emphasized repeatedly that "Uncle Ludwig" meant much to him and, in the opinion of others, was one "root of my strength."[78]

What impressed him most deeply was Gerlach's linking of legal and theological thinking. He was "among jurists the best theologian and among theologians the best jurist," Reinhold wrote. "The Kingdom of God encompassed, in his eyes, state and church alike."[79] There was no room in that for free churches.

It is all but certain that under these circumstances the younger Thadden had direct knowledge of the differences of opinion and eventual estrangement between his father and Ernst-Ludwig von Gerlach. He knew that Trieglaff's break with the established church oppressed the latter. It goes without saying that he was familiar with Gerlach's assertion, concerning his father, that it was painful "to part ways with him, after we have gone along together for 30 years closely allied, on a vital question in our time—and perhaps not in time alone."[80] Gerlach's memorial composition on "Neolutheranism" of 1851 would not have been unknown to him either. According to it, "a Christianity centered exclusively within" is "not Christianity, but mysticism." Separations detracted from that common stance that was commanded of all Christians and confessions against the looming secularization movement.[81]

So the younger generation, torn between the two starkly diverging viewpoints of the older, had to survive a test. In Reinhold's case, this test was intensified by his marriage to Marie Witte, whose father Karl held romantic, pan-German, and Italophile convictions. Marie's mother, Auguste Hentschel von Gilgenheimb, who came from Silesia, had been Catholic until her daughter's confirmation. Upon moving to Trieglaff in 1858, Marie cultivated close, also musical, contacts with Pastor Nagel's successor Rudel. He in turn was connected to the family of the shepherd Wangerin. These Old Lutheran sympathies notwithstanding, she remained with the Landeskirche and did her part to keep Trieglaff from succumbing entirely to the pull of the "separatists." Over the long term she would—owing in part to her long life, lasting until 1922—show herself to be a sturdy pillar of the colorful, intense family.[82]

Reinhold and Marie built their house on the adjacent estate of Batzwitz, which had been acquired in 1855 using the Romberg dowry. The elder Thadden leased it to them for a manageable sum. With that a triangle of Thadden estates emerged. Because of its size, it mattered, even in the District of Greifenberg, which had a wealth of estates in any case. Trieglaff, the largest estate with its 2,095 acres (848 hectares), remained in the possession of the senior Thadden for another fourteen years. Batzwitz, with 1,050 acres (425 hectares), was in the hands of the elder son Reinhold, and Vahnerow, at 1,035 acres (419 hectares), went to the younger son Gerhard (Figure 9). All three were manorial estates, formally recognized "Rittergüter," but they varied in importance.[83]

By the mid-nineteenth century, these estates could claim only a few privileges denied others. With their petty judicial powers suspended and even enforcement of policing penalties within their bounds under attack, few limitations remained on acquisition of estates that once had been passed along according to hereditary, class-bound norms. The limitations had fallen away by 1867, soon after Bismarck founded his German Empire (das Deutsche Reich).[84] After 1854, they still offered estate holders a few advantages only with respect to voting rights in elections to the Herrenhaus, the upper house of the Prussian parliament, in that ownership by a family for at least one hundred years, or else permanent establishment of ownership in the form of a legally indivisible primogeniture, was mandatory.[85]

This was, of course, supposed to strengthen the position of the traditional landed nobility. For decades though it had been the case that by no means all estate proprietors were able to claim noble status. By 1856, 43.1 percent of the 12,339 manorial estates in Prussia east of the Elbe were owned by non-aristocratic families.[86] And middle-class ownership had increased even in the province of Pomerania, which with its high count of farming people included a higher percentage of manors than East Prussia. Of the 37 manorial estates in the District of Greifenberg in 1857, 23 were, in fact, in middle-class ownership and only 14 still in aristocratic.[87] It must be noted, however, that an aristocratic owner in Pomerania held on average 3,074 acres, and a non-aristocratic one by comparison only 1,448 acres.[88]

This is not to say that the revised legal and social situation by itself determined the whole reality of life. Of equal importance was its perception by the people, accustomed for generations to live, if things were going well, with provident estate holders mostly conscious that their superordi-

Figure 9. The new manor house at Vahnerow, built by Gerhard von Thadden in 1856

nate status imposed obligations. The high regard in which a "Herrschaft" was held, as venerated lord and master of the locality, played a considerable role. It could endure well beyond the lifetime of the person upon whom it centered.[89]

When the brothers Reinhold and Gerhard von Thadden took over their comparatively small manorial estates at Batzwitz and Vahnerow, both unquestionably still profited in every way from the extraordinary respect that their father, Adolph, continued to enjoy in the vicinity. At the same time they also had to establish their own competence and independence. For the elder brother, management of agricultural operations did not always come easily, and for years the senior Thadden tended to intervene reactively in decisions. A whole stockpile of letters demonstrates that the suggestions he offered in doing so were best taken to heart, down to the details of the purchase of equipment and the hiring of personnel.[90]

In one letter, though, it was not the father who shone but one of the sons. The younger brother Gerhard came forward with an idea that testifies to powers of originality. In a note to Reinhold, he suggested a new method of sheep shearing that would yield more than the customary method did. It was advisable, he elaborated, "to shear the sheep unwashed and to wash the wool taken that way, factory-like, in the country, and then take it to market." His reasoning was simple: the method of washing sheep that was in place was "a gruesome ordeal for man and beast," and was more expensive besides. "The entire wool trade would really profit significantly from the sale of wool washed as in a factory, and thereby a gain would accrue to the seller."[91]

Gerhard was thinking in terms of economization. Yet in doing so he did not appear to challenge the rank of others, and certainly not that held by the principal estate. Trieglaff, after all, remained the hub of the area. The village, following the confessional division, had two churches, whereas Batzwitz had just one and Vahnerow none at all. In addition, it had a well-built school where, by 1870, thirty-four children were taught by a teacher who was simultaneously employed as sexton. Vahnerow lost its school in 1870, supposedly because the number of children was too small. In Batzwitz, a poorly paid teacher taught lessons.[92]

Further contributing to Trieglaff's preeminence was the presence of an independent gristmill, which ground grain for all the surrounding villages. The mill was also at the disposal of the farm people, and because Trieglaff and Batzwitz had smaller farmsteads independent of the estate—unlike Vahnerow—it lent importance to the place.[93] Last but not least, Trieglaff's two large lakes were uniquely valuable, for they enabled a small fishery to carry on business.

Given this regional significance, it is unsurprising that some vivid legends wove themselves about the place. In Fontane's *Stechlin*, the lake was possessed of mysterious depths from which a red rooster sometimes appeared.[94] Similarly, in the fantasy world of Trieglaff's homespun tales, the image of the old Wend god Triglaw was ubiquitous. Three-headed, he was thought to have been worshipped at the place where the medieval village church was later erected within a grove of primeval oaks. This wonderful legend was nourished in a treasured presentation by the Pomeranian reformer Johannes Bugenhagen, who in describing the Christianization of the land under Bishop Otto of Bamberg wrote:

> When the images of the gods were destroyed the priests stole the idol of Triglav and hid it with a widow in the country, in a farmhouse, as some presumed, that today is named Trieglaff near Greifenberg. She wrapped it in a heavy cloth covering, put it into the trunk of a tree, and left only a small opening into which incense and sacrificial offerings could be placed.[95]

A memory of Slavic people having once lived at this place attached itself to these stories as they were repeated again and again, especially during long winter evenings. Surviving alongside them was the caricature in Fontane's Stechlin (the setting of the novel of the same name) of an old Triglaff maiden with "outsized fantasies of Triglaff."[96] A conviction took hold that Trieglaff was something special, or at least more than a place on the map no different from other Pomeranian places.

Wonderful legends snuggled themselves into the family history of the Thaddens as well. For example, the assumption that the name Thadden was traceable to that of the Biblical apostle Thaddeus made its way from generation to generation in stories. The Polish form of the name, Tadeusz, is also found in a reproduction of the oldest family document, from the year 1334.[97] So one might ask whether inspiration for this association was not supplied also by the title of a literary work, *Pan Tadeusz*, by the great Polish national writer Adam Mickiewicz, which was very well known at the time of the Thaddens' tenure. Be that as it may, the world of a nineteenth-century Pomeranian aristocratic family could have been found to be closely replicated there, for the epic is set in the rural life of formerly Polish Lithuania.[98]

To be sure, little was known about Poland in the part of Pomerania that lay within Stettin's jurisdiction. Occasional reports about the Polish uprisings against czarist Russia in 1863 would have been heard only from neighboring Posen, which belonged at the time to Prussia. In particular, occasional reports about the politics of that old family friend Bismarck, in support of the Russian position, would have reached there.[99] But this was a topic of discussion for the young generation, not the old.

For from the early 1860s on, significant differences came about with respect to conditions of ownership in the Trieglaff triumvirate of properties. At the same time, changes arising in "large-scale politics" too affected the Thaddens critically. The romantic-thinking King Frederick William IV died in 1861, followed shortly thereafter by Adjutant-General Leopold, older brother of the strict and inflexible Ernst-Ludwig von Gerlach. Then in 1862, Otto von Bismarck assumed leadership of the Prussian government, introducing a new epoch of European history.[100] How did the Trieglaff world react to these events?

In the wake of the fundamental controversies unsettling the camp of their fellow conservatives, it should not be surprising that debates went on inside the Thadden family about the right course for Prussian politics.[101] The brothers Reinhold and Gerhard in particular held divergent opinions about Bismarck's political path and carried on an intensive correspondence during these decisive years.[102] Whereas it shows Reinhold proceeding in line with the Gerlachs as usual, being opposed in principle to Prussian politics directed against Austria, Gerhard emerges as a confirmed adherent of Bismarck who defends his course with considered arguments.

Gerhard was committed to the Bismarck family well before Otto's appointment as prime minister in October 1862. Like his brother Reinhold initially, he was among the friends of Johanna von Puttkamer, even before her marriage to Bismarck, as numerous letters testify.[103] But from the beginning of the 1860s on, he adopted a political stance more and more often when he felt there was cause to defend Bismarck's political direction within the Trieglaff family group. In early March 1862, he wrote to his brother Reinhold from Berlin that he had "the pleasure of seeing Bismarck almost daily,"[104] being a member of the intimate circle that Bismarck gathered about himself in the evenings.

In the lead-up to the Seven Weeks' War between Prussia and Austria in summer 1866, Gerhard explicitly informed Reinhold that he did not at all agree with Gerlach's criticism of Bismarck. Bismarck would "not be the kind of man to frivolously bring about a war in which rivers of blood might flow." In addition, obstruction "of peace is being fostered by Uncle Ludwig Gerlach, too, with his article in the *Kreuzzeitung*, because it stiffens the Austrian attitude if they see that B. is being abandoned by his most faithful!"[105]

The article, about war and reform of the German Confederation (Deutscher Bund), split not only the Thadden family but the camp of the Prussian conservatives as well.[106] It emphatically warned against war as a means of settling differences with the brother nation, Austria, and against destruction of the founding document of the Confederation. That basis had "provided fifty years of peace and flowering prosperity to Germany." Besides, war was "elementarily destructive," exceeding even "the material harm which follows upon every war."[107]

The domestic political argument for reform of the Confederation seemed to Gerlach to be of equal importance. Here Bismarck had taken a step that the conservatives could only see as revolutionary: he had demanded of the German Bundestag in Frankfurt that a federated parliament be formed on the basis of general, equal, and direct elections.[108] In Gerlach's eyes, Bismarck thus had contradicted fundamental conservative principles in the struggle against the Revolution. The article closed uncompromisingly: "A universal right to vote is political bankruptcy."

Reinhold Thadden was on Gerlach's side.[109] And he received letters from his uncle justifying the "circumstances into which you and I have come with beloved and respected persons" and stating his unwillingness to see "[t]he German fatherland—and more than anything the Prussian fatherland in particular ... besmirch itself with sin and injustice ... and on top of that the murky future, darker almost if Prussia is victorious than if it is defeated."[110] To undergird his argument, Gerlach appended a detailed exposition of the prehistory of the war, a *status causae* that chiefly blamed Prussia for aggravating the conflict with Austria.[111]

Reinhold plainly found the political tensions, which also reached over into the Trieglaff family, difficult to bear. He provided a telling explanation of his ready compliance with orders to report to the royal army in a letter to his wife Marie:

> The more I guard myself within against any sympathy with our political direction, the more incisively I feel myself impelled to intervene by joining in the military action. It's the only way that I think that I can earn the right as a son of the fatherland to oppose it on its wrong path.[112]

So Reinhold escaped into military duty in order to avoid disagreeable discussions at home while at the same time he strengthened his position in the family. Now he, like his brother Gerhard, stood "upon the field of honor" and could start over again as opportunity offered, should circumstances demand it.

He did exactly that after victory in this war against Austria wished for by Bismarck. At the end of the year he justified himself in a letter to his mentor Gerlach: "I want to give the present an opportunity to reconcile itself with me. I am tracing a long line underneath the past and will begin, as of the 1st of January, a new textbook of world history."[113] Gerlach noted sarcastically in the margin of the letter, "Just so he doesn't reconcile himself with the present!" But Reinhold did not hesitate to lay out his efforts toward adaptation even more openly:

> It seems to me the task is to begin afresh, and bravely, upon a new foundation.... New facts that I have to continue working with lie before me, whether rubble or freshly-hewn block, I am not the master builder, only the hod carrier.[114]

The younger brother Gerhard was no hod carrier—quite the contrary. He approached Reinhold in another manner: "Recently I wrote Uncle Ludwig Gerlach my first letter—of loving reproaches. He replied today and invited me over. I can't."[115] Because Gerhard considered the discussion still open, despite the military decision in favor of Bismarck's and against Austria's German policies, he set about drafting a further letter to Reinhold, this time very detailed, summarizing once more his reasons for opposing Gerlach's position.[116] He opened by saying that the letters by Gerlach that had been forwarded to him did "not convince" him; nor did their appendix, the *status causae* mentioned earlier: "I have my reservations about each one of the items of complaint."

Gerhard first repudiated Prussia's guilt for aggravating a conflict with Schleswig-Holstein in 1864–1865, since Austria had supported the Augustenburg party from the beginning:[117] "Here is where the origin of the war lies buried." After that, Austria—in contrast to Prussia—had engaged the German Confederation in support of the Augustenburg party and thereby made a common policy for both of the German great powers impossible. Bismarck's threat that he would call for a federated German parliament on the basis of general, equal, and direct elections was thus an answer to the Austrian threat to engage the bureaucratic organs of the German Confederation in Frankfurt. Gerhard summarized his argumentation, including some additional points, with a clear sentence: "I do not understand how Bismarck can be condemned as guilty of peace-breaking in such a way with such certainty?!? At any rate the whole thing is not 'simple.'"[118]

Inside the Thadden family, conditions were not simple either, especially now that a further element had entered with Reinhold's wife, Marie, from the Witte family. Upon her marriage she had integrated herself quite warmly into the Trieglaff world and followed along with independent judgment as it participated in the political debates of the country. In doing so she had not lost her attachment to the academic background and experience of her family home in Halle, having kept up a vivacious, extended correspondence with her father. Particularly since the Revolution of 1848, he, like the Trieglaffers, held opinions about the course of politics. His views had grown and ripened with time.[119]

The Wittes, like all Prussian conservatives of the time, espoused the European order that had been created by the Congress of Vienna of 1815 in response to Napoleonic France's struggle for hegemony. In central Europe this order had been organized as the German Confederation, with its two great powers Austria and Prussia. But through Dante scholar Karl Witte's acquaintance with Italy, the family brought in an extra-German perspective that distinguished their judgment of Bismarck. They took the growing national pressure toward unification more seriously. What Italian Prime Minister Cavour did to unify his country ought not to be simply forbidden to the Prussian Bismarck and Germany.[120]

Differences of opinion between father and daughter soon came to light in family discussions. While the former opposed conflict between Austria and Prussia under any conditions, the latter sympathized increasingly with Bismarck's policy of faulting Austria. The father wrote:

> To your question pertaining to Bismarck I reply that I regard him highly, but salvation for Prussia and Germany is to be found not in enmity with, but only in concord with Austria, and for that he doesn't yet seem to have what it takes.[121]

And the daughter answered:

> Your worries about his position vs. Austria are, sadly, probably too well-founded.... However, for our particular Prussian circumstances, Bismarck is surely the right man. Had his strong shoulders not arrived for support, where, given this liberal chamber, would the Kingdom of God's Grace be now![122]

This letter mirrored the concerns Marie felt together with all the Thaddens in Trieglaff, Vahnerow, and Batzwitz. The Prussian monarchy, unwilling to make any parliamentary concessions, found itself in a difficult position.

But at the same time, the letter makes obvious that she set greater store by the judgment of her brother-in-law Gerhard than that of her husband Reinhold. And so she endeavored from then on to win her husband, and her father as well, over to Bismarck's policies. Shortly before the outbreak of war against Austria in June 1866, she wrote to her father, who continued to be critical of Bismarck: "Today just a few political words to convince you, if possible, that Bismarck tried honestly right up to the very end to maintain peace."[123] Her foremost authority was Moritz von Blanckenburg from Zimmerhausen, esteemed by all, who had been the husband of her sister-in-law Marie from Trieglaff, who died so young. He later became leader of the conservatives in the Prussian state parliament (Landtag).[124]

Blanckenburg also maintained connections with Ernst-Ludwig von Gerlach, the person so influential for Reinhold. Gerlach looked up Bismarck personally once more. Marie wrote that "Moritz was most unhappy with Uncle Ludwig for continuing to trust and believe an enemy more than a friend." But there follows an item of information that had significance for peace in the family:

> Reinhold has been brought around somewhat by the news from Moritz, at least he is no longer arguing about Bismarck. He only continues to pity the poor Austrians, who will not be able to escape their plight honorably except through war.[125]

In fact, these Trieglaff friends of Austria were genuinely brought around only by Bismarckian Prussia's victory over the Habsburg monarchy. The elderly Karl Witte gave thoughtful expression to this shift in thinking—this reorientation—in a letter addressed "to spouse and children" shortly before the definitive Peace of Prague.[126] It appeared that

> in the drama of world history the curtain is rising on a new act: *Magnus ab integro saeculorum volvitur orbis* (the great cycle of epochs revolves anew). But the germ of the new must already have been present and, despite every opposition, been pushed forth into the light and to life by its inner strength, not concerned for the organisms that it destroyed in breaking through its hull. It is this manifest destiny with which I now justify for myself what has taken place.[127]

Notes

1. Cf. Martin Wehrmann, *Geschichte von Pommern,* 2nd ed. (1921; repr. Würzburg, 1982), 2: 310f.

2. *MICHEL-Briefmarken-katalog* [stamp catalog] (Unterschleißheim, 2008), section "Preußen."

3. Heinrich Stephan, *Geschichte der Preußischen Post von ihrem Ursprunge bis auf die Gegenwart* (Berlin, 1859), vff. Regarding Stephan, see Hermann von Petersdorff, "Heinrich (v.) Stephan," *ADB,* vol. 54 (Leipzig, 1908).

4. Stephan, *Geschichte der Preußischen Post,* 376.

5. Ibid., Reports on the mails in Pomerania in the seventeenth and eighteenth centuries, 95, 149.

6. Cf. Wolfgang Klee, *Preußische Eisenbahngeschichte* (Stuttgart, 1982), 49ff., 61f.

7. *Verhandlungen der evangelischen General-Synode zu Berlin vom 2. Juni bis zum 29. August 1846* [Proceedings....] (Berlin, 1846), 118f.

8. Cf. Rudolf von Thadden, *Prussia,* 105–106. A note by Adolph's son Reinhold about his father participating at the general synod is to be found in the carton for Reinhold von Thadden, FA.

9. Von Thadden's speech at the Generalsynode on 30 July 1846, reprinted in Reuß, *Adolf von Thadden,* 267f.

10. Ibid., 268.

11. Undated letter by Gerlach in Reuß, *Adolf von Thadden*, 76. Also handwritten in the carton for Adolph von Thadden, FA.

12. Cf. on this Hans-Christof Kraus, *Ernst-Ludwig von Gerlach* (Göttingen, 1994), part 1, 362ff.

13. Cf. Rudolf von Thadden, *Prussia*, 105ff.

14. Ibid. Cf. on this Huber, *Deutsche Verfassungsgeschichte*, 2: 492ff.

15. Cf. on this Erich Marcks, *Bismarcks Jugend 1815–1848* (Stuttgart and Berlin, 1909), 391ff.; Lothar Gall, *Bismarck. Der weiße Revolutionär* (Frankfurt am Main, 1980), 68f.; E. Engelberg, *Bismarck*, 243ff.

16. Marcks, *Bismarcks Jugend*, 267ff.; Gall, *Bismarck*, 50ff.; E. Engelberg, *Bismarck*, 231f.

17. Letter by Bismarck, 21 December 1846, in Bismarck, *Otto von Bismarck. Die gesammelten Werke* [hereafter *GW*] (Berlin, 1933), 14/1: 47. Also in Hans Rothfels, ed., *Bismarck-Briefe* (Göttingen, 1955), 58.

18. Bismarck, *GW*, 14/1: 47, Rothfels, 58.

19. As does Reinold von Thadden-Trieglaff, *War Bismarck Christ?* (Hamburg, 1950), 19f.

20. Waltraut Engelberg, *Otto und Johanna von Bismarck* (Berlin, 1990), 27.

21. Letter by Marie, lacking exact date, from the year 1845, in carton for Adolph von Thadden, FA; additionally, excerpts in Petrich, *Adolf und Henriette*, 91.

22. Speech by Bismarck, 15 June 1847, in *GW*, 10: 8ff. Also in Eduard Bleich, ed., *Der Erste Vereinigte Landtag in Berlin 1847* (1847; repr., Vaduz, 1977), 4: 1783ff.

23. Reuß, *Adolf von Thadden*, 87f.

24. Cf. E. Engelberg, *Bismarck*, 246f. Also Marcks, *Bismarcks Jugend*, 417f.

25. Marcks, *Bismarcks Jugend*, 414f.

26. Cited in Reuß, *Adolf von Thadden*, 85.

27. Cf. Thomas Stamm-Kuhlmann, "Pommern 1815–1875," in Buchholz, *Pommern*, 406. Further, Treue, "Wirtschafts- und Sozialgeschichte Deutschlands," 3: 326. And above all, Wilhelm Abel, *Massenarmut und Hungerkrisen im vorindustriellen Europa* (Hamburg and Berlin, 1974), 365ff.

28. Letter by Bismarck, 28 April 1847, in *GW*, 14/1: 84. Also in Rothfels, *Bismarck-Briefe*, 97f.

29. On this, Arthur. L. Rabenhorst, *Family Lines* (private printing, 2008), 20.

30. Cf. Wienfort, *Patrimonialgerichte in Preußen*, 134ff.

31. Ibid., 15.

32. Cited per Reuß, *Adolf von Thadden*, 223.

33. Cf. Marcks, *Bismarcks Jugend*, 429ff.

34. Cf. Wolfgang J. Mommsen, *1848. Die ungewollte Revolution* (Frankfurt am Main, 1998), 104. Further, E. Engelberg, *Bismarck*, 251f.

35. Cf. Reinhart Koselleck, "Wie europäisch war die Revolution von 1848/49?" in Kosellek, ed., *Europäische Umrisse deutscher Geschichte* (Heidelberg, 1999), 9ff.

36. Cf. Huber, *Deutsche Verfassungsgeschichte*, 2: 582.

37. Ibid., 583. Further, Reuß, *Adolf von Thadden*, 91.

38. Cf. on this Huber, *Deutsche Verfassungsgeschichte* 2: 583, n. 47.

39. *Werke*-edition of "Erinnerung und Gedanke," in *GW*, 15: 28. Further, Knaur edition, *Gedanken und Erinnerungen* (Munich, 1952), 61. Cf. on this E. Engelberg, *Bismarck*, 282f.

40. Cf. Kraus, *Ernst-Ludwig von Gerlach*, 1: 287ff.

41. Letter of 5 April 1848, in Gerhard Ritter, ed., "Altersbriefe Ludwig von Gerlachs," *Deutsche Revue* 36, no. 1 (1911): 43f.

42. Cf. Kraus, *Ernst-Ludwig von Gerlach*, 1: 118, n. 76. Kraus says here that Gerlach was neither greatly knowledgeable about nor friends with Bonald.

43. Cf. on this the introductory contribution by Theodor Eschenburg, "Tocquevilles Wirkung in Deutschland," in the unfinished German edition of *Alexis de Tocqueville. Werke und Briefe*, ed. J. P. Mayer together with Theodor Eschenburg and Hans Zbinden (Stuttgart, 1959), 1: xviiff.

44. Alexis de Tocqueville, *Über did Demokratie in Amerika*, ibid., 5. [Found also in a number of English translations of Tocqueville's work, among them that by George Lawrence, *Democracy in America*, ed. J. P. Mayer (New York, 1969), 9.]

45. Tocqueville, *Democracy in America*, 12.

46. Reuß, *Adolf von Thadden*, 95.

47. Cf. Reinhart Koselleck, *Preußen zwischen Reform und Revolution* (Stuttgart, 1967), 487ff.

48. Ibid., 499.

49. Letter by Pritzlaff, 23 April 1842, reprinted in Lieselotte Clemens, *Die Auswanderung der pommerschen Altlutheraner in die USA* (Hamburg, 1976), 83ff. Further on this, Helbich et al, *Briefe aus Amerika*, 290ff. [This work, elaborated, exists in English translation: Walter Kamphoefner, Wolfgang Helbich, and Ulrike Sommer, eds., *News from the Land of Freedom*, trans. Susan Carter Vogel (Ithaca and London, 1988). Chapter 9, pp. 299–318, features an extensive sequence of letters by Pritzlaff, including the one from which the quote is taken.] On Johann Pritzlaff's journey to the United States and his astonishing ascent founding an extremely successful iron products business of his own in Milwaukee, correspondence between the author and Pritzlaff's great-great-grandson James H. Koch of New York can be found in the carton *Amerikanische Briefe* [correspondence], FA. Also present there is a letter by Koch of 15 December 1978 containing the following sentence about the pioneer spirit of Trieglaff: "So you see the pioneering spirit and dedication generated at Trieglaf among the Old Lutherans continued in the New World!"

50. Cited from Kamphoefner et al., *News*, 306; German translation in Clemens, *Die Auswanderung*, 84.

51. Rabenhorst, *Family Lines*, 19.

52. *The Kiekhaefer Family Register* (private printing, 1979), 5, FA.

53. Ibid. Additionally, Stephan, *Geschichte der Preußischen Post*, 650ff.

54. Tocqueville, *Democracy in America*, 18.

55. Cf. Koselleck, *Preußen zwischen Reform und Revolution*, 507.

56. Reuß, *Adolf von Thadden*, 103; Petrich, *Adolf und Henriette*, 78.

57. See chapter 1 of this volume.

58. Petrich, *Adolf und Henriette*, 77. Further, Hermann T. Wangemann, *Sieben Bücher preußischer Kirchengeschichte* (Berlin, 1860), 2: 418ff.

59. Reuß, *Adolf von Thadden*, 102.

60. Petrich, *Adolf und Henriette*, 78.

61. Reproduction presented to the author in Wisconsin, in the carton *Amerikanische Briefe*, FA.

62. Cf. Petrich, *Adolf und Henriette*, 78.

63. On the beginning phase of the separation, ibid.

64. See chapter 1 of this volume.

65. Cf. Reuß, *Adolf von Thadden*, 53f.; Petrich, *Adolf und Henriette*, 79.

66. Petrich, *Adolf und Henriette*, 81f.

67. Cf. Ulrich, *Chronik des Kreises Greifenberg*, 416.

68. Personal experience, author.

69. "Geschichtliche Meditation über die altlutherische Bewegung," in carton for Reinhold von Thadden, FA.

70. Ibid.

71. *Generalkonzession von 1845*, reproduced in Wangemann, *Sieben Bücher*, 2: 407f. The foremost subject here is people's right to form their own congregations.

72. "Geschichtliche Meditation," 4, FA.

73. See chapter 1 of this volume.

74. "Geschichtliche Meditation," 5, FA.

75. Cf. Hermann Witte and Hans Haupt, *Karl Witte. Ein Leben für Dante* (Hamburg, 1971), 163, 236.

76. "Geschichtliche Meditation," 8, FA.

77. Ibid.

78. Undated notes (presumably from the 1870s) about Ernst Ludwig von Gerlach, in the carton for Reinhold von Thadden, FA.

79. Ibid., 18.

80. Cited from Reuß, *Adolf von Thadden*, 103.

81. Memorandum concerning "Neolutheranism" of 1851 in the carton for Gerlach, FA. Reproduced also in Hellmut Diwald, ed., Ernst Ludwig von Gerlach papers: *Von der Revolution zum Norddeutschen Bund*, part 2, *Briefe, Denkschriften, Aufzeichnungen* (Göttingen, 1970), 773ff.

82. Cf. Witte and Haupt, *Karl Witte*, 248f.

83. These figures are given in Morgen in Ulrich, *Chronik*, 354f., 289. [In modern usage, 1 Morgen = 1 acre.]

84. Cf. Wagner, *Bauern, Junker und Beamte*, 42. Further, Wienfort, *Patrimonialgerichte in Preußen*, 322ff.

85. Cf. Hartwin Spenkuch, "Herrenhaus und Rittergut," *Geschichte und Gesellschaft* 3 (1999): 385ff.

86. Cf. Wagner, *Bauern, Junker und Beamte*, 43.

87. Ulrich, *Chronik*, 273.

88. Cf. Ilona Buchsteiner, "Wirtschaftlicher und sozialer Wandel in ostdeutschen Gutswirtschaften vor 1914," *Archiv für Sozialgeschichte* 36 (1996): 93.

89. Cf. Heinz Reif, *Westfälischer Adel 1770–1860* (Göttingen, 1979), 41ff., 176ff.

90. In the carton for Adolph von Thadden, FA. According to the letters, Reinhold was in particular need of advice because he was not held to be a good businessman. Contrariwise, his wife Marie proved herself an uncommonly adept businesswoman who even took over bookkeeping for the estate when necessary.

91. Letter by Gerhard (undated, presumably from the beginning of the 1860s) in the carton of Vahnerow materials, FA.

92. Ulrich, *Chronik,* 436, 420.

93. Ibid., 376.

94. Theodor Fontane, *Der Stechlin,* ed. Helmuth Nürnberger, dtv (Deutscher Taschenbuch Verlag) edition, 3rd ed. (Munich, 1998), 7.

95. Bugenhagen, *Pomerania,* 156.

96. Fontane, *Stechlin,* 91.

97. In the carton for genealogy, FA.

98. A. Mickiewicz, *Pan Tadeusz,* Polish edition 1834, first German translation 1836, 2nd edition translated Siegfried Lipiner under the title *Herr Thaddäus oder der letzte Einritt in Litauen* (Leipzig, 1882).

99. Alvensleben Konvention of 1863 between Russia and Prussia for mutual support in politics relating to Poland, in *Vertragsplotz,* ed. Helmuth Roennesarth (Bielefeld, 1953), p 168f.

100. Cf. on this E. Engelberg, *Bismarck,* 525ff.; Gall, *Bismarck,* 244ff.

101. Correspondence between Leopold von Gerlach and Bismarck, particularly Bismarck's letters of 2 May 1857 and 30 May 1857, in *Briefwechsel Leopold von Gerlach/Otto von Bismarck,* ed. Horst Kohl, 2nd ed. (Berlin, 1893), 333ff. Further, the letters of General Leopold von Gerlach to Bismarck, particularly those from 6 May 1857 and 21 May 1857, in Leopold von Gerlach, *Briefe des Generals Leopold von Gerlach an Otto von Bismarck,* ed. Horst Kohl (Stuttgart and Berlin, 1912), 208ff.

102. In the carton of Vahnerow materials, FA.

103. Six letters by Johanna von Puttkamer to Reinhold from the years 1846 and 1847, in the carton of Vahnerow materials, FA.

104. Ibid., letter by Gerhard of 2 March 1862.

105. Ibid., letter by Gerhard of 12 May 1866.

106. Ernst Ludwig von Gerlach, *Neue Preußische Zeitung,* no. 105 (8 May 1866). Cf. on this also Kraus, *Ernst-Ludwig von Gerlach,* 2: 805f.

107. Gerlach, article of 8 May 1866, *Neue Preußische Zeitung,* no. 105.

108. Bill of 9 April 1866, in *Dokumente zur deutschen Verfassungsgeschichte,* ed. Ernst R. Huber, 3rd ed. (Stuttgart, Berlin, and Cologne, 1986), 2: 223ff.

109. Letter of 22 May 1866 by Gerlach to his nephew Jacob: R[einhold] Th., "Who in sharp contrast to his father and Moritz Blanckenburg enthusiastically agrees with me," in Diwald, *Briefe, Denkschriften, Aufzeichnungen,* part 2, 1291.

110. Letter by Gerlach of 23 June 1866, reproduced in Gerhard Ritter, *Die preußischen Konservativen und Bismarcks deutsche Politik 1858 bis 1876* (Heidelberg, 1913, repr. 1976), 383ff.

111. In Diwald, *Briefe, Denkschriften, Aufzeichnungen,* part 2, 1314ff.

112. Excerpt quoted from a letter of 20 July 1866 by Reinhold von Thadden to Gerlach, ibid., 1327f.

113. Letter of 28 December 1866 by Reinhold, ibid., 1375f.

114. Ibid.

115. Letter of 13 April 1867 by Gerhard, in the carton of Vahnerow materials, FA.

116. Letter of 9 February 1867 by Gerhard, ibid.

117. Cf. on this E. Engelberg, *Bismarck,* 546ff.; Gall, *Bismarck,* 305ff.

118. Letter of 9 February 1867 by Gerhard, FA.

119. Hermann Witte, ed., *Bismarck und die Konservativen. Briefe aus Trieglaff,* in *Deutsche Rundschau* 149 (1911): 334ff.

120. Karl Witte, "Preußen und die italienische Frage," *Die Neue Preußische Zeitung* (February 1859).

121. Letter of 17 March 1863 by Karl Witte, in Witte and Haupt, *Karl Witte,* 254.

122. Letter of 23 March 1863 by Marie, in H. Witte, *Bismarck und die Konservativen,* 336.

123. Letter by Marie from early June 1866, ibid., 238.

124. Cf. Ritter, *Die preußischen Konservativen,* 157ff.

125. Letter by Marie from early June 1866, in Witte, *Bismarck und die Konservativen,* 334ff.

126. Cf. E. Engelberg, *Bismarck,* 619; Gall, *Bismarck,* 374f.

127. Letter of 15 August 1866 by Karl Witte, in Witte and Haupt, *Karl Witte,* 262.

Chapter 3

Generations in Transition

Feelers toward the Liberals

The wars that brought Prussia to dominance within Germany also touched Trieglaff. Several members of the Thadden family and numerous inhabitants of the village took part in them as soldiers. And the process of founding the Reich shifted the balance of public interest from Prussian to German affairs, threatening to push especially the provinces east of the Elbe to the fringes of the political world. How important, after all, was Pomerania in a German Empire that now extended as far as Bavaria and into Alsace?[1]

In light of the people's recollections of the Napoleonic occupation of their land, it is hardly astonishing that motivation for war against France was incomparably greater than that for a "war between brothers" against Austria in 1866. In 1870 even "those Gerlachs" thrilled to the thought of military successes in the Franco-Prussian War.[2] No one outdid either Reinhold or Gerhard as the brothers recounted with pride participating in the advance of their armies in their letters from France.[3]

Trieglaffers were equally preoccupied with the domestic political developments leading to election of a pan-German Reichstag (parliament) alongside the regional Prussian Abgeordnetenhaus (assembly/lower house). This warranted some thought, for whereas the members of the Prussian lower house assembled as before on the basis of the three-class arrangement of voting rights of 1849, the Reichstag was shaped according to universal and equal voting rights. So although the aristocracy maintained its unassailable status in Prussia, in the empire, on the contrary, it receded noticeably to a position behind the middle class.[4]

Awareness of such things may have contributed to one Thadden's willingness to permit his own election to the Reichstag. Gerhard, Bismarck's friend, had agreed in 1867 to stand as candidate for the Reichstag of the North German Confederation; then in 1871 he consented to be put up for election in the new German Empire. The result was that he became one of the fourteen Pomeranian members of the national legislative body.[5]

The older brother Reinhold, who to this point had been critical of Bismarck, deemed his brother's political career remarkable enough to earn his somewhat distanced, yet accepting, assessment in a biographical sketch (*Lebensbild*) composed later. He emphasized that "Gerhard, like brother-in-law Moritz Blanckenburg from Zimmerhausen," belonged, of course, on the right in the Reichstag. "But he earned for himself also the affection of members at the edges of other parties, e.g., Lasker's."[6]

This relationship was unusual for Pomeranian conservatives, for Eduard Lasker was one of the leaders of the National Liberal Party (Nationalliberale Partei). After initial resistance, he had privately wrestled his way through to support of the Bismarckian politics of imperial unity and pursued the goal of strengthening the parliamentary rights of the Reichstag. Additionally, he was of Jewish origin and he came from Jarotschin in the province of Posen, where it was being discussed vigorously whether and how far a Pole could assent to a unitary German nation.[7]

Lasker was a resolute advocate of defeudalization in the eastern provinces of the Prussian state that were so characterized by feudal structures. By modernizing government toward self-governance in districts and local communities, he wanted to strengthen a "state affording constitutional rights" also at lower levels of the monarchy, "so that Prussia preserves itself at the head of Germany."[8] Prussia was not supposed to be the last light to blink on when it came to constitutional policy in the new German Empire.

This thinking appears to have impressed Reichstag Member Gerhard von Thadden, who, according to his brother Reinhold, was "immensely taken by the potential for accomplishment of the National Liberals." Also "in voting and customs questions" there were "utterances by him carrying undertones of the liberal faction."[9]

So what were these liberal tendencies? And what essential liberal reform concepts pertaining to flatland Pomerania had to be of interest to a Pomeranian estate holder? After the debates during the years of the founding of the empire, they had to do especially with proposals for district restructuring that were intended to accommodate political realities to social realities, the latter changed for decades already. Because a third of all agricultural operations larger than 200 hectares (some 500 acres) were no longer part of manorial estates, it was high time to revise voting conditions in the local bodies of self-government in the region.[10]

The liberal conservatives—the so-called Free Conservatives—knew this too. For a considerable time they had warned of the consequences of the collapse of the feudal order. One of their spokesmen, Count Bethusy-Huc, with whom Gerhard von Thadden was in contact,[11] said openly in the Abgeordnetenhaus: "Since the privilege of purchasing manorial estates has been suspended for the aristocracy, a reason to leave political rights attached to these estates no longer exists. It makes those rights absolutely saleable." The conservatives would have to seek their future by finding a base in "the collectivity of larger landowners"—whether these were estate holders belonging to the nobility, those lacking this formal status, or large-scale farmers—while also counting on the well-to-do middle class in regional towns and cities.[12]

These ideas led to a breakdown of the contrasts between the various rural landholding elites and contributed to the formation of a sort of "gentry," or what might be called a "commonized" landed aristocracy, after the English model. The objective was to create a stimulus to social climbers that was oriented to ownership of land, to represent the interests of the old aristocracy. Thereby points of departure for modernization of rural life and living would be established. The trans-Elbe region was to adopt the perspective of a society without feudal structures.[13]

It is not known how far Gerhard von Thadden was prepared to pursue these thoughts. What is evident in his letters is no more than that he sought contact with Reichstag members who were critical of the old conservative concepts of social order. He did write that during a session debating a law to limit usury,[14] he "became pretty well upset, as our party is doing bad things here—I would have preferred to speak on the opposing side."[15]

Whatever the course of the discussions between the various conservative wings, thoroughgoing reform of district affairs in East Elbian Prussia indeed became a reality upon conclusion of the partisan disputes. At top stood the requirement to do away with the *"Virilstimmen"*[16] of landed aristocrats in the district councils. Most important, according to the liberals—Lasker not least among them—was to grant independent farmers (formerly dependent peasants) a share of the district elective seats proportional to their number. But the larger towns, too, with their traditions of self-governance, were to be given greater weight.[17]

Notwithstanding considerable resistance mounted by traditional conservative forces, a district restructuring (*Kreisordnung*) was passed on 9 December 1872 with the aim of seriously altering the balance of power in rural areas. The number of seats in district councils was now distributed between the larger towns and the rural areas of the district in such a way that the towns could contribute at most half of the delegates. At the same time, rural areas had to see to the interests of voting associations of large land ownership and of the rural "precincts" in a one-to-one ratio. Rural precincts (*Landgemeinden*) were the primary local units of formal civil organization in sparsely settled areas. Thus three economic interest groups were represented in district councils, according to established proportions.[18]

This also held for district commissions. Their duties lay, on the one hand, in active management and oversight of governance within a district. On the other hand, they served as the first judicial instance within the framework of a newly inaugurated administrative justice. Each commission was made up of seven members in all. The district council (*Kreistag*) selected three representatives from the towns and three from the rural precincts. The Landrat, who was the state-approved administrator of the district, was the seventh member and chair and as such could potentially serve as counterweight to both state bureaucracy and remnants of class dominance.[19]

By and large the arrangement reflected the ideas of Eduard Lasker, but also those of the Free Conservatives and above all of Interior Minister Count Friedrich Eulenburg. The concept reached far beyond Bismarck's intentions.[20] Within the arrangement, the districts (the governmental units a step below Prussian provinces such as Pomerania) were to be strengthened as self-governing regional corporations. This would provide a supplemental level of responsible activity to the ordinarily weak rural precincts. These, existing where working village organization was absent, were weakly developed east of the Elbe. By contrast, the more or less independent manorial estates as civil units (*Gutsbezirke*), with their lingering postfeudal traditions of autonomous internal governance, were in a historically well-developed and well-established position. The two existed side by side. Buttressing the responsibilities of rural precincts was thus a worthy accomplishment of the revamped district organizational structure.

What did all this imply for Trieglaff? First, it was a decisive turning point in conventional legal arrangements. Despite all the transformations respecting economic development, legal conditions were still characterized by a class-based conceptualization of social order, so the question of the status of smaller, half-dependent farmers arose insistently. Like the peasantry before them, these farmers, up to that time, had lacked the access to governmental institutions that would enable them to pursue their particular interests. Might they now hit upon the idea of playing an independent role between large landowners and the middle class of the regional towns?[21]

From the reports in the *Stettiner Amtsblatt*, the official provincial news organ circulating from Greifenberg while the new district organization was being enacted, one gains the impression that local political elements of the organizational scheme played at least as great a role as those pertaining to the entire district. This was true above all in the matter of the new provisions for the rural precincts, which endowed constituencies with the right to vote for their precinct supervisor (*Gemeindevorsteher*) and the two assessors appointed as assistants to him. The supervisors, elected for a term of six years, were subject to confirmation by the Landrat, but they originated without exception from the farmers' group. On the estates, on the other hand, it was the estate holders who, in the event they did not wish to fill the office themselves, selected a supervisor.[22]

At the level above the rural precincts and manor precincts it became more difficult to establish civil entities, or *Amtsbezirke* ("wards," as they might be called), which were to be made up of multiple rural precincts together with one or more estates. This step became necessary because police powers, as a onetime entitlement of landed estate holders, had long been under attack and now were suspended; hence other agencies were needed to exercise those powers. Accordingly, it was essential to find an adequately qualified and respected honorary superintendent (*Amtsvorsteher*) for these larger civil entities. It had to be someone who enjoyed the confidence of the district council and could secure support of the president of the Province of Pomerania as well.[23]

Problems soon arose, not just in the selection of suitable individuals, but in the shape and size of the bounds of such jurisdictions. Each was to include 800 to 3,000 inhabitants to ensure it was large enough to bear a major part of the administrative costs. Combining the three Thadden properties Trieglaff, Batzwitz, and Vahnerow with their rural precincts of farm people and augmenting them with the adjacent estate village Barkow brought the population count up to a level that met the size requirements for such an official administrative unit.[24]

But though agreement was reached on joint affiliation in a ward, the problem of selecting a superintendent was by no means resolved thereby. The brothers Reinhold and Gerhard were disinclined to merge their estate governance with the rural precincts of farm people, and their elderly father was simply beyond consideration for the role anymore. The opinion of Hugo von Kleist-Retzow, their old conservative party ally, certainly held for them. He protested against "becoming superintendent on both of his Pomeranian estates, plus several rural precincts."[25]

Reinhold was nevertheless chosen superintendent, possibly having been pressured to take the post.[26] Obviously Gerhard could have been considered too within the context of this innovated district organization that he had gone along with so sympathetically. But he would probably not have found it easy to exchange the responsibilities of membership in the Reichstag for those of a member of the Greifenberg district council or a Trieglaff superintendent. Moreover, he had to withstand political tensions that extended well beyond differences of opinion having to do with district reform.

Implementing these reforms, namely, would be falling into a period of conflict that demanded immeasurably greater energy: the time of the so-called *Kulturkampf*[27] between the new empire and both the Catholic and Protestant churches. It had European dimensions. Supremacy of the state over the church itself, fought for by the liberals, was at stake. In the course of it, Bismarck and his friend of many years, Moritz von Blanckenburg, became distanced to the extent that a breach opened between them. Blanckenburg condemned Bismarck's policies as detrimental to the church's place in society, while the chancellor, in his function as Prussian prime minister, in turn advocated above all the recognition of civil marriage and the abolition of church supervision of schools.[28]

This conflict touched also the devout house of the Thaddens at Trieglaff. Reinhold and his wife Marie agreed with Moritz von Blanckenburg that this conflict of cultures was a betrayal of the spiritual legacy of Lutheranism.[29] Gerhard suffered enough from these tensions between his friend Bismarck and his brother-in-law Blanckenburg to weary of politics. In November of 1872 he decided to give up his seat in the Reichstag—purportedly, as his brother later explained, "on account of his business affairs."[30]

The year 1873 concluded with two tragedies, of very different nature. One involved the estrangement between Bismarck and Blanckenburg, which took on such dimensions that Blanckenburg was provoked into destroying every last letter to him from Bismarck, who for so long had traveled life's roads together with him. On an evening visit to neighboring Zimmerhausen, Reinhold and Marie Thadden were witnesses to an act born of despair and rage: Blanckenburg's burning of innumerable letters going back to the 1840s. The record of lifelong political connections along Prussia's great path to German national unity that was lost thereby is of inestimable value.[31]

In the other, Gerhard von Thadden suffered a fatal accident at the silver wedding anniversary of a relative on the nearby estate of Witzmitz, tearing open a void in the family and in the whole neighborhood that could not be filled. He had represented renewal of conservatism and had shown, more than most other Pomeranian estate holders, readiness to adopt liberal thought. Those members of the family who were of a modern bent remembered him gratefully.[32] Bismarck was particularly shaken by Gerhard's death. Directly upon receipt of the news of mourning, he wrote in a touching personal letter to Gerhard's wife:

> I am unable to attempt during this difficult and sudden turn of fate to hope to comfort you with words. I can only say to you that this unexpected blow will probably not be felt by anyone outside your closest circle of kin so painfully as by Johanna and me. I have not been acquainted with many people in my life upon whose loyal friendship, in jesting and in earnest, and upon whose continual affectionate devotion I counted as certainly as upon Gerhard's—and the number of my friends can scarcely be called a number anymore. From his childhood on I have felt genuinely happy as often as he appeared, within the most varied situations of life, and regretted when he left. I do not recall a moment that might have been capable of leaving behind any trace of unfriendliness, and that is weighty testimony to an endearment lasting through 30 years of eventful life.[33]

Once again Trieglaff was impoverished. This prompted a swap of homes and estates that had been planned for some time. In the summer of 1874, the elder Thadden moved to Batzwitz with his wife, Eleonore née Baroness von Romberg, and his daughter from this second marriage, Gertrud. Reinhold, and his household with its many children, took over the main estate of Trieglaff.[34] Vahnerow became a widow's residence for Gerhard's childless wife Eugenie. Custodial management of that estate went into the hands of Reinhold.

The further history of Vahnerow would be incomplete though without some attention to an individual who was virtually indispensable to functioning of practical business: the chief shepherd Hermann Wangerin, a striking personality. He was the second son of that legendary shepherd Friedrich Wangerin, who had triggered conflict with the established church by seeking baptism administered in proper faith for his eldest son, Johann.[35]

Unlike his elder brother Johann, who emigrated to Wisconsin in 1866, Hermann remained in Germany and founded a substantial branch of the Wangerin family that is expressly portrayed and recognized in the family history authored by "the Americans."[36] He was married to Caroline Kiekhäfer, who came from the part of Trieglaff inhabited by farm people. It was conjectured that she descended from the estate's prior occupant, Heinrich von Oertzen.[37] Following the death of Gerhard von Thadden, Hermann grew into the role of supervisor (*Inspektor*) at Vahnerow. Eventually he took his place beside Gerhard's brother Reinhold at Batzwitz also. And at last he came to Trieglaff—in a relationship "as friends rather than as employer/employee," as the culture of memories of the Wangerin family words it.[38]

But the story of the generations goes further. Hermann Wangerin had a son named Julius who was regarded as exceptionally capable and had received an education, specializing in agriculture. Several places were competing for him, and he was a serious candidate for a position as Inspektor on an estate in the surrounding area. With this in mind, the elderly Adolf von Thadden wrote to his son Reinhold that everything possible ought to be done to get Julius: "I would have been really happy if he had become a dynamic successor to the invalid Trieglaff Inspektor, particularly on account of the good influence which his father could exercise from nearby Vahnerow."[39]

In another letter the senior Thadden went even more forcefully into detail and suggested a transitional solution, just to be safe:

> As J. Wangerin is also sought after elsewhere … will probably be kept in Barkow now too, I would be very happy if young Eleve Bülow would occupy the position for the time being. Nothing definite needs to be promised him yet about the future.[40]

Thus the Thaddens were interested in Julius Wangerin, but for family reasons as well: Julius was about to marry Lydia, a daughter of the Old Lutheran pastor Rudel, who had long been a close friend of the family. He was the one who had certified the baptisms of the four children of Johann Wangerin, who emigrated in 1866. Even today, a number of Wangerin's descendants in Wisconsin treasure a portrait of Rudel that they have.[41]

Following his father Hermann's retirement from active work on the estate, Trieglaff once more offered Julius the position of Inspektor. But he preferred to remain in the position he already held. Of his four children, three went so far as to become teachers at Gymnasiums, the secondary schools that qualify students for university entrance. He named his oldest son Gerhard after Gerhard von Thadden, owner of the Vahnerow estate during his childhood, now deceased.[42]

The connection with those Wangerins who had emigrated to the United States was sustained into the next generation. On the Thadden side, though, it was now cultivated less from Vahnerow than from Batzwitz, where Gertrud, daughter of the elderly Adolph's second marriage, kept up a personal, pious correspondence. After her marriage in September 1878 to Baron Karl Senfft von Pilsach, she corresponded regularly with her erstwhile attendant and intimate, Ulrike Dorn, who had married Hermann Wangerin's cousin Albert and emigrated with him to Wisconsin in 1867. Up to the beginning of the twentieth century, they exchanged news and pictures that offer lively impressions of the living conditions of the time.[43]

And what became of Trieglaff's pious world? What attracts notice is that, in the maelstrom of the Kulturkampf, the points of emphasis in religious engagement underwent a certain shift. On the one hand the Thaddens, like other traditional conservatives, rejected the liberal policies calling for secularization of the social order. On the other they declined to be drawn into any kind of dispute concerning the ecclesiastical-political reforms affecting the established Protestant Church at the margins of the Kulturkampf. Reinhold's wife Marie, a vivaciously collaborative thinker, gave especially eloquent expression to this stance. In 1873, a year of heated conflicts, she wrote to her father in Halle: "The Catholic Church is still better off than we Protestants, whose devout segment is going to be squeezed over to the Old Lutheran free church."[44]

Meanwhile, interest in developments in the established Church of the Prussian Union was very obviously receding. Yet these developments deserved notice at just this time, for parallel to the new district restructuring, a reform of the constitution of the Protestant Church was undertaken that should, in part at least, have prompted a gratified reaction from the Trieglaffers. A following wind of liberal legal thought and Bismarck's express support made it possible to introduce new regulations for the church. These opened up a right of participation to laymen and in principle secured, for the first time within the eastern provinces of Prussia, the election of church representative bodies. The congregational and synodal organization promulgated on 10 September 1873 (Kirchengemeinde- und Synodalordnung) guaranteed a right of church self-governance to the congregations and district synods.[45]

With it, a congregational council (*Gemeindekirchenrat*) was formed in every congregation, consisting of the pastor as chair and several elders who were elected by the congregation. In estate congregations, where patronage obtained, the estate owner-patron was authorized to designate a congregational member as elder if he did not care to become part of the congregational council himself.[46] Formation of synods was provided for at the level of the districts. To these were to belong, under the chairmanship of a superintendent, all the clergymen of the district holding a pastorate, as well as double their number of elected lay members.[47]

For Trieglaff this meant that the master of the estate, as patron, had the right to belong to this newly constituted congregational council. He could also, if he wished, be elected to the district's synod as a lay member, which in actuality required little expenditure of time as the synod met only once annually. Similarly, he could put forth efforts to be elected from the district's synod to the provincial synod, called together every three years by the consistory.[48]

In Trieglaff, Reinhold von Thadden exercised his rights of patronage and nothing further. But his wife also maintained contact with the local Old Lutheran congregation, whose members included the Vahnerow widow Eugenie and the Blanckenburgs from neighboring Zimmerhausen. Congregational and communal affiliations were independent of each other.

The old patriarch Adolph accepted this development with humor and the wisdom of age. He attended worship services held by pastors he esteemed to be good and no longer engaged in church politics. He died in November 1882, universally revered as the senior family member and as representative, renowned countrywide, of the last generation still shaped according to the social order of the prerevolutionary ancien régime.[49] Even to the present day, the Trieglaffers who emigrated to the United States have not forgotten him.[50]

But history did not stand still. Agriculture, too, pushed beyond conditions of earlier times and soon caused Bismarck's generation to appear dated to the one that followed it. Industry's adoption of technology was increasingly felt in the rural work world as well, as machines advanced into the farthest corners of Eastern Pomerania. Above all the steam engine, and particularly the steam plow co-invented by Max Eyth, revamped farming operations by enabling significant acceleration and intensification of tillage of large acreages.[51]

Equally significant was the introduction of the threshing machine. It led not only to further growth in productivity, but also to modification of the activities of workers on the land, with significant savings of time. With mechanical threshing, the manual threshing that traditionally had been done during the long winter months became unnecessary. Labor that was spared commonly migrated to the large cities, especially those in western Germany, and was replaced by seasonal workers recruited from Polish regions of the czarist empire, who needed to be paid only in the summer.[52]

Lastly, the use of chemical fertilizers—founded upon the research of Justus Liebig[53]—brought about considerable increases in land productivity. This went hand in hand with discontinuation of the former three-field agriculture and its nonproductive fallow fields as part of crop rotation. One beneficiary was a newly important food- and feedstuff, the potato. In the last quarter of the nineteenth century in Trieglaff, potato cultivation almost equaled that of grain in terms of land area used. It profited from a spur off the rail line running from Stettin to Kolberg that was completed in 1882, facilitating transportation.[54]

Naturally, all this modernization was associated with costs. More than anything, acquisition of machines burdened the budgets of estate businesses that were already increasingly indebted as a consequence of the depression that began in 1873.[55] Credit agencies were called for which could make loans available on favorable terms. For independent farming businesses, these were primarily the newly established *Raiffeisen-Kassen*. The manorial estates continued relying on the *"Landschaften"* created by Frederick the Great. As aristocratic credit associations, the latter made advances of capital backed by mortgages available to estate holders who needed money.[56]

In the case of the Thadden estates' business, membership in a Landschaft became pertinent. Reinhold was elected early on to the Landschaft board in the Treptow region. Service was voluntary, with a certain associated prestige. Nevertheless, keeping in mind the indebtedness of the estates, there was a yawning gap between appearances—given the high-flown title—and the actual performance capacity of the Landschaft.

Despite frequent reversals, Pomeranian agriculture, in Trieglaff as elsewhere, ultimately underwent a process of modernization that altered conditions of life. But modernization and the step-by-step defeudalization accompanying it did not automatically signify liberalization, either economically or politically. The depression of the 1870s brought free trade to its limits, so that everywhere a demand grew for protectionist measures. Finally, in 1878, Bismarck turned to a policy of protective tariffs that was supposed to shield the domestic market against foreign competition.[58]

Politically, fear of a labor movement that was gaining momentum grew more intense. Up to this time the movement had been confined to the large cities, but now it was on the verge of spreading to the countryside. Here, too, Bismarck gained sympathy with his innovative policy of socialist legislation.[59] Latitude for liberal movements was becoming narrower, to say the least, but it would be too simple to trace the country's growing antiliberal mood solely to the economic and sociopolitical conflicts of the time. Even if certain fears have to be taken seriously as part of the reality of life, they cannot explain adequately why Pomerania, and Trieglaff particularly, were less ready than East Prussia, for example, to grant some chance, even limited, to liberal ideas of social order.[60]

To understand this, some things that are linked to experiences and traditions specific to Trieglaff must be borne in mind. The Kulturkampf, for one, affected the pietistic world of the Thaddens more forcefully than it did worlds less molded by Christianity. Precisely because people in Trieglaff thought of themselves as having contributed to the church's renewal through their pietistic intensification of the life of faith, they regarded the new governmental regulations unfavorably, particularly the one abolishing supervision of schools by the clergy. The regulations were going to rob them of the harvest from seed sown during the decades of the awakening movement.[61]

People undoubtedly were disappointed that Bismarck had turned away from his earlier experience of Pietism in Trieglaff. In the imperial chancellor's assertion, for example, that, "A new effort is being made with the new church regulations ... to overcome indifference of the masses toward the church by involving lay people more vigorously than before in church governance and business,"[62] the Trieglaffers of the second generation saw merely further steps toward secularization and loss of spiritual substance. They wished to keep the secular world away from the church, whereas Bismarck aimed to bring more world into the church.[63]

It is noteworthy that in Trieglaff, people belonging to the Witte family stoked the fears of secularization especially intensely. As the elderly Karl wrote to his daughter Marie: "Vatican insolence had pretty well eradicated my old Catholic sympathies. But Bismarck and liberal Culture Minister Falk are operating so effectively that these are gradually beginning to germinate again."[64] And a few months before that he had written, in direct confrontation of Bismarck, about "this petty, narrow minded war, nominally against Jesuitism, but in fact not against the Catholic Church alone, but just as much against the Protestant also, yes, against believing Christianity itself, but substantively for the sake of glorious freemasonry."[65]

But it was not exclusively fears of secularization awakened by the Kulturkampf that strengthened these antiliberal positions. Older defensive attitudes were casting shadows as well. Hence Marie Thadden-Witte composed a note about the most influential liberal scholar and politician of his time, Dahlmann,[66] which—while granting full recognition of the man's courage—permits perception of distinct reservations:

> I am, to be sure, not so foolish as to want to hatch out the egg that is hidden in the oath of Dahlmann and the other gentlemen of Göttingen, but have sincere admiration for men who, true to their oaths, always keep their lives in harmony with their principles.[67]

This delimitation of her political stance vis-à-vis Dahlmann's evidenced its vitality also following the establishment of the empire. As spokesman for the Prussia-friendly Kleindeutsche Partei (for smaller borders excluding Austria) in the Frankfurt Assembly of 1848 (Frankfurter Nationalversammlung), Dahlmann had advocated moderately liberal constitutional goals. Marie was no friend of liberal reforms (Figure 10).

Caution, then, is warranted over against propositions, frequently found in modern research, that in this society molded by aristocracy the growth of middle-class forces inevitably led to proliferation of liberal ideas of social order.[68] Growth in the number of middle-class estate holders in the District of Greifenberg did not make it more liberal.[69] On the contrary, in many cases middle-class persons took on feudal manners of living and in doing so provoked "the folks" in the village. Increased middle-class composition of this population was not equivalent to defeudalization.[70]

But the dismantling of feudalism, multilayered as it was, had to bring along with it risks to the modern economic world that could not be postponed and uncertainties that could lead into blind alleys. Thus, in a crumbling feudal society people asked what future perspectives a renewed conservativism might have, in Trieglaff not least of all. It was no longer enough, after the success of Bismarck's establishment of the Reich, merely to prop themselves upon the fundaments of national order and think German in place of Prussian.[71] Optimistic sociopolitical conceptualizations of order had to be visualized too.

In this search for novel orientations, a powerfully effective but ambiguous figure succeeded in garnering public attention, especially in Christian circles. The court and cathedral preacher Adolf Stoecker,[72] offspring of common people, was a socially conservative thinker to whom many of the middle-class and academic traits of the Lutheran pietistic movement were foreign. In the conflicts of the Kulturkampf, he had sensed as threatening the loss of ties to the church in the Protestant population. He had seen in liberalism, no less than in the ascent of social democracy, a danger to the Christian foundations of social order. Influenced by the strong decline in church marriages and baptisms following the introduction of civil marriage, he had taken over leadership of the Berlin City Mission with the goal of once again bringing Christian faith to the people. He also meant to take action against waning church involvement. A popular (folk) church (Volkskirche) was more important to him than a state church (Staatskirche).[73]

Unsurprisingly, Stoecker also exerted an attractive force upon Trieglaff. Particularly in the transition phase following the end of the liberal era, he won sympathy with his social ideas—no longer even class-based—in the mixed aristocratic/burgher home of the Thaddens, that is, in a home that was already known for placing social thinking above liberal thinking. What pleased the Trieglaffers most was his advocacy of a program for taking the government out of the church, one that affected people belonging to the established church (so-called Landeskirchler) and to the free church (Freikirchler) in equal measure. A "folk church," or "people's church," (Volkskirche) promised to subsume all.[74]

It merits more than marginal comment that here, too, initiatives lay on the Witte side. Karl Witte wrote to his daughter Marie: "The emergence, apparently successful, of the Christian-social group is gratifying too, and Stöcker, Wangemann, etc. deserve the highest recognition for their courage."[75] Shortly thereafter, Marie and her husband opened the hall that her father-in-law, Adolph Thadden, had built for the Trieglaff Conferences[76]

Figure 10. Reinhold von Thadden (1825–1903) and Marie von Thadden née Witte (1834–1922) at a game of chess in the Trieglaff castle gardens

to Stoecker so that he could read his lectures for the Inner Mission and the Christian-social movement there. Her brother Leopold appears to have been associated with Stoecker, too.[77]

The relationship with Stoecker carried into the following generation. Marie and Reinhold's daughter-in-law, Ehrengard née von Gerlach, chose this Volkskirche pastor to baptize her son Reinold; he would later play an important role in Protestant church history.[78] Stoecker himself had in the meantime become renowned, controversially, beyond Prussian borders. These intricate historical threads, scarcely comprehensible anymore today, demonstrate connections reaching across generations.

Yet they too were controversial. Stoecker gave cause for concern when he first emerged in the public eye, for in the interest of his Christian-social movement he did not shy away from anti-Semitic slogans and utilized populist and demagogic methods. Indeed, in the 1880s these tactics scared away many adherents of the Conservative Party in the cities as well as in the country.[79] More than anything though, he increasingly aroused the displeasure of Bismarck, who worried about the impression the bustling court preacher's activity made on the young heir to the throne, Prince William, later Emperor William II. It went so far that the old chancellor felt compelled to warn the crown prince against overly close connections to Stoecker, and to give him political instruction about the relationship between state and church spheres of interest in government.

"I have," Bismarck wrote,

> nothing against Stöcker; he has for me only the one fault as a politician, that he is a priest, and as a priest, that he practices politics.... The Lutheran priest is, as soon as he feels himself strong enough for it, just as inclined toward theocracy as the Catholic. Meanwhile, it is harder to manage him because he has no Pope above him. I am a believing Christian, but I fear that I could go astray in my faith if I, like the Catholic person, were restricted to priestly mediation to God.[80]

Thus did Bismarck almost echo Adolph von Thadden's critique of the church at the Prussian General Synod of 1846.[81]

Nothing of these ecclesiastical-political disputes at the highest level trickled down to the daily life of the village inhabitants of Trieglaff, Vahnerow, and Batzwitz. Here the congregational members awaited that their pastors should attend to worship using the traditional liturgy and to official functions that were proper. The church was responsible for the ceremonial execution of the great family events, weddings, baptisms, confirmations, and above all funerals, in which the entire village participated.[82] The many hymns by Luther and Paul Gerhardt particularly have remained fixed in the memory of the Pomeranians who emigrated to the United States. These hymns are still found today, in older and newer hymnals kept with great care, in English translation as well as in bilingual editions. Pomeranian *Gesangbücher*—hymnals, songbooks—have not been forgotten in Wisconsin.

Notes

1. Cf. Wolfgang J. Mommsen, *Das Ringen um den nationalen Staat* (Berlin, 1993), 7/1: 248ff.

2. Cf. Kraus, *Ernst-Ludwig von Gerlach,* 860f.

3. Letters by Reinhold and Gerhard von Thadden from the years 1870–1871 concerning negotiations in Versailles, in carton for Reinhold von Thadden, FA. Further, letter by Gerhard of 20 February 1871 about negotiations in Versailles, reprinted in Fritz Stern, *Gold und Eisen,* 2nd ed. (Hamburg, 2000), 232 (absent in FA).

4. Cf. Rudolf von Thadden, *Prussia,* 90.

5. Cf. Buchsteiner, "Wirtschaftlicher und sozialer Wandel," 195.

6. Biographical sketch of Gerhard von Thadden composed by his brother Reinhold, p. 13, in carton for Reinhold von Thadden, FA.

7. Cf. Adolf Laufs, *Eduard Lasker. Ein Leben für den Rechtsstaat* (Göttingen, 1984), 15ff.

8. Address by Lasker of November 1872, ibid., 77f.

9. Biographical sketch of Gerhard von Thadden, p. 15, in carton for Reinhold von Thadden, FA.

10. Cf. Wagner, *Bauern, Junker und Beamte,* 41. Further, Huber, *Deutsche Verfassungsgeschichte,* 4: 352ff.

11. Undated letter by Gerhard von Thadden from his time in parliament, in carton for Gerhard von Thadden, FA.

12. Quoted from Wagner, *Bauern, Junker und Beamte,* 317f.

13. Ibid.

14. Treue, "Wirtschafts- und Sozialgeschichte Deutschlands," 3: 328.

15. Undated letter by Gerhard von Thadden, FA.

16. *Virilstimmen* were individual votes of estate holders as a prerogative of ownership.

17. Cf. Wagner, *Bauern, Junker und Beamte,* 321.

18. Ibid., 323f.

19. Ibid., 325. Further, Huber, *Deutsche Verfassungsgeschichte,* 4: 358.

20. Pertinent, Otto von Bismarck, "Erinnerung und Gedanke," in Bismarck, *GW,* 15: 347, 366f. Gerhard von Thadden reported on conversations with Lasker in an undated letter (see n. 11 above).

21. Cf. Wagner, *Bauern, Junker und Beamte,* 328.

22. *Amts-Blatt der Königlichen Regierung zu Stettin* [official organ of the royal government at Stettin] of December 1872. Further, Wagner, *Bauern, Junker und Beamte,* 322f.

23. Wagner, *Bauern, Junker und Beamte,* 323.

24. Cf. Ulrich, *Chronik des Kreises Greifenberg,* 279ff., 281ff., 351ff., 354f.

25. Quoted from Wagner, *Bauern, Junker und Beamte,* 344.

26. This is suggested by an official writing of 19 October 1894 in which Reinhold requests release from duty as commission chairman, found in carton for Reinhold von Thadden, FA.

27. Cf. Karl E. Born, "Epochen der preußischen Geschichte seit 1871," in *Handbuch der Preußischen Geschichte,* ed. Wolfgang Neugebauer (Berlin, 2001), 3: 78ff., 82ff. Further, Rudolf von Thadden, "Die Geschichte der Kirchen und Konfessionen," in *Handbuch der Preußischen Geschichte* 3: 596ff.

28. In "Erinnerung und Gedanke," Bismarck expresses the following judgment concerning Moritz von Blanckenburg: "Blanckenburg lacked a capacity to judge the historical progression of German and European politics in a broad scope. He was without ambition himself and free of the sickness of many old Prussian class comrades, envy of me; but his political judgment had difficulty breaking free from the Prussian-particularist, even Pomeranian-Lutheran viewpoint. He was not uninfluenced by the residue of the struggles of the 'unfortunate Lutherans,' the 'Old Lutherans,' whom Blanckenburg was at one with during the thirties," in Bismarck, *GW,* 15: 341f.

29. Letter by Marie to her father from the year 1873 (undated), in H. Witte, *Bismarck und die Konservativen,* 347.

30. Biographical sketch of Gerhard von Thadden, p. 15, in carton for Reinhold von Thadden, FA.

31. Report by H. Witte, in *Bismarck und die Konservativen,* 348.

32. Biographical sketch of Gerhard von Thadden, 18ff., in carton for Reinhold von Thadden, FA.

33. Letter of 14 October 1873 from Bismarck to Eugenie von Thadden, in Bismarck, *GW,* 14/2: 855. Further, a letter by Johanna von Bismarck to Adolph von Thadden from 14 October 1873, in carton of Vahnerow materials, FA.

34. Reuß, *Adolf von Thadden,* 154f.

35. See chapter 1 of this volume.

36. Wangerin, *Family Wangerin,* 57ff. (FA).

37. Ibid. Further, see chapter 1 of this volume.

38. Wangerin, *Family Wangerin,* 57ff. (FA).

39. Letter of 1 March 1878 by Adolph von Thadden, in carton for Reinhold von Thadden, FA.

40. Second letter of 1 March 1878 by Adolph von Thadden, in carton for Reinhold von Thadden, FA.

41. In holdings of FA, as gift. Document reproduced in Wangerin, *Family Wangerin,* 40 (FA).

42. Family tree in Wangerin, *Family Wangerin,* 55 (FA).

43. Copies from Wisconsin, presented to the author, in the carton of the U.S. letters, FA.

44. Letter by Marie to her father from the year 1873 (undated), in H. Witte, *Bismarck und die Konservativen,* 347.

45. Cf. Huber, *Deutsche Verfassungsgeschichte,* 4: 849ff. Further, Rudolf von Thadden, "Geschichte der Kirchen," 602f.

46. §§ 2, 3, 6 of "Kirchengemeinde- und Synodalordnung," in Ernst R. & Wolfgang Huber, *Staat und Kirche im 19. und 20. Jahrhundert: Dokumente zur Geschichte des deutschen Staatskirchenrechts,* vol. 2, *Staat und Kirche im Zeitalter des Hochkonstitutionalismus und des Kulturkampfs 1848–1890,* 2nd ed. (Berlin, 1990), 933.

47. Ibid., 936.

48. Ibid., 939f.
49. Reuß, *Adolf von Thadden*, 162ff.
50. Natzke, Foreword, *The Nobleman Among the Brothers;* see above, chap. 1, n. 9.
51. On Max Eyth see article "Max Eyth" in *NDB*, 4: 714f. Eyth authored the tale *Hinter Pflug und Schraubstock*, much read in its time. Cf. also Treue, "Wirtschafts- und Sozialgeschichte," 329f., and Christian Graf von Krockow, *Die Reise nach Pommern* (Stuttgart, 1985), 73ff.
52. Cf. Mommsen, *Ringen*, 290ff.
53. On Justus Liebig, see the articles in *ADB* 18: 589ff and *NDB* 14: 497ff.
54. Cf. Krockow, *Reise*, 63f.; Mommsen, *Ringen*, 291.
55. In Pomerania in 1896, 60 percent of the large estates were indebted to 60 percent of their estimated value, Mommsen, *Ringen*, 295.
56. Cf. Ilona Buchsteiner, *Großgrundbesitz in Pommern 1871–1914* (Berlin, 1993), 258.
57. In Pomerania there were four regions, each with two councillors and a regional director. These in turn selected two general councillors and a general director for Pomerania. Cf. Buchsteiner, *Großgrundbesitz*, 259.
58. Cf. Thomas Nipperdey, *Deutsche Geschichte 1866–1918*, vol. 1, *Arbeitswelt und Bürgergeist* (Munich, 1990), 192ff. Cf. also Rita Aldenhoff-Hübinger, *Agrarpolitik und Protektionismus* (Göttingen, 2002), 71ff.
59. Cf. E. Engelberg, *Bismarck*, 2: 297ff.; Gall, *Bismarck*, 551ff., 574ff.
60. Cf. Wagner, *Bauern, Junker und Beamte*, 511f., 581f.
61. See chapter 1 of this volume.
62. Report by Bismarck to highest levels, 4 June 1877, in Bismarck, *GW*, 6c: 82.
63. Cf. Rudolf von Thadden, "Bismarck—ein Lutheraner?" in *Weltliche Kirchengeschichte. Ausgewählte Aufsätze*, ed. Rudolf von Thadden (Göttingen, 1989), 154.
64. Letter of 17 March 1873 by Karl Witte, in Witte and Haupt, *Karl Witte*, 267.
65. Letter of 27 December 1872 by K. Witte to Reumont, ibid., 266.
66. Cf. Hermann Heimpel, "Friedrich Christoph Dahlmann," in *Die Großen Deutschen* (Berlin, 1957), 5: 236. Further, Rudolf von Thadden, "Mut zum Dissens. Dahlmann und Gervinus im Spannungsfeld von Geschichte und Politik," in *Weltliche Kirchengeschichte. Ausgewählte Aufsätze*, ed. Rudolf von Thadden (Göttingen, 1989), 43ff.
67. Undated note, presumably from the 1860s, in carton for Reinhold v. Thadden, FA. This has to do with a reference to the liberal protest of the "Göttingen seven" opposed to the absolutistic demeanor of the Hanoverian king in 1837.
68. On this—more critical of aristocracy than of class—Hans-Ulrich Wehler, *Deutsche Gesellschaftsgeschichte*, vol. 3, *Von der "Deutschen Doppelrevolution" bis zum Beginn des Ersten Weltkrieges 1849–1914* (Munich, 1995), 816.
69. See chapter 2 of this volume.
70. Cf. Arno J. Mayer, *Adelsmacht und Bürgertum* (Munich, 1984), 19. Further, Nipperdey, *Deutsche Geschichte*, 1: 211.
71. Nipperdey, *Deutsche Geschichte*, 2: 333f.
72. Cf. Günter Brakelmann, Martin Greschat, and Werner Jochmann, *Protestantismus und Politik. Werk und Wirkung Adolf Steockers* (Hamburg, 1982), 19ff., 123ff.

73. Cf. Rudolf von Thadden, "Geschichte der Kirchen," 605.
74. Cf. Nipperdey, *Deutsche Geschichte*, 2: 334f.
75. Letter of 9 April 1878 by Karl Witte, in Witte and Haupt, *Karl Witte*, 268.
76. See chapter 1 of this volume.
77. Witte and Haupt, *Karl Witte*, 163.
78. Note in family album, part 3, FA.
79. Cf. Nipperdey, *Deutsche Geschichte*, 2: 335.
80. Letter of 6 January 1888 by Bismarck, in *GW*, 15: 467f.
81. See chapter 2 of this volume.
82. Krockow, *Reise*, 86ff.

Chapter 4

The Wilhelminian Generation

Modernization within Traditions

S eldom, perhaps, have hopes for a renewal of social and political life coincided with a perception of generational change so forcefully as after Bismarck's dismissal in 1890. The country breathed a collective sigh of relief when the young Kaiser William II proclaimed a "new course" that did away with the Anti-Socialist Laws of 1878 directed against the labor movement in a series of measures that introduced broadened social policies meant to improve legislative protections for labor and to restrict work hours for people under sixteen years of age. Expectations were high in Pomerania as elsewhere.[1]

Indeed, running counter to this sense of a new departure was an unusually sharp critique of the traditional ruling class in the East Elbian lands, including Pomerania. Formulated during the 1890s by Hugo Preuß (Preuss), a leading mind of the leftist liberals and later father of the Weimar Constitution of 1919,[2] it held the Junkers, titled landowners, accountable for the Prussian state's dwindling susceptibility to reform and accused them of myopically subordinating the interests of the state to their own class interests. "All attempts to transform the Junker class into a modern political nobility were and are bound to remain fruitless," for "the conditions favoring the survival of this Junker class are rooted at all times in outdated economic forms."[3]

With this political challenge, Preuß was leveling criticism that broadly reflected the view of liberals from urban regions. He proceeded from the assumption that the class of farm people (*Bauernstand*) east of the Elbe shared the interests of middle-class society in towns and cities in opposition to the landed aristocracy:

> The fact that Junkers are the enemy of middle class people and farm people alike is what the history of centuries teaches on every page. But farmers are in the end not historians. They have to experience historical facts directly upon their bodies.[4]

According to Preuß, then, farmers needed to catch up and become familiar with historical reality.

But what if farmers' own experiences did not coincide with the theories of academic historians? It might be the case that in situations of great conflict, like the Revolution of 1848, farmers and the urban middle class could engage in struggle side by side for the sake of common interests. Yet they did not for that reason have to join forces under all circumstances with the liberal representatives of the urban middle class in the East Elbian district councils, especially since these groups themselves were by no means always aligned politically. Local interests clearly had a weight of their own.[5]

At the start of the 1890s, during the time of the "new course" following Bismarck's "dismissal by resignation," fear was mounting that advancing industrialization of society, centering on large cities, would wrest primacy from agriculture. Consistent with this, an association of agriculturists, the Agrarian League, was founded in 1893 to represent the interests of the agricultural "country" versus the cities oriented toward an industrial economy.[6] As a result, farm people ended up on the side of the large landholders, diminishing their potential for common cause with the urban middle class. Alliance against established feudal structures, as liberals conceived it, thus became harder.[7]

In that situation the new government under Imperial Chancellor Caprivi[8] launched a legislative project that had long been on the agenda and was thought to be overdue: the law for structural reform of the rural precincts,[9] having importance for Trieglaff. This step of reform had been put aside when district structures were revamped in 1872[10] because it had become enmeshed in the tangle of conflicts of interest between conservatives and liberals in the Prussian lower house. But now prospects for its realization looked more favorable, especially because the new minister of the interior, Ludwig Herrfurth, had signaled that he was inclined toward reform.[11]

The innovative restructuring of rural precincts dating from 3 July 1891 had the goal of creating viable communal structures while doing away with the earlier widespread fractionalization into too-small precincts. Accordingly, it undertook to fuse rural precincts of farm people with estates as much as possible, and to equip the emerging entities, at a size of at least forty eligible voters, with representative bodies capable of functioning (*Gemeindevertretung*).[12]

It would not have been Prussia if the law had made it through the Abgeordnetenhaus without abridgements. The conservative faction forced attention in the direction of the interests of estate holders and demanded that the reform be enacted only with the support of those affected or of district commissions, which was tantamount to veto power for the large landowners. The outcome in the East Elbian provinces was that between 1892 and 1907, only 29 estates lost their autonomous civil status while 787 were brought together with other communal entities.[13]

Trieglaff counted among the estates that retained their status. Combined with its outlying farmsteads Gruchow and Idashof, the village was large enough to claim a representative body for itself, one representing more than just the population of farm people and businesspeople such as the proprietor of the mill and the innkeeper: for the first time, unpropertied laborers meeting a certain tax status were also included. The smaller estate village, Vahnerow, which had no independent farms, was in contrast adjoined to the nearest rural precinct, Batzwitz, a move prompted in part by its belonging to the parish there. In both instances a supervisor was elected, but he had to be confirmed by the Landrat, the district administrator.[14]

This precinct organization, which included newly introduced, circumscribed rights for day laborers, took into consideration a social situation that had been obscured in the district restructuring of 1872: the rural population comprised not just estate holders and farmers, but also agricultural workers who owned no property. These people in fact worked primarily on estate premises, but more and more they were employed by farm businesses and had to be taken seriously in elections as an important component of the world of village life.[15]

These day laborers on estates, now entitled to vote, were as a rule paid partly in kind. They received part of their wages in products of the estate and had the use of some two-thirds of an acre of land (1 Morgen) per family. They were entitled to have a cow, two pigs, and four sheep, and received the necessary feed for them. In addition, they could keep a certain number of chickens and ducks.[16]

Among the scant sources that treat this central theme of rural social history, one provides particularly vivid information about the relationship between farm people and day laborers. It originated in the nearer environs of Trieglaff from the pen of a local author, Elisabeth von Oertzen, the eldest daughter of Reinhold and Marie von Thadden and wife of the estate holder Karl von Oertzen. This storyteller, who hailed from Dorow in the neighboring district of Regenwalde, described the rural Pomeranian way of life in books widely read at the time. In a piece entitled "My Cow" ("Meine Kuh"), she graphically portrayed the story of a woman with two daughters, one of whom pledges herself to the son of a farmer while the other marries a laborer.

In the first instance the mother refuses to give her consent, arguing, "Over my dead body my daughter'll get looked down on, livin' on a farm. We're poor folks, we wanta be left alone. You won't be no farm wife; I'm not standin' for it, 'n' you ain't marryin' 'im."[17] In the second instance she welcomes the marriage because it is within their own class, and they will get to keep a cow of their own besides: "A cow was special property conferring social position, lending it honor and prestige."[18]

But the story takes a dramatic course. After some time, the cow dies, diminishing the mother's position and the new family's means of support. The son-in-law starts to drink and is fired. When at last he manages to find a different job in another village, he leaves his mother-in-law behind. Happily, though, she is taken into the home of the older daughter on the farm, and so escapes destitution.[19]

Portrayals besides this one do exist. Anna Lange, the wife of the Trieglaff cartwright, wrote to her Aunt Ulrike Wangerin in the United States that "the cows of laborers and of workers getting part of their wages in farm goods are housed in a single barn," but "the feed for them … is thin and pathetic," so that "each person has to take a beating, in the milk-pail, according to their circumstances, and many a person is compelled to put out a lot of money for lard." "Our cow," the letter continues, "has been standing with no milk or butter for a long time now already, things that can't be gotten easily here either because the gentlefolk who have the estate don't sell anything to us ordinary folks like they did before; milk is transported every day to the dairy in Plathe."[20]

The so-called modernization of business enterprises, then, had negative aspects too. Previously, milk had stayed in the village and at times could even be generously distributed. Now it was taken to a central dairy in the nearby town of Plathe and was thus withdrawn from local consumption—a further step on the way from a needs-based to an acquisitive society.

At first this did not change the relationship between day laborers and farmers. An unspoken social order, which found no embodiment in legislation, continued to be maintained in villages. Deeply rooted modes of behavior prevailed without regard for census categories—indeed, they applied as much as, or even more than, written regulations. In moments of distress they could attain an unexpected measure of significance.[21]

Given this background of complicated social conditions and half-hearted institutional reforms accompanying the dismantling of the feudal order, how was the region actually administered and governed? There were, to be sure, supervisors (Gemeindevorsteher) and superintendents (Amtsvorsteher) now, the latter assigned registrars to record births and deaths and conduct civil marriages. But the traditional estate owners still had substantial responsibilities, which generated uncertainties in instances of conflict. Who, for example, was accountable for road building, who for regulation of boundary disputes between independent farms and traditional estates?

A glance into the records shows that one office, that of Landrat or district administrator, acquired central importance for these interconnections.[22] It was situated at the intersection of state governance and local-interest politics. But it was also the agency for everything that could be called modernization and improvement in economic life. In many respects one might characterize it as nothing less than the engine of developmental policy for the rural sphere.[23]

Beginning in the 1890s, even more tasks for promoting effective administration fell upon these district administrators. For example, they decided cases conducted by district commissions involving the accident insurance that covered agricultural workers; they decided on applications for disability pension; and from 1911 on they became, as a rule, chiefs of the local insurance bureaus. Whoever became entangled in rules and regulations went to the office of the Landrat.[24]

But it was not only ordinary petitioners who sought contact with the district administrator. Local officials who came up short on administrative experience and found themselves without an office did, too. Hence superintendents and supervisors were in many instances dependent upon help from his office. Above all, supervisors were in a state of dependency, because they required the Landrat's endorsement for their election. Critical observers claimed that "a Gemeindevorsteher would take no important step without the Herr Landrat." A Landrat even reported that all precinct resolutions requiring approval "are worked out in my office."[25]

It calls for no special imagination to recognize that a Landrat could, given this state of affairs, easily exert political influence. It was hardly thinkable that in elections to the Landtag (provincial legislative body) or to the Reichstag a supervisor might not proceed in the interest of the government. At any rate, there were no Social Democratic representatives from the rural precincts in East Elbian Prussia in the time of William II's rule.[26]

Intense demands were placed upon a district administrator. He had to be politically reliable and be in a position to effectively represent the government's direction in public. At the same time he had to be able to master the mechanisms of the state bureaucracy and assert himself relative to them. Finally, he had to enjoy prestige with the social elites of his district.

This meant, concretely, that to qualify the Landrat had to have passed the second civil service examination, had to present several years of experience in administration in local government offices in districts and provinces, and was required to own real property in the district of his appointment. These were criteria that not many candidates met.[27]

But one person who did meet them very adequately was Adolf von Thadden, the only son of Landschaft board member Reinhold (Figure 11). He had passed all his law exams with very high marks, beyond that had earned his doctorate, and had accumulated experience as a young Landrat in the prestigious District of Mohrungen in East Prussia, where the family of Count and later Prince Dohna-Schlobitten had its seat. Finally, he was claimant to possession of the Trieglaff estate in the District of Greifenberg, which would become his eventually. Hence he belonged to the landed aristocracy of the region. No one could contest his qualifications for the office.[28]

Adolf von Thadden soon proved to be an extremely imaginative and active entrepreneur. When he assumed his office in Greifenberg in 1895, he immediately undertook projects to improve the infrastructure of the district. Main highways and paved country roads came first, but next in line were plans to extend the rail network that envisioned narrow-gauge lines as extensions of the Prussian state-run railway. These branch lines came into the custody of the district. By the beginning of World War I in 1914, a dense network of branch lines would be completed in Greifenberg— with freight-rail connections to Trieglaff.[29]

Figure 11. Adolf von Thadden (1858–1932), Administrator (Landrat), District of Greifenberg

Cultivation of hoed crops had proven to be unexpectedly profitable since the 1880s, and only a sugar beet processing plant was still needed to push returns even higher. Together with other estate holders of the district, Adolf von Thadden undertook construction of a sugar beet factory in Greifenberg that soon had great significance for the agriculture of the region. Sales increased markedly.[30]

This progress in the economic life of the district, however, did not at all alter the fact that emigration of farm workers held steady. Compared to earlier times, the only difference was that emigrants now were no longer going to the United States but to the large cities of the Ruhr region or the Berlin area, where better prospects for employment had opened up. The loss of labor, leading to a veritable flight from the land, aroused concern in Pomerania.[31]

Trieglaff families let their relatives in the United States know about this too. In a letter to his great-aunt Ulrike Wangerin, the third son of the cartwright Gustav Lange wrote:

> This spring 11 families of laborers moved away from Trieglaff…; they are moving mostly to the towns, especially to Greifenberg. With the partial sale of the neighboring estate Cardemin the laborers there were mostly dismissed. 4 families from there have hired on here. Otherwise, 4 dwellings here would have stood empty.[32]

Continuing, the letter elaborated that several homes were empty in the outlying properties of Idashof and Gruchow. "There, too, people aren't staying for longer than a year." Then follows a reflective passage: "This urge to move around is not the rule just for our people here; it is taking place on many other estates in this area, too. It all stems from everyone's believing they will be better off someplace else."[33]

The outcome? Gustav Lange brought up a development that had already alarmed families of farm workers in earlier years, when threshing machines were being introduced.[34] "The cultivation of sugar beets around here is done by Russian-Polish workers. There are 40 individuals right here this year."[35] And living space had to be provided for them, as was accomplished through construction of a new building, a so-called "reapers' barracks."

These problems of flight from the land took on quite another timbre in the mouth of the mistress of the estate, the wife of Landrat Adolf von Thadden. She was a granddaughter of the court chaplain Otto von Gerlach, brother of Bismarck's archconservative opponents Leopold and Ernst-Ludwig.[36] In a note headed "Auch Landflucht" (Also flight from the land), she spoke in melancholy tones about the "wheel of history" that "is moving off the land, away to the large cities, overfilled with people." She complained that "in distant eastern rural areas we are getting almost nothing now anymore but servant girls who we know in advance will be wholly unsuited and inadequate for the tasks and demands that our culturally advanced times place upon them." She also criticized the educational practices in rural areas as counterproductive for society east of the Elbe: "The educating that we do doesn't take place for our own homes and for the future, but for the wife of some commerce and finance bigwig in the Thiergartenstrasse in Berlin."[37]

Signs of a romantically tinged rootedness in the land are detectable in her husband too. In an address in Greifenberg on the occasion of the eightieth birthday of Otto von Bismarck, he accentuated Bismarck's bonds with the land emphatically and gushed, "We sense still his aversion for the big city, this desert of walls and cobblestones, his affection for country life and his genuinely German love for German forests."[38]

In contrast to his wife, however, who was of a brooding nature, the Landrat still had a sound sense of the reality of this country life, subjected increasingly to industrialization. He reacted to the departure of numerous workers from his estate by building new houses for the farm workers. These replaced the old straw-roofed, timbered clay-built cottages and were distinguished by a generous layout of rooms and an attractive little fenced garden in front. A detailed report in an anniversary volume about Trieglaff concludes, "Such friendly white houses as these, wood trim colorfully done up, are a powerful attraction to the country people, and seem specially suited to counter the flight from the land. It has never been difficult to find occupants for these dwellings."[39]

The families of farm workers were of the same opinion. "Here in Trieglaff, since the Landrath has arrived," Anna Lange, wife of the cartwright, writes to the United States,

> much is being improved and built. A workers' house for 2 families is being built, from the manor to the red path, mentioned before, a new fence has been made, and the interior space is planted with roses and groups of fir trees. It looks real pretty. In general the Landrat is very much in favor of improvement and beautification, for which his wealth is very useful to him. It is said that he married into 80 thousand Thaler.[40]

For the workers at Trieglaff—called, as always, "our people" by the Thaddens—the time "since the Landrath got here" counted for much, even though he had served as Landrat of the District of Greifenberg starting in 1895 and so had been present in a political, administrative sense. It was only as heir to the Trieglaff estate that he had not exercised any responsibility. His father, Reinhold, lived until 1903, so for a time the generations overlapped. Grandparents, parents, and already five grandchildren lived very near to each other, though not under the same roof, and gave the Thaddens a pronounced presence in the district.

The level of this prominence was demonstrated at the funeral of the older gentleman, as an exceptionally long procession paid him last respects. "The wreath-laying," the teacher Ramthun wrote in a detailed letter to relatives in the United States,

> was unusually bountiful. The district and town of Greifenberg, the district assembly and representatives of the precinct, the community of farmers and the workers—all exhibited their love for the deceased with sometimes large, splendid wreaths. Of them all ... none made the family so happy as the wreath that v. Th's. loyal group of workers laid at the casket.[41]

Ramthun highlights particularly that a laurel wreath had even been sent by the emperor:

> So it could be seen that the old Thadden line was honored far beyond the bounds of our home here. Herr von Thadden was, personally, someone very willing to help. ... If ill befell a worker or he had some other concern, he appealed to the master, and the matter was taken care of in the shortest time. This was that old trait still, a legacy from the former master. We don't know how things look in Trieglaff at present.[42]

Before long, the first changes made their appearance. First, elderly Frau von Thadden moved with her unmarried daughter Marie to Bayreuther St. in Berlin. "This move is hard for her," wrote Anna Lange, "you can see it on her. She invited all the women who live below her, even the oldest farm women, for coffee on Sunday. Each got a Christian book as memento."[43] Her brother, Reinhold Ramthun, supplemented that a year later: "The manor house is standing empty now and makes a really desolate impression with its shuttered windows. It is so genuinely an image of human nothingness.[44]

But then new ways of living asserted themselves. The young Landrat decided to build a new house in the magnificent style that corresponded with the spirit of the times (see Figure 12). The young generation of workers was deeply impressed by it. "The new castle for our noble gentry," the oldest son of Anna Lang, Otto, wrote, "is completed that far already, that it can be finished off on the outside. The finishers came right from Berlin. If you look at the castle from the front, it looks just real grand and magnificent." Next he describes the details with evident pleasure: "To the right on the front of the building ... a 26 m high tower rises. Stand up there and you have a wide, splendid view into the whole surroundings."[45]

Yet Otto Lange did not stop at externalities. As a fourteen-year-old youth he was interested in the interior furnishings of the new castle, too, and especially in technical details. "In the basement accommodations are steam heating facilities and equipment for electric lighting."[46] This was a launch into the modern world.

Figure 12. The new castle at Trieglaff, built 1903–1906

In the mode of expression used in the letter, it is striking that Otto Lange, like all his peers, spoke about a "castle" as a matter of course. He referred to the old manor house as the "Herrenhaus," invoking aristocracy. Its time was clearly past. In keeping with this, he reported soberly that other buildings were being torn down, and that "our workshop" — the cartwright's — had to be relocated.

The letter testifies to a highly gifted youth, which poses the question about prospects for his further education. From the letter we learn that he, together with his twin brother Reinhold, "went to the municipal school in Plathe" after finishing at the Trieglaff village school, and was to be accepted next to the royal preparatory school (*Königliche Präparanden Anstalt*) in Plathe. "In total, 52 applied to take the entrance exam; of those about 20 have been accepted, we are among them."[47]

These plans were abetted particularly by the two youths' uncle, the teacher Ramthun. He knew the weaknesses of the Prussian primary school system well and regarded attendance at the Plathe municipal school as advisable, in order to be able to "venture it with the entrance exam for the preparatory school." "Of course, we all want badly for them to accomplish some real learning." They would not have had to become teachers necessarily, but "they need to achieve more than the primary school offers."[48]

How realistic were such desires? Materially, the situation with the schools was much improved during the time of William II. From 1888 on the state had taken over payment of teachers' salaries and thereby put aside the old system of hiring by the local constituency obligated to pay school taxes. Now teachers were civil servants entitled to a pension, and their prestige mounted observably among the general population. In the two decades prior to 1911 their salaries doubled.[49] But by the same token, teachers now became more dependent on the state. From this point on, formal communications passed via the Landrat to the education bureau of the administrative district (*Regierungspräsidium*), where commentary was added. Teachers were integrated into the hierarchy of state officials.[50]

This went hand in hand with a process of secularization. Most teachers welcomed their integration into the system of public officials because they eluded the influence of the church in this way. Even religious teachers like Ramthun were inclined toward sharper separation between ecclesiastical and public matters. "Our public school here," he wrote,

> has to give instruction in religion, too. In doing so, distinctions between the Lutheran and the Reformed confessions are little observed, oftentimes not even those between Lutheran and Catholic. But we teachers like the situation in America best: Religion ought to be taken out of the public schools and placed into special religious schools. True and genuine religion would only gain thereby.[51]

Ramthun's criticism was not confined to the relationship between state and church in the schools, however. It also took aim at dubious social conditions, as when he wrote to his U.S. relatives that many persons in the conservative party of the large landowners "begrudge the workers, who are below them, the physical and intellectual development which they claim for themselves and their children. That is why the aristocrats out here in the country take such poor care of their schools."[52]

Class-determined policy interests of the gentry in affairs of education were a particular thorn in Ramthun's side. He wrote: "They don't send their own children to the local school. They consider their own children too good for that. They are supposed to go to the Gymnasium at least, so that later they are capable of holding a higher public office."[53] "To be sure, though," he continued,

> these landholders will not be denied appointing the teacher for the local school.... Here too our teacher N. was once selected by Herr von Thadden and the Union pastor, by precisely those two family fathers whose children do not attend the village school.[54]

Indeed, the Landrat and his four sisters had received their elementary education from tutors at home. Later he himself attended and graduated from the Greifenberg Gymnasium. For his five children it was another matter, since during their elementary years they lived in Greifenberg, not Trieglaff. Not until the next generation was attendance at public schools mandatory from the start.[55]

An outstanding example of education surpassing village potential is the case of Hildegard, the Landrat's highly gifted youngest sister (Figure 13), who was governess at the court of the emperor in the early twentieth century and from 1908 provost of a girls' boarding school, the Magdalene Girls' School (Freiadliges Magdalenenstift), in Altenburg in Thuringia. She seems to have received private instruction in the home of relatives in

the Altmark and then—according to word-of-mouth reports within the family—passed a qualifying exam for women teachers, something that was still rare for landed aristocracy at the time.[56]

Yet it was not this educational pathway that drew the attention of the emperor's court to Hildegard, but the public success that she found with a little novel entitled *Ikarus*, about a trip to Rome in the year 1894,[57] which appeared in four editions. This novel of personal development evinces impressive knowledge of the Roman world of art and culture and may be taken as interesting testimony of how cultured Protestantism perceived papal Rome.[58]

Of greater importance for Hildegard's summons to the imperial court was, of course, descent from her Trieglaff family. Rather fortunately, she combined the capabilities of both of her grandfathers: the broadminded piety of the patriarch Adolph von Thadden, and the

Figure 13. Hildegard von Thadden (1866–1955), provost, Magdalene Girls' School in Altenburg

broad education of the famed Dante scholar Karl Witte. Supplementing this was the pronounced fealty to the crown for which the Trieglaff family was known.[59]

In 1901, when the court approached Hildegard to win her for this assignment with its heavy responsibilities, she exhibited her style in an exchange of letters about prominent pedagogical ideas. "When so-called knowledge goes hand in hand with experience," she wrote to the imperial lady-in-waiting, Countess Keller, "both first acquire value for the quiet, constant development of the whole person.... Both ought to be of benefit to the person—and not as knowledge for its own sake: instruction, and free time."[60]

After a few years, her evident conviction of the worth of personal independence left its imprint in a confrontation with the empress that ultimately led to her dismissal as governess from the imperial court. Following differences of opinion about the limits of freedom to be granted to the princess—e.g., also permission to romp around in piles of hay[61]— conflict arose over the particular mode of saying good night. Hildegard learned, in a roundabout way from a nurse accountable to her, that the empress desired a change that would constrict her as governess, whereupon she wrote, with uncommon directness:

> Should Your Majesty, in fact, no longer wish my free access to the bedchamber of the princess, something that is, after all, of great importance for my whole relationship with the princess ... then I request that Your Majesty might most graciously wish to relieve me of my highly responsible office as soon as possible, as there is surely a person more suited to these difficult conditions than I am.[62]

This decision took all observers completely by surprise. A court governess's request for dismissal could be overlooked if it could be communicated to society without damage to those involved. But there was a want of this sort of bearing on the part of the imperial couple. News of Hildegard's supposed ill health was spread, then, and at last reached the population of the villagers in Trieglaff. Probing for reasons for the otherwise incomprehensible event, Anna Lange wrote as follows to her aunt in the United States: "Well, Frau von Thadden's youngest daughter, Hildegard, was the princess's governess. She's supposed to be dismissed on account of illness everybody's saying. Whether that's the case, nobody knows."[63]

Little is known of Hildegard von Thadden's years at the imperial court. There is, however, an exchange of letters with the lady-in-waiting Countess Keller. Though it makes clear that Hildegard's understanding of her task was very strongly shaped by a model of reformist pedagogy for personality growth, it is not as if she evidences closeness to the women's movement of the time in the exchange. Not a trace remains of a diary she supposedly kept that was often a subject of conversation in the family.[64]

It was scarcely imaginable that an esteemed individual like Hildegard would remain inactive for any length of time. So it was no cause for surprise when, only a few years after leaving the court in 1908, she was recommended for a leading position in a school with a rich tradition. This was the office of provost at the Freiadliges Magdalenenstift, a Lutheran boarding school for girls.[65] The Duke of Sachsen-Altenburg, who personally took up her cause, was determined to remove an obstruction that in those times still always had to be considered: by the standards of the aristocracy, Hildegard was not "institutionally qualified" (*Stiftsfähig*).

Why, and to what degree, did the question even play a role by this time? This is worth pursuing, given the commonly expressed opinion that modernizing developments had made outmoded concepts of society politically irrelevant. Such developments appeared everywhere in the empire of William II as it strove for international standing. The process of defeudalization was supposedly so far advanced on the eve of World War I that elements of feudal class structuring no longer had any real significance.[66]

However, the reservations about the qualifications of the prospective provost demonstrate that the matter was not so simple. Someone was "institutionally qualified" only if all sixteen of that person's great-grandparents belonged to the nobility—that is, if the candidate could claim an "unassailable" family tree. In addition, according to the statutes, the provost had to be "a Christian, decent, virtuous aristocrat—or a widow or single woman of noble extraction."[67]

Hildegard was unable to meet those qualifications. Her mother had come from a middle-class home, and even though the grandmother qualified as nobility, a quarter of the requisite sixteen ancestors were nevertheless middle-class. So the then provost at the school called attention to the legal problems arising with Hildegard's appointment.[68] Fortunately, the duke was in a position to dismiss the provost's reservations. Correspondence addressed to him by the minister of state for Sachsen-Anhalt reads:

> In view of the abundance of important duties associated with the office of provost, there can be no doubt that predominant weight is to be placed upon personal qualities. Having been selected following a long search by the imperial couple to direct the training of the imperial princess, Fräulein von Thadden has proven herself fully equal to these duties and responsibilities.[69]

The appointment of Hildegard von Thadden as provost of the Magdalenenstift in Altenburg—an office she would occupy until 1932—coincidentally took place in the same year as enactment of the Prussian stipulations for a revised structure of higher education for girls (Bestim-mungen über die Neuordnung des höheren Mädchenschulwesens).[70] This promulgation, which opened the way to university study for women, went far beyond the educational concepts of the Altenburg institute but fell short of altogether fulfilling the hopes of the German women's move-ment, which demanded rights of education for girls on a par with those for boys. In that area, reform was still needed.

Very little from these discussions reached the ears of the people in the world of Trieglaff. Following the death of her husband, elderly Grand-mother Marie lived in Berlin. Her sister-in-law Eugenie, widow of Ger-hard von Thadden, who had died young, made her home in Vahnerow, and Gertrud, the half-sister of Eugenie's husband, who had close bonds with "the Americans," lived with her spouse Karl Senfft von Pilsach in neighboring Batzwitz. That amounted to a dominance of the older gen-eration, further reinforced by the fact that Ehrengard, the wife of Landrat Adolf von Thadden, now in possession of Trieglaff, was in ill health and seldom made an appearance in the world and life of the estates.

People in the villages mused about the circumstances. The wife of the teacher at Vahnerow, Marie Hackbarth, a daughter of the now deceased head shepherd Hermann Wangerin, wrote to her relatives in Wisconsin:

> The wife of the Landrat is a woman much too sickly for Trieglaff; a lot will be missing there. Frau Baroness Gertrud in Batzwitz is doing quite well now, she has traveled to Berlin with her daughter for a quarter of a year; those we serve simply regard that as necessary for the education of their daughter.[71]

Marie Hackbarth expressed some concern about Vahnerow. Old Frau Eug-enie was very lonely: "Our daughter visits Frau von Thadden every after-noon to read to her and to keep her company; I'd be glad if it does some good."[72] Otherwise, she reported, the old lady liked to travel to Italy for rest and relaxation and for that reason was often absent from Vahnerow. "Correspondingly, the beautiful estate has deteriorated so much that it is a pity." But now it belonged to the Landrat, who "is fixing up what needs to be done, so that it looks better again."[73]

The circumstances of the church caused Marie Hackbarth particular worry. "It has changed a lot here since the last century; our Old Lutheran church here does not have many members anymore; the path toward church has gotten pretty empty."[74] She was entirely unable to get over the secularization in progress: "Unbelief is becoming so widespread, and at the secondary schools and educational facilities, of all places, the young souls get so ruined; I have two nephews who are teachers, what ever hap-pened to faith?"[75]

Something was coming to an end in Trieglaff and its way of life. That became obvious as well when four deaths occurred within the circle of persons immediate to our account. First Ehrengard, the wife of Trieglaff's Landrat, died in the spring of 1909 at the age of only forty-one. There followed the Batzwitz brother-in-law, Karl Senfft von Pilsach, then Ulrike Wangerin, who had maintained the bond between the U.S. emigrants and their Pomeranian relatives. Finally, Eugenie, the widow of Gerhard von Thadden, having grown old at Vahnerow, succumbed to her prolonged illness in Italy in the summer of 1910. A new generation took the stage.

Notes

1. Cf. Thomas Nipperdey, *Deutsche Geschichte 1866–1918,* vol. 2, *Machtstaat vor der Demokratie* (Munich, 1992), 699ff.

2. Manfred Friedrich, "Hugo Preuß," in *NDB,* vol. 20 (Berlin, 2001), 708–710.

3. Hugo Preuß, "Die Junkerfrage, 1897," in *Gesammelte Schriften,* vol. 1, *Politik und Gesellschaft im Kaiserreich,* ed. Lothar Albertin (Tübingen, 2007), 202.

4. Ibid., 200.

5. Cf. Wagner, *Bauern, Junker und Beamte,* 526.

6. Hans-Jürgen Puhle, *Agrarische Interessenpolitik und preußischer Konservatismus im wilhelminischen Reich (1893–1914),* 2nd ed. (Bonn, 1975), 37ff.

7. Cf. Wagner, *Bauern, Junker und Beamte,* 405, 451.

8. Cf. John C. G. Röhl, *Wilhelm II. Der Aufbau der persönlichen Monarchie 1888–1900* (Munich, 2001), 365ff.

9. Cf. Huber, *Deutsche Verfassungsgeschichte seit 1789,* 4: 362f.

10. See chapter 3 of this volume.

11. Cf. Wagner, *Bauern, Junker und Beamte,* 538ff.

12. Ibid., 551.

13. Ibid., 540, 543.

14. Ibid., 553. Further, Ulrich, *Chronik des Kreises Greifenberg,* 354.

15. In southern Germany other circumstances prevailed. There it was the small-holding and sub-farming strata of hired workers (*Söldner*) that constituted the reserve of labor. Cf. Hans Medick, *Weben und Überleben in Laichingen 1650–1900. Lokalgeschichte als Allgemeine Geschichte* (Göttingen, 1996), 264ff.

16. Comment by the earlier estate secretary at Vahnerow, Barbara Fox née von Thadden, in the carton for Vahnerow materials, FA.

17. Elisabeth von Oertzen, *Entenrike und andere pommersche Geschichten* (1903; repr. Hamburg, 1956), 67.

18. Ibid., 71.

19. Ibid., 84ff.

20. Letter of 4 January 1908 to Ulrike Wangerin née Dorn, in the carton for U.S. letters, FA.

21. See below, chapter 5.

22. Cf. Christiane Eifert, *Paternalismus und Politik. Preußische Landräte im 19. Jahrhundert* (Münster, 2003), 50ff., 96ff., 153ff., 211ff., with emphasis on Brandenburg district administrators. In addition, Dieter Stüttgen, revision of *Grundriß zur deutschen Verwaltungsgeschichte 1815–1945,* vol. 3, *Pommern,* 65f; Wagner, *Bauern, Junker und Beamte,* 412ff.

23. Wagner, *Bauern, Junker und Beamte,* 415f.

24. Ibid., 419.

25. Quoted from Wagner, *Bauern, Junker und Beamte,* 563.

26. Ibid., 555.

27. Ibid., 429.

28. Obituaries for Adolf von Thadden in the year of his death, 1932, in the carton for Landrat Adolf von Thadden, FA.

29. On this, Wolfgang Bäumer and Siegfried Bufe, *Eisenbahnen in Pommern* (Egglham, 1988), 195ff.; Andreas Geissler, "Nutzung regionaler Handlungsspielräume," in *Pommern im 19. Jahrhundert,* ed. Thomas Stamm-Kuhlmann (Cologne, 2007), 275ff., 285ff.

30. Ulrich, *Chronik,* 84f.

31. Cf. Klaus J. Bade, "Massenwanderung und Arbeitsmarkt im deutschen Nordosten," *Archiv für Sozialgeschichte* 20 (1980): 265ff.

32. Letter of 6 April 1908 to Ulrike Wangerin, in the carton for U.S. letters, FA.

33. Ibid., 6f.

34. See chapter 3 above.

35. Letter of 6 April 1908, 7f., as in n. 32. That there were forty individuals indicates that the seasonal workers brought their families along.

36. See above, chapter 2.

37. Ehrengard von Thadden, "Auch Landflucht," written ca 1900, in the carton for letters of E. von Gerlach, FA.

38. Address of 4 April 1895, in *Greifenberger Kreisblatt* 41, in the carton for Landrat Adolf von Thadden, FA.

39. Contribution on "Trieglaff" by unidentified writer, in *Die deutsche Landwirtschaft unter Kaiser Wilhelm II,* vol. 1 (1913), 97ff., in the carton for Landrat Adolf von Thadden, FA.

40. Letter of 2 June 1907 by Anna Lange to Ulrike Wangerin, in the carton for U.S. letters, FA. Note that the Mark, not the Thaler, was the official currency in Prussia and Germany at this time.

41. Letter of 8 April 1903 by Reinhold Ramthun (a brother to Anna Lange) to his Aunt Ulrike Wangerin, ibid.

42. Ibid.

43. Letter of 8 December 1903 by Anna Lange to Ulrike Wangerin, ibid.

44. Letter of 29 December 1904 by Reinhold Ramthun, ibid.

45. Letter of 13 September 1905 (not 1903, as mistakenly written in the letter) by Otto Lange to his great-aunt Ulrike Wangerin, ibid.

46. Ibid.

47. Ibid. Folkert Meyer, *Schule der Untertanen. Lehrer und Politik in Preußen 1848–1900* (Hamburg, 1976), 72f., gives information about the preparatory schools

(*Präprandenanstalten*): "The general guidelines (*Allgemeine Bestimmungen*) in Prussia attempted to make the system of preparatory education for the position of teacher more efficient and to control it more closely through bureaucratic furtherance of preparatory institutions in which persons interested in education at a teachers' college were prepared for the appropriate exam."

48. Letter of 29 December 1904 by Ramthun to Ulrike Wangerin, in the carton for U.S. letters, FA.

49. Wagner, *Bauern, Junker und Beamte*, 565.

50. Ibid., 566.

51. Letter of 6 December 1907 by Ramthun, FA.

52. Letter of 28 July 1903 by Ramthun, FA.

53. Ibid.

54. Ibid.

55. Cf. Meyer, *Schule der Untertanen*, 166ff. Further, Heinz Butzlaff, *Geschichte des Friedrich-Wilhelms-Gymnasiums Greifenberg in Pommern* (Hamburg, 1984), 19ff., 35ff.

56. Writing by Wiebke von Thadden, in the carton for Hildegard von Thadden, FA.

57. H. Mellin, *Ikarus. Eine Reisenovelle* (Wolfenbüttel, 1896). In the fourth printing she identifies as *H. Mellin* (Hildegard von Thadden).

58. Writing by Wiebke von Thadden, 23ff., in the carton for Hildegard von Thadden, FA.

59. A judgment of the Princess, later Duchess, of Braunschweig, Victoria Luise, in *Herzogin Viktoria Luise. Ein Leben als Tochter des Kaisers* (Göttingen and Hanover, 1965), 21ff.: "She was a fantastic woman, very intelligent and cultivated. But she was, in fact, not young anymore either. I believe it would have been better if she had not entered my life until my later years."

60. Letter of 17 March 1901 by Hildegard von Thadden to Countess Keller, in the carton for Hildegard von Thadden, FA.

61. Cf. Barbara Fox née von Thadden, *Finding a Way Home: Recollections of a Family in Pomerania* (York, private printing, 2001), 11, FA.

62. Letter of October 1903 (copy lacking exact date) by Hildegard von Thadden to the empress, in Victoria Luise, *Herzogin Viktoria Luise*, 122.

63. Letter of 8 December 1903 by Anna Lange to Ulrike Wangerin, in the carton for U.S. letters, FA.

64. The journal in question was apparently never finished. "Tante Hildegard" [Aunt Hildegard], highly regarded in the family, is supposed to have said that she intended to get to writing it down following completion of her stint as provost of the training institute in Altenburg in 1932. In the Nazi era that followed, she was presumably not in a state to come to grips personally with the affairs of the imperial household. And after dissolution of the Prussian state in 1947, she likely no longer had the strength to write down her observations concerning a sunken world.

65. Cf. on this Reinhild von Capitaine, *Unser liebes Stift. 267 Jahre Mädchenerziehung im Magdalenenstift in Altenburg/Thüringen* (Altenburg, 2005), 178ff., 199.

66. On this, first and foremost, the work by Arno J. Mayer calling for a rethinking of things, *Adelsmacht und Bürgertum,* 9ff.

67. Capitaine, *Unser liebes Stift,* 202.

68. Ibid., 201f.

69. Written 16 April 1908. Reprinted in Capitaine, *Unser liebes Stift,* 202.

70. Hans-Georg Herrlitz, Wulf Hopf, and Harmut Titze, *Deutsche Schulgeschichte von 1800 bis zur Gegenwart,* 2nd ed. (Weinheim and Munich, 1998), 99ff.

71. Letter of 24 January 1905 to Ulrike Wangerin, in the carton for U.S. letters, FA.

72. Letter of 22 January 1909 to Ulrike Wangerin, in the carton for U.S. letters, FA.

73. Letter of 30 November 1908 to Ulrike Wangerin, in the carton for U.S. letters, FA.

74. Letter of 24 January 1905 to Ulrike Wangerin, in the carton for U.S. letters, FA.

75. Letter of 22 January 1909 to Ulrike Wangerin, in the carton for U.S. letters, FA.

Chapter 5

The Generation of the World Wars, 1912–1922

Paths at the Close of the Old Era

On the eve of World War I, people in Trieglaff were reading Fontane's *Effi Briest* through lenses unlike those in use in most conservative families in the Prusso-German Empire, for in Trieglaff, as in the book, people had had to live through an affair involving a duel. It had a different ending than the one in Fontane's great novel, however. In Trieglaff, convention did not win out, dissent did.

What was it about the story that kept people in suspense? Or in Fontane's words: "Why any of it then?" Instetten, whose honor had been sullied by the seduction of his wife Effi, replied:

> Because it has to be, regardless.... In living together with people, a thing, whatever it is, takes shape that's simply there. We become used to judging everything, others and ourselves, by its clauses and paragraphs. Going contrary to it is not allowed. Society despises us, and in the end we ourselves do, and can't stand it, and put a bullet through our head.[1]

In Fontane, the "social something tyrannizing us" keeps the upper hand. Individuals whose ideas and conceptions are inconsistent with it have to subordinate themselves to it. In Trieglaff in 1912, a situation of conflict brought the norms of Wilhelminian society into question when the only son of the esteemed Landrat Adolf von Thadden, Reinold, future heir to

Trieglaff, spurned convention by refusing a challenge to a duel. Effects extended far beyond the world war.

The event must be related in detail, because in the end the whole region—"Gegend," for the Pomeranians—was gossiped about. As luck would have it, an exchange of letters documenting the event in its social and cultural details has survived. According to it, a Korpsstudent (ROTC student essentially) belonging to a dueling fraternity challenged Reinold von Thadden and Jürgen von Blanckenburg, son of the landowning family on the neighboring estate of Zimmerhausen, to a saber duel because of a conflict brought about by their forthright answers to an absurd question. The question was:

> Did you, while at home on vacation within your family circle ... make insulting statements with regard to our coarse manners, moral or religious views, that would motivate separation from our company at the table?[2]

In both cases the answer was a brief, clear yes—though with a difference that led to serious consequences. Jürgen von Blanckenburg took up the challenge to the duel, but Reinold von Thadden declined it, and unconditionally, for reasons of conscience. Given the concepts of honor in place at the time, it was evident that Thadden's reputation was badly marred. Whoever as a member of the Prussian nobility refused a duel was seen as a dodger, a coward. He had committed social suicide.[3]

A few days after receiving this news, dated 11 October 1912, his elderly grandmother, Marie von Thadden, wrote, in elementary revolt, to her daughter Hildegard:

> You've told yourself what the consequences are for our Reinold.... A thorny time in the military, he can't become an officer in the reserves (*Reserveoffizier*), hardly accepted into governments, and defenseless against rowdies, who can go unpunished for striking him in the face with their whips.

And what did she see as the alternative?

> Peace of conscience and union with a living God, togetherness with Christian friends, and tasks in the Kingdom of God that make life worth living.[4]

So now the curtain had been rent asunder. People had to decide, and in deciding they kept consequences in mind.

The full implications of the event became apparent, in fact, only as "society" took it up and began to talk about it. Without public attention it would have led only to Reinold von Thadden's exclusion from his fraternity, but with the growth of chatter, privacy was lost. How the rural society was sorting itself out and what convention still meant for the behavior of families soon became perceptible. Who was prepared to display solidarity with Reinold?

The discussion spread first to relatives in Dorow, who were considered emphatically nationalistic.[5] The mother of the family there, a sister of Landrat Adolf von Thadden at Trieglaff who had made a name for herself as a local author,[6] stood up outspokenly for the Korpsstudenten and evinced no sympathy of any kind for Reinold's refusal to duel. Indeed, she went so far as to accuse the Trieglaffers of betraying family tradition, understanding herself to be the custodian of the traditional conservative legacy. "She sees herself," the elderly mother Marie wrote to her youngest daughter Hildegard, "as bearer of the Thadden ideals and Reinold as the deviant one who insults but doesn't give satisfaction."[7]

Trieglaff did not fail to react. Landrat Adolf exhibited full solidarity with his son Reinold against his sister Elisabeth von Oertzen and aligned himself with the "handful of Pietists" who otherwise had been rather distant.[8] In addition he turned to Rudolf von Valentini, the head of the kaiser's private civil cabinet (Geheimes Zivilkabinett) in Berlin, with whom he was acquainted, as well as to the then undersecretary of state in the Prussian finance ministry, Georg Michaelis, who was a friend, in hopes that they would bring their influence to bear at court.[9] And his mother Marie wrote to her daughter in Dorow that she had to retract her "bad" words, "or else things cannot be made right again."[10]

The conflict widened as the relatives from Batzwitz followed those from Dorow. With them went the Senfft von Pilsach family, likewise related to the Thaddens.[11] The Blanckenburgs of Zimmerhausen too, whose son Jürgen was embroiled in the affair, were unwilling to put themselves entirely on the side of Reinold. There remained the Normanns in Barkow, with connections to Landrat Adolf, and—the name attracts notice—Ewald von Kleist-Schmenzin, who was close to Reinold Thadden from student days and was closely associated with him later as well, into the years of their resistance to National Socialism.[12]

Widely differing conservative attitudes had now been delineated in Pomerania. Besides those having a militaristic cast, there were the ones that did not hold "civilian" to be a derogatory term or look to the "Casino-Leutnant" as the model for social worth. "The greatest hero in this drama," in the elderly matron Marie's assessment, "is for my tastes Kleist, who took Reinold's part fully, accepting every consequence of it for himself." She did, however, add that "I don't believe that the Canitzers with whom Reinold held membership will, as a fraternity, distance themselves from their mistaken principles; a majority of unprincipled people is too powerful for that."[13]

Yet where might one find those principles that could serve to persuade the people who thought otherwise? For Reinold von Thadden it appeared obvious that they should be sought in the family tradition. Thus he recalled an address by his great-grandfather about dueling in relation to war. The respected Trieglaff patriarch Adolph von Thadden had delivered it at the Berlin pastoral conference in June 1848. This talk was reprinted in Princess Eleonore Reuß's memorial volume and hence was well known in the Trieglaff household.[14]

In it, the elder Thadden distinguished between justified and unjustified settlement of conflicts by duel. He sharply condemned "the conventional duel for personal honor," which desires to shed blood "in order to fend off the disgrace of cowardice." Equally unjustified for him were "all those affairs in which the contest is solely for an injured ego, for one's individual property." And lastly, "vengeance" seemed to him to be a "reprehensible motive for dueling … any fighting whatsoever for wretched ego." For him, honor could become an idol.[15]

Reinold von Thadden was just twenty-one years old when he came to grips with these issues.[16] Following two semesters in Paris and Leipzig, he had taken up the study of law in the Pomeranian provincial university at Greifswald. There he had cultivated contacts with the fraternity of the Canitzers—without distinguishing fraternity colors—as well as with the World Student Christian Federation (Deutscher Christlicher Studentenverein), a Christian student group. Preparing for examinations preliminary to graduation remained his priority.

Retrospectively, he emphasized that the matter of the duel did not affect him particularly at first. But then it became clear to him that he had to take a position "against this caricature of honor expressed in such challenges." He said, literally, in a conversation that was recorded after World War II, "A genuine expression of faith just had to be put forward."[17]

But first it was necessary to get through World War I. According to surviving family correspondence, in Trieglaff, just as in all of Germany, the war was greeted by a mood of national revitalization.[18] It was merely striking that no one was hewing to the old Prussian tradition of opposing war with czarist Russia. Memories of the confederation of Prussia and Russia against Napoleon seemed to have faded.

Instead, and in fact from the onset of military confrontations, a different war experience was occupying the family at this time. Reinold von Thadden would not be able to become an officer. During his training at Gnesen in the province of Posen in the months prior to the war's outbreak, he had already been socially isolated within his group of first-year volunteers (Einjährig-Freiwillige), who were mostly fellow Korpsstudenten.[19] After the start of the war, though, the early weeks of which he spent in Belgium, he experienced discrimination in his military career as well. While his comrades of the same age were promoted to *Vize-Wachtmeister* (junior sergeant), he remained the single exception (Figure 14).

He told his admired Aunt Hildegard, provost in Altenburg, about this event in a detailed letter:

> For me the biggest event recently was my conversation yesterday with my commanding officer in Lagny, in which Maltzahn informed me kindly but decisively that he did wish to promote me on 1 November to junior sergeant and officer candidate qualified to become a reserve officer, but could not and did not want to keep me in the regiment, demanding instead that I present myself after the war (during the campaign I would not in any case become an officer) to some other regiment for selection as a reserve officer.

Reinold Thadden then comes to his conclusion:

> And so, despite all my efforts during the past year, staying in the regiment for the longer term is not to be; and even the war is not capable of earning for me a claim to a place within its ranks. That is painful! Now where will I with my dark past find a new regiment that will accept me as reserve officer unconditionally, when my old regiment did not want to keep me?[20]

A short time later, the group of junior sergeants of the same age as Thadden were promoted to second lieutenant, while he remained in the group of noncommissioned officers. At that point his father, the loyal district administrator, bypassed bureaucratic channels by directing a petition to the kaiser. He gathered signatures of influential friends and traveled personally to military and governmental headquarters at Charleville. There he succeeded in speaking with Rudolf von Valentini, head of the private civil cabinet, and in the end pushed further, to Imperial Chancellor von Bethmann Hollweg. He gave each person he spoke to a copy of his petition to the kaiser.[21]

The Landrat returned home feeling he had accomplished something for his son. But he was wrong. The military had a structure of its own. First, Thadden's regiment was moved from the western to the eastern front. Next, it was assigned a new commander, who wanted the case of the uncomfortable Vize-Wachtmeister to be presented to him once more. Reinold reported about this to his Aunt Hildegard in a postcard from the field dated 8 December 1914:

> Yesterday I was called before Commander von Bülow to give the fatal answer to that question about my stance regarding dueling. After I had finished speaking, as I was obliged to, the commander concluded, "then

I cannot submit your name and you will not become a reserve officer!" Lord help me now—it is not going to be nice for me now, when the other first-year people are all lieutenants and I stay behind, as the only one in the subordinate rank of noncommissioned officer. It's curious how differently people experience the war.[22]

Following this report, his grandmother Marie felt compelled to provide her siblings with a summary and analysis. Yet prior to Christmas she wrote:

The dice were thrown some 14 days ago. That it came to this is probably due to the persistent efforts of the fraternity—as we know from a wholly reliable source. The cavalry regiments are riddled with fraternity men and law clerks (*Referendare*), and Reinold's case became a cause célèbre.[23]

After that she described details of the process. Reinold was excluded from the officers' table and had to stay with the troops. Further, he had to stand at attention before volunteers and the former junior sergeants, who had all been promoted to officer. The worst was that the noncommissioned officers and troops could make neither rhyme nor reason of the affair.

To his grandmother Marie, however, the affair did seem clear:

How it all fits together has to be sought exclusively within the Korps.... We know from insiders that from the beginning it was a foregone matter with them to thwart Reinold's becoming an officer. And those frat men have enormous influence up to the very top.[24]

Under these circumstances Adolf's petition to the Kaiser would hardly change anything either: "The Kaiser stands opposed to the military cabinet,

Figure 14. Reinold von Thadden (1891–1976) at time of failed promotion to officer from junior sergeant, 1915, at Włocławek on the Vistula

and the regiments are sovereign in the choice of their officers! Oh, how long is the war still going to last?"[25]

But the war was going to last a long time. "Following peace," Grandmother Marie commented,

> we will get over it all right that Reinold is not becoming an officer.... Michaelis says we will come to learn to be grateful for what R. has suffered for something like this—it will still have to be battled out vigorously after the war, because things just can't stay this way.[26]

In another letter to her brother Leopold, she wrote with sober insight into the current state of affairs: "It's simply so, that everything rests with the Militärkabinett." The civil authorities did not have much to say anymore. "Militarism is a word of reproof around here"—something that "used to be so precious."[27]

Then, unexpectedly, the head of the Militärkabinett, General von Lyncker, did decide—differently, to be sure, than many believed he would. He wrote to Landrat Adolf on 22 January 1915 from headquarters at Charleville:

> His Majesty the Kaiser and King have deigned to express themselves in reply to Your Highborn's petition of 26 November 1914 that they are compelled to abide by the principle of permitting promotion to officer to take place only on the basis of preliminary selection by the officers' corps. The question posed to the officer candidate concerning what position he takes regarding the custom of defending honor by duel is, however, not admissible. His Majesty have, therefore, ordered reassignment of your son to the Mecklenburg Dragoon Regiment No. 17, where he will undergo another evaluation.[28]

This was how people thought the long-smoldering conflict could be resolved. Regulations of the Prussian military had not been meddled with. An expedient external to Prussia was sought instead. The German Reich was, remarkably, offering possibilities that the old Prussian monarchy dared not resort to. With three-class voting rights exerting pressure, not even the emperor appeared to have the power to enact sensible changes within his own military. But in Mecklenburg Reinold von Thadden finally became a reserve officer.

The villagers in Trieglaff most likely did not learn anything to speak of concerning these turbulent events. The growing number of the fallen in their own families was more important to them than the estate owning family's exasperation with the Prussian military over the effects of a nonsensical affair about dueling. Hence it falls within the realm of the possible, in view of the large number of casualties, that not all of Anna Lange's sons attained their hoped-for career goals as teachers, noncommissioned officers, and cartwrights.[29] In the related family of the shepherd Albert Lange in Gruchow, the oldest son, Otto, suffered a serious war wound and, unable to remain in the military, shifted over to join the administration of the state-run railroad. At the end of the war, the slate of the fallen in front of the Trieglaff church displayed a full thirty names.[30]

Similarly depressing, particularly for economic life, was the large number of farm workers pulled into military service. Although the shortage of labor could be offset in part with soldiers from prisoner-of-war camps, it was hard to replace the missing specialized workers who could maintain the machines in use everywhere. Added to that was a growing shortage of foodstuffs that extended even to the agriculturally rich province of Pomerania. From 1915 on, bread could be had only in exchange for bread coupons, and a few months later other important foodstuffs such as butter, sugar, and meat were rationed as well. Even potatoes came under rationing.[31]

An ancillary effect of the war was that the flow of information between emigrants and their relatives who had remained in Pomerania quickly came to a complete standstill. Transatlantic correspondence had already diminished markedly since the death of Ulrike Wangerin in 1909. But after a German U-boat sank the passenger steamship *Lusitania* on 7 May 1915 and unrestricted submarine warfare was declared on 1 February 1917, relations with the United States worsened so dramatically that writing between the U.S. and the German Trieglaffers ceased almost entirely. An important source of information about the everyday life of the population of Trieglaff during the years of World War I is therefore missing.[32]

So the information found in the correspondence of Elisabeth, eldest daughter of Landrat Adolf von Thadden, becomes all the more important. As early as spring 1915, she began expressing worries about developments in agriculture—to be sure, along with admiration for the organizational accomplishments of Undersecretary of State Georg Michaelis, a person bound in friendship to the family:

> How the people in agriculture are howling up a storm now again in their usual way you can't even imagine to yourself … they ought to just wait and see whether this difficult and most magnificent of all organizing efforts, monopolizing of bread grains, proves good in such a way that the English plan of starving us into submission is brought to naught … and without great sacrifice victory in the domain of agriculture cannot be attained either.[33]

Apart from this, Elisabeth also had an eye for the social dimension of the war:

The war has decisively bridged a chasm that was still there previously between us and our people, and it happened very naturally. The women needed us for military field addresses, they needed warm things for their sons and husbands, we all knitted together every Sunday and shared the same worries and cares. ...[34]

With these thoughts Elisabeth came close to discovering the *Volksgemeinschaft* (united national community) as a power for transcending class contrasts, a notion that developed into a conservative guiding concept during this time and later.[35] These ideas had an enduring effect in determining her thinking and acting. In her own words, "It is by all means necessary now to hold on to what has been won, also after the war, so that the social gain actually endures for us."[36]

In Trieglaff in 1915, it was not yet determined whether the social gain could give rise to a political gain, too. Doing away with the allotment of voting rights among three classes in Prussia was presumably not yet being considered. But people suspected that they would not emerge from this burgeoning war without drastic changes: "We have just got to sacrifice, then, and if it can't be said it's for the fatherland, then at least for ourselves, to free us dyed-in-the-wool Junkers from things that still seem too important to us."[37] Elisabeth's thoughts in this vein became ever more intense throughout the years in which the war would necessarily entail consequences for the transformation of conditions inside Germany. And so she wrote in November 1915:

It is probably clear to all reflecting persons from within their camp—Papa for sure, Reinold too!—that conservatives perhaps have to change first. We were in full agreement too recently with Undersecretary of State Michaelis about the necessity—in your sense of compromise—for both sides to reach out to each other![38]

The critical thoughts Elisabeth now increasingly had about the future of the world east of the Elbe also had to do with her reading. Deeply impressed, she reported:

Now I've read an excellent book by a Social Democrat, Anton Fendrich, *Mit dem Auto an der Front* [By car at the front]. It isn't what he sees, but how he sees it and what he thinks that moves a person's heart. On this basis we can surely build bridges over to the Reds.[39]

She was especially impressed by a book that, at the time, had a great impact upon the public, Friedrich Naumann's *Mitteleuropa* (Central Europe).[40] She found not only the content convincing, because it "strikes down numerous internal contradictions," but also its style and construction, which seemed to her "artistically beautiful." Naumann failed to convert Elisabeth to liberalism. But doubts did begin to assail her about the ethnicity-centered *"völkisch"* national future so highly praised in conservative circles. Still fending off these doubts, she asked, "Could we be at the end of our potential for development; might we have exceeded the pinnacle of our existence and of our capacities?"[41]

In this phase of misgivings about established models of thinking, Elisabeth von Thadden became acquainted with someone who would acquire central meaning in her further life, the Berlin clergyman Friedrich Siegmund-Schultze.[42] He was known for his uncommon career path and nonconformist convictions. As a young theologian he had given up a highly regarded pastorate at the Friedenskirche (Church of Peace) in Potsdam, attended by the empress, in favor of a position in the east of Berlin in order to do social work there and to establish a "social working group" (*Soziale Arbeitsgemeinschaft*, SAG) in the middle of the workers' quarter.

Aside from this, he had placed himself at the disposal of a church committee for the cultivation of friendly relations between Great Britain and Germany, serving as secretary. The group co-sponsored the first World Conference of Churches for Peace (Weltkonferenz der Kirchen für den Frieden) in Constance, coinciding with, of all days, that of the outbreak of war on 1 August 1914. This meant he had made a name for himself in a world of competitive arming and nationalistic passions.[43]

Siegmund-Schultze entered Elisabeth von Thadden's field of vision at the Michaelis home in Berlin. During the war years he held regular Bible studies there with higher officials and other houseguests, among whom the Trieglaff Thaddens were often to be found. It followed, then, almost of itself, that he also received an invitation to Trieglaff. In 1916 he preached there in the village church, on the occasion of the thanksgiving harvest festival. Afterward, at the fireside in the manor house, he described his activity with the SAG in the east of Berlin.[44]

This encounter must have made a strong impression upon Elisabeth, for right after it she wrote Siegmund-Schultze a letter that went well beyond being a note of thanks:

> What you told us here on 1 Oct. I am pondering a lot in my heart. And I would like to turn these thoughts into deeds with the enclosed bit of aid for your work. —— In case I have no further obligations toward my father later on, I would like to do social work in your sense of it![45]

Social work in Trieglaff—now what shape would that take? In the deprivation-stricken winter of war from 1916 to 1917, there was a need existing before all eyes that could be diminished with the help of this agrarian countryside: city children's need for adequate nourishment. Here is where Elisabeth believed she could do meaningful work. But Siegmund-Schultze was aiming farther. He wanted to develop a huge program of evacuating children that reached abroad, into neutral nations. Was that not a bit too much for Trieglaff?

Elisabeth overcame her reservations and in summer 1917 invited several groups of children to the estate as well as to the adjacent estates. They were—as they were fond of saying in Trieglaff—to build themselves up in the country, breathing healthy air and eating good food. But in that same summer, political conflicts in Berlin intensified between forces targeting a negotiated peace and those favoring a peace following victory. Bethmann Hollweg had to resign as chancellor under pressure from the top military leadership.[46]

In these circumstances, the fatherly friend of the Trieglaff household, Georg Michaelis, was called, wholly unexpectedly, to be chancellor of the empire. He could not endure the test of the political tensions and fragmentation for very long, to be sure, and was dismissed after just a few months. Following his hapless departure, Elisabeth, somewhat baffled, commented on the event:

> I am still too nearsighted to understand why everything had to come to this with His Excellency Michaelis! ... If this man is to be entirely shut out now, if Germany rejects one of its best like this, well, then you don't actually feel like reflecting on things anymore, for it tears your heart apart![47]

But Elisabeth did reflect further. In the same letter she asked Siegmund-Schultze for clarification and insight into the thinking of his "workers":

> In this area a demand is heard, which I join, to hear more about the goals and the makeup of the Social Democrats, because after all it's necessary for us to familiarize ourselves with the fact that 'the gang' will be ruling us.

Hence her direct question, "Would it perhaps be possible for you, for the sake of a party truce, to give us a lecture on this subject?"[48]

The answer was affirmative. Siegmund-Schultze came to Trieglaff at the end of November and explained the development of German social democracy during the war to the Pomeranian estate holders. Landrat Adolf von Thadden subsequently invited him to a conference in the summer of 1918 that was not only designated "Trieglaff Conference" but was also plainly intended to be seen in the tradition of the old Trieglaff Conferences that Adolph, Elisabeth's great-grandfather, had organized during the 1830s and 1840s. Trieglaff, indeed, site once again of uncommon conferences and meetings (Figure 15).[49]

Elisabeth von Thadden was interested above all in inviting Social Democratic members of the Reichstag. It was "agreeable" to her father too to have a progressive and some National Liberal gentleman there, maybe Friedrich Naumann. But most importantly, Elisabeth regarded it as significant for people to make themselves knowledgeable in preparation for the meeting:

> We want so badly to educate ourselves about social democracy before the 3 Red members of the Reichstag come here. … Have they written anything worth reading? Is there a good text about unions, cooperatives, and similar important social democratic things that does not get too detailed?[50]

The themes of the conference were to deal with social and religious issues. Foremost were problems of the relationship between the cities and the country and the divergence of the two groups' lives. Then there were the problems of flight from the land and "resettlement" of the unemployed. Lastly, there were the plans for a "people's house" (*Volkshaus*) in the east of Berlin, that is, a community home where workers and youth groups could shape their free time.[51]

These proposed issues had no revolutionary features, but given circumstances in Pomerania they caused a stir. They offered a glimpse into the social and political changes coming to the rural regions, however true it was that numerous participants at the conference were doubtless still

Figure 15. Trieglaff Conference, summer 1918, with Pastor Siegmund-Schultze (4th from left) and Elisabeth von Thadden (6th from left)

stuck in the conceptual world of traditional Prussia. It was not possible to exit what had constituted the ancien régime in Europe in a single leap.[52]

Historical events, however, could very well sweep over people. And so they did in November 1918 in Pomerania, when a revolutionary uprising shook the old order and swept away the monarchy in just a few days. For the largely conservative-leaning inhabitants of the province, an entire world was shattered.[53]

Just one day after the kaiser's abdication as emperor on 9 November, workers' and soldiers' councils were formed in many Pomeranian towns. They established themselves as co-governments alongside the official state bureaus and commissions.[54] Understandably, Stettin took the lead, but councils were formed in all the district seats in rapid succession. By the year's end, they had been spontaneously formed in 231 Pomeranian towns and rural communities—hence also in some of the villages—serving by order of "the people's government."[55]

As for policies for personnel, little changed at first. As a rule the councils functioned together with administrative organs to tackle the most important problems. The president of the provincial government of Pomerania, Georg Michaelis, who had ties to the Trieglaff manor house, showed himself to be especially cooperative, so that most of the conservative district administrators could remain in office. Only five of twenty-one Landräte in Pomerania were replaced in 1919.[56]

In Michaelis's view, "the members of the Stettin workers' and soldiers' council had no conception of what they actually wanted to do and ought to do":[57]

> Individual persons, particularly radical ones, gave bombastic speeches about upholding rule by the people ... the moderate elements, especially the leaders of the unions, had a better understanding and took up the suggestion that a commission consisting of three men should be formed as superior provincial presidium, to exercise control over whether there was just, popular governing.[58]

Cooperation came about somewhat less peaceably in the small towns and in many of the rural communities. There, according to Michaelis, it was "nonlocal soldiers who forcibly assumed rule, showing up as friends of some comrade or other following disbanding of the troops."[59] "They interfered in the supply of foodstuffs, confiscated foodstuffs in the country without legal basis, and sold them at low prices in order to earn favor for themselves with the urban population."[60]

Under these circumstances the district administrators had a hard time of it. Taken to be the actual bearers of the old governmental authority, they were made responsible for all the accumulated problems of food supply left by the chaos of war. For that reason a great deal depended upon the personal reputation commanded by an individual Landrat.

Adolf von Thadden appears to have been among those whom people "abode well," as people were accustomed to saying in the Pomeranian dialect. He not only managed to remain in office but also found a manageable way to cooperate with the Greifenberg workers' and soldiers' council. Thus he and the local chairman of this council signed official notices together—for example, the one concerning regulation of conditions for a war economy, which was to remain "in force for the time being in the interest of economic demobilization" following the military capitulation of November 1918.[61] And in everyday practice he shared space with the "new bosses" and saw to it that files were laid before them in sufficient numbers. Funds were scarcely available anyway anymore.[62]

Matters came to a head in January 1919 following the assassination of the Spartacist leaders Rosa Luxemburg and Karl Liebknecht.[63] Fearing that the council movement would now be eliminated, the radical forces attempted to secure as many of their "acquisitions" as possible, and all the more energetically as elections to the Weimar National Assembly (Weimarer Nationalversammlung, for drafting a constitution) were imminent. According to the will of the moderate social democratic majority, these elections were to lead to the establishment of a parliamentary government in the new republic—a parting of ways, therefore, for parliamentary democracy and council democracy.[64]

The roll of the dice was slated for 19 January 1919. Whereas the majority Social Democrats won barely 38 percent of the votes in the empire and the left "independents," the Independent Social Democratic Party of Germany (Unabhängige Sozialdemokratische Partei Deutschlands, USPD), got 7.6 percent, in Pomerania the former attained a sensational 41 percent of the votes and the latter only 1.9 percent. That had consequences for the workers' councils. Apart from this, the traditional conservative party in leadership in the province, which now called itself the DNVP, the Deutschnationale Volkspartei (German National People's Party), took only 23.9 percent, which in fact was double its average for the empire (10.3 percent). The left-leaning liberals, the newly founded Deutsche Demokratische Partei, the DDP, won—astonishingly for Pomeranian circumstances—21.7 percent, while the right-leaning liberals, the Deutsche Volkspartei (German People's Party) made it to 10.9 percent. The Catholic Zentrum (Center Party) played no role in Pomerania.[65]

In the District of Greifenberg, the numbers shifted proportionately leftward. In both of the larger towns, the majority Social Democrats received far above 30 percent of the votes for the first time: 35 percent in Treptow and even 45 percent in Greifenberg. On the other hand, the left-leaning liberal DDP won an astonishing 29 percent in Treptow, while its tally in Greifenberg only reached 17 percent. The right-leaning liberal DVP fell significantly behind its sister party's results, with 8 percent in Treptow and 14 percent in Greifenberg. This showing could not be offset by votes for the conservative DNVP, which, most unusually for circumstances in Pomerania, did not win 30 percent in either Treptow or in Greifenberg. In the case of the former it attained 28 percent; in the latter, only 21.5 percent.[66]

It might be possible to explain these surprising election results by citing altered voting rights, depicting the outcome as an aftereffect of the elimination of three-class voting rights in Prussia that carried over to the level of the empire. But the transformed electoral-political landscape in the rural precincts can be understood only by taking into consideration the DDP—urban middle-class in its origins—and its new claim to be representative of the interests of the farming population as well.[67]

Only the left-leaning liberals' political ambition explains how, for the first time, large segments of the farm population in Pomerania voted for a party that could scarcely be said to be rooted in the rural setting. They did not care to vote for the DNVP because it was regarded as the party of the estate holders. And the SPD did not come into consideration because it represented the interests of workers and day laborers. Meetings of the DDP were well attended in Greifenberg.[68]

These election politics were concretely manifested in the Thadden estate villages. Whereas in Trieglaff with its large proportion of farm people more votes were cast for the DDP candidate than for the DNVP candidate, 45 to 39, in Vahnerow, devoid of farmers, only 2 voted for the DDP as opposed to 31 for the DNVP. The SPD candidates won only 16 and 15 votes in Trieglaff and Vahnerow respectively.[69]

The elections to the Prussian Constitutional Assembly (Preußische Landesversammlung), held one week after those for the Weimar National Assembly at the Reich level, were equally important for the Trieglaffers.[70] They eliminated their fears that the state of Prussia might be dissolved in the wake of the November revolution and confirmed that the Social Democrats too were acting to perpetuate the Hohenzollern government, little loved by them until then. "A free Prussia," as the first Social Democratic prime minister, Paul Hirsch, said,

> is no longer that bugaboo from days past that people attacked using the timeworn slogan about the dangerous predominance of Prussia over Germany. Dangerous for Germany was only the old Prussia of the world of Junkers and of reactionary attitudes. The new Prussia of a free people is to be a blessing for the entire German fatherland.[71]

To what extent were the Trieglaffers ready, against this backdrop, to give to the new republican Prussia a chance, possibly even to support it? Written sources contain no statements about the stance of the village population. Here we can only rely on the oral reports of members of the families of laborers, all of which testify to a strong bond with the Prussian state. Into the years prior to World War I, return addresses on letters to U.S. relatives still frequently read, "Trieglaff, Kreis Greifenberg, Prussia." "Germany" appeared much less frequently.[72]

In the manor house, of course, the Thadden family clung to the Prussian state. But there were discussions on the question whether and how far one might assent to its becoming republicanized. The provost of the Altenburger institute, Hildegard, and her Landrat brother Adolf were thoroughly loyal to kaiser and king. They accepted an invitation to the kaiser's place of exile in Doorn, Holland, in 1922 and remained in contact with the court in other ways as well.[73]

Elisabeth proved more open to issues regarding the new state of affairs. She pushed for continuation of the Trieglaff Conferences and desired a deepening of the debate about the social question. Accordingly, she sent invitations to a second conference in June 1919, for which more than 150 participants enrolled, from the most varied callings. Among them were social workers, publicists, pastors, higher-level officials, members of parliament, and of course, estate owners from the vicinity.[74]

A number of well-known women were noticeably present this time: Alice Salomon, founder and principal of the Soziale Frauenschule Berlin (the Social Women's School in Berlin); Alix Westerkamp, lecturer at the Soziale Frauenschule der Inneren Mission in Berlin; and Renate Lepsius from the Berlin family of scholars, who had been involved in protest against the Turkish genocide of Armenians. Participants with well-known names included Anton Erkelenz—the workers' secretary for the German association of labor unions and a member of the Weimar National Assembly—as well as former Imperial Chancellor Georg Michaelis.[75]

In comparison with the first conference, the topics now had somewhat more of a "red," that is, a socialist, tinge. Peculiarly for Trieglaff ears, they dealt with "class contradictions and moods in the city and in the country," "the socialization of agricultural and industrial concerns," and "the moral-social tasks of the coming period."[76] One utterance heard in the discussion was that the social question was not just one of bread, but also one of education.[77]

While Elisabeth was following a socially conservative line more intensively here, her younger brother Reinold, back from the war, pursued the nonconformist path that had already been perceptible in 1914.[78] He soon set out to complete a doctoral thesis with the faculty of law at the

University of Greifswald. He devoted it to a topic that must have come as a challenge to most conservative German nationals of the time, as it was very controversial in recently defeated Germany: "International Law and the League of Nations" ("Völkerrecht und Völkerbund").[79] Taking off from the Bismarck-critical tradition of the Gerlach brothers and the work on the politics of peace by the internationally recognized student of international law Walther Schücking,[80] he advocated a positive response to the idea of a League of Nations, in obstinate disregard of all reservations vis-à-vis realities of the League of Nations as created by the Treaty of Versailles.

The unique feature of this work was that it was consistently oriented around the idea of supranational solidarity, palpable in Christianity as well as in the workers' movement. It took the position that

> the significance of intellectual forces that find neither their roots nor their bounds in the national has grown colossally for international relations in the past five years. That we Germans did not recognize that sooner and act accordingly was our misfortune. The countries of the Entente knew more about it.[81]

What was noteworthy about the argumentation in the thesis was how it accentuated statements and judgments from the ecumenical world that were not German, especially Anglo-Saxon ones. So it cited a resolution by English friendship groups from February 1919, by which "the special interests of nations must be subordinated to general interests of humanity."[82] And from a call put forth by some U.S. Christians, he emphasized that peace could be preserved solely by means of "a spirit that is international, which finds a footing not upon trade and class advantages, but upon warmhearted brotherhood in faith."[83]

And yet Thadden's work did not focus exclusively on Christian utterances mandating solidarity. It also brought similar proclamations of intent by socialists into its argumentation. Pointing to resolutions passed by the International Federation of Trade Unions in Amsterdam in July 1919 and a subsequent conference of international social democracy in Lucerne, it counseled a positive evaluation of these associations toiling for solidarity and asserted, "The force of the international workers' movement has without doubt experienced such strengthening under the burden of the World War that it will soon play a positive part in shaping relations between countries."[84]

That Reinold von Thadden, a member of a conservative family, did not shy away from resort to Marxist thought is unusual. For him, it clearly was important to recall earlier stances of the workers' movement, too. He cited, from the founding Congress of the Socialist Internationale assembled by Karl Marx in Geneva in 1866, that all efforts directed toward economic emancipation of the working classes have to this point broken down from a deficiency of solidarity amongst the numerous branches of labor in each country and from the absence of a fraternal bond of unity between the working classes of the various countries.[85]

This is not at all to say that Thadden was a religious socialist, although he was acquainted with the piece on "The Revolution of Christianity," published before World War I by the Swiss social democratic clergyman Hermann Kutter,[86] and made affirmative mention of it.[87] For him, the spirit of universalistic human rights was of decisive significance. It enables the conclusion in his doctoral thesis that "[t]he bond of nationality, of race, or of continental contiguity is simply not the most all-inclusive one binding people together. There is a superordinate *societas* [a community ethos]."[88]

Reinold von Thadden's fundamental criticism of the perverse nature of nationalism was not to remain just theory. Just a few weeks after publication of his dissertation, it was put to the test by a political event that direly imperiled the new republican national entity, namely, the so-called Kapp-Putsch in March 1920. This was nothing but an act of counterrevolution against the Social Democrat–led government in Berlin.[89]

Why had it come to such a revolt by antidemocratic, nationalistic forces, gripping the entire country and making its effects felt as far as the world of Trieglaff? To understand this, a glimpse is necessary into the consequences of the oppressive Versailles Treaty, ratified at the beginning of 1920. There it had been set down that the army of millions mustered during World War I had to be reduced to 100,000 men, including all the units of volunteers (*Freikorps*) that had formed, mainly in the east of Germany. How can it be wondered at, then, that some units under radically nationalistic leaders refused to disarm and sought to take matters into their own hands?

In keeping with this impetus, on 13 March a marine brigade under Captain Ehrhardt, his back covered by General von Lüttwitz, moved to topple the elected government of the Social Democratic Reich's Chancellor Bauer and lay the groundwork for a counterrevolutionary government in Berlin under the general director of the manorial credit agency, Generallandschaftsdirektor Kapp from East Prussia, whose political orientation skewed to the extreme right. Over the course of that day, the Bauer government saw fit to withdraw to Dresden.[90]

At first people in Trieglaff and the neighboring villages reacted with uncertainty. But coincidentally, Reinold von Thadden was in Berlin during these very days and witnessed events in the east of Berlin. Worried about possible misperceptions, he wrote a letter, rich in its content, to his father, Landrat Adolf:

As there are no newspapers being published, you are probably poorly informed about events here in Berlin. … But we are experiencing planes dropping pamphlets … thousands of people standing and debating in the Wilhelmsplatz, soldiers running around with anti-Semitic swastikas on their helmets, and Berlin lying in darkness at night.[91]

Reinold continued the letter the next day:

Today the general strike is taking place that was called for by the former government just shortly before it fled to Dresden, and it has become reality to the full extent. Everything is shut down, even the city rail system … is no longer operating, and since this forenoon long-distance trains are inactive, too. On the other hand, the streets suddenly came alive. Out of factories which in the early morning had still taken in their workers to vote on the general strike poured the dark hordes of strikers, who filled and are now filling the streets in endless streams.[92]

What impressed Reinold particularly was the powerlessness of the putsch participants:

You can't spot a trace of the new people in power; no member of the troops that marched in has made it to our part of town; no one interferes when people bunch together in excited groups to talk, when independent or communist speakers urge battle against a "white terror" and preach dictatorship of the proletariat in opposition to "militarism's domination by saber." One gets the impression that the rule of Reich's Chancellor Kapp doesn't extend much further than from the avenue Unter den Linden to Leipziger Straße.[93]

A paragraph follows then that emphatically describes the realities in Berlin:

There is hardly any doubt that the labor force senses the counterrevolution as a slap in the face, as a challenge to which it is in no way inclined to submit. If it is conducting itself relatively quietly nevertheless, it is probably attributable to the rock-solid faith that the putsch … can only be a transient episode. Of course, if the reactionaries do not disappear from the scene again soon, then woe to middle class people![94]

The letter closes with no less than a supplication to reason:

If sensible people do not very soon gain the upper hand and convince Herr Kapp with his comrades that the German people can no longer be ruled in this manner today, I am personally convinced that we are driving irrecoverably toward Bolshevism.[95]

In Trieglaff this letter may well have met with bewilderment. In the living environment there, people felt more anxiety about radicalization of the workers than about the reactionary aspirations of the Kapp-putschists. And so Hildegard von Blanckenburg from neighboring Zimmerhausen, the young wife of the master of the estate, recalled that following the miscarriage of the putsch—"ventured" with an intent to restore the monarchy—communist-influenced "Plebs" from nearby Plathe, the town with the dairy, "ganged together" to demand the "owners' firearms" kept in the manor house. "Thereupon, several of our faithful workers made their way into our entrance hall to stand by us in an emergency."[96]

Typical for rural life in Pomerania at that point were the efforts on both sides toward unity. A worker known to be a "Red" came to an agreement with the estate holder that it was desirable to disable the weapons by taking the bolts out of them: "With the bolts in a small basket that they carried together, the two went over to the Old Pond and sank the bolts."[97]

But that still did not end the uprising. A "bunch of Reds" from Plathe who would not be deterred attempted to incite the farm workers at Zimmerhausen. "When the people from Plathe saw that they wouldn't accomplish anything, they desisted from their intentions." They were supposed to have said later that they felt sorry for "a few young women in the family who had been so scared."[98]

No such incidents at Trieglaff and Vahnerow have been passed along to us. But we know from a vivid report about the district seat Greifenberg how things played out there.

> On Thursday, 18 March, in the morning, the biggest share of the working men here went into a 48-hour walkout, which afterward was reduced to 24 hours. With a band in the lead and with a red flag waving, the strikers paraded through the city, drawing up later in the market square. From here several of the strikers entered the district office building (*Kreishaus*) and voiced a request that the flag of the old government be raised. After their wish was fulfilled and they had hailed the flag with shouts, there followed the march off to their group meeting place. The peace was not disturbed.[99]

Furthermore, real consequences of the disarmament provisions of the Versailles Treaty now came into play, affecting the social conditions of many residents in these localities. The third son of Trieglaff's Lange family, Gustav, was affected by the demobilization provisions in that he could not continue his military career via the noncommissioned officers' school in Greifenberg. The oldest son of the Lange family at Gruchow, Otto, having been seriously wounded, took up service with the Reichsbahn, the national railroad.[100]

People in Pomerania adjusted to the close of the postwar period in other ways as well. Reichstag elections scheduled for 6 June 1920 accentuated this. According to the resolutions of the National Assembly of 1919, they were urgently needed. But in fact, the results differed greatly from what was expected. In the Reich overall, the parties of the so-called Weimar Coalition lost the majority installed by the democratic parliamentary system of the new Weimar Republic.[101] On the left, the radical USPD gained an additional 10 percent (now 17.8 percent), while the SPD gave up over 16 percent (now 21.7 percent). On the right, votes for the DNVP increased by 5 percent to reach 15 percent, and those for the right-leaning liberal DVP went up too by almost 10 percent, to 13.9 percent, at the expense of the left-leaning liberal DDP, which sank from 18.5 percent to 8.2 percent. The Catholic center, not significant in Pomerania, also lost 6 percent of its votes (13.6 percent).[102]

Political shifts were even more pronounced in the District of Greifenberg. The SPD sank to 16.7 percent, the USPD climbed to 8 percent, and the DNVP hit prewar levels, attaining an absolute majority with 53.8 percent. The DVP raised its share of votes to a noteworthy 17.7 percent. Lastly, the DDP faded by 2.7 percent, a result far below those at the national level. In comparison with the figures for the whole district, the parties on the left made a somewhat better showing in the towns of Greifenberg and Treptow. There the SPD and USPD together approximately matched the strength of the DNVP.[103]

In Trieglaff and Vahnerow, election results might have been cause for reflection. Here, in contrast to the other villages in the District of Greifenberg, numerous voters turned away from the DNVP, regarded as friendly to the estate holders, and voted for parties that were not conservative: in Trieglaff for the SPD, in Vahnerow for the DDP. In Trieglaff with its many farmers and 380 inhabitants, 141 of the voting citizens gave their vote to the DNVP, while 52 still marked their "X" for the SPD, and in one instance even for the radical USPD. Alongside that, 8 voted for the left-liberal DDP and 6 for the right-liberal DVP. In smaller, farmerless Vahnerow with its 110 inhabitants, the traditional DNVP received, by contrast, only 35 votes, whereas the DDP, regarded as urban middle-class, got a striking 21. Votes remaining for the SPD numbered only 7, and for the DVP a mere 5.[104]

These proportions, not typical for the area, cannot be explained merely by pointing to candidates with great appeal. It seems somewhat more pertinent in this case to consider factors that acquired significance in that year. In Trieglaff, it was the activity of estate holder Adolf von Thadden as Landrat in Greifenberg, which was not satisfactory to everyone politically. In Vahnerow, it was the nearly fifty-year absence of a proprietor who concerned himself with the place. Workers quite plainly felt this to be neglect of this secondary estate. Contact with the teacher Ramthun may also have played a role in the attitude taken by many people in Vahnerow. His critical judgment about deficient manorial solicitude for schooling possibly contributed to a number of voters' becoming open to a liberal party.[105]

The conservatives were nevertheless able to breathe a sigh of relief in the District of Greifenberg. In any case, the shock from the spring carried over, so that at least in Trieglaff people were disinclined to deviate from the direction of the social conferences of recent years. The third Trieglaff Conference was held before the end of June 1920, that is, a few weeks after the elections.[106]

As before, Elisabeth was the driving force. She pushed for broadening the range of topics offered and strove for examination of politically controversial issues. Three themes stood at the center of the conference: "1. Planned agricultural economy, 2. Proletarization of the rural population, 3. The leadership and the masses."[107] All three topics were to be dealt with in argument-counterargument fashion by conservative and left-oriented speakers.

Again the conference enjoyed a lively resonance plainly not limited to mere agreement. Thus the elderly but ever alert and active Grandmother Marie wrote to Siegmund-Schultze, who apparently was unable to participate, "The waves went so high that destinations took on new, uncertain contours."[108] This judgment corresponded to an altered mood in the country that permitted recognition of a stronger polarization of political forces. In any case the "model worker" for Siegmund-Schultze's social working group SAG, Wenzel Holek, expressed himself rather critically about the worldview of the estate owners:

> The stimuli to the current movement among the workers on the land are not simply show and personal party interest. They lie grounded deeply, upon a long sociological development, of which the Junkers have caught neither a sound nor a glimpse.[109]

What *was* recognized, on the other hand, was something that transcended class differences: the prominent participation of women at the conference. Here again it was the grandmother, Marie, who put the observation into words: one of the participants had, despite all her great successes in her career, "remained so femininely charming that one may look forward to women's progress with confidence. So it is possible to remain human, even while practicing a man's occupation."[110] The women in the von Thadden family would confirm the correctness of this judgment.

But first, other important events in Trieglaff proved to be of even greater consequence, perhaps, than the increasingly problematic conferences. Among these were the almost parallel engagements of the father Adolf and his son Reinold in July and August of 1920. The exciting political events of the same year had by themselves provided enough material for a dramatic production, but the family events that followed might have inspired Fontane. Woldemar's marriage in *Stechlin* is innocence itself by comparison.

A few weeks after the third Trieglaff Conference, 62-year-old Adolf surprised the family with the news that he wanted to put an end to his extended life as a widower and bind himself once more in marriage. A 25-year-old friend of Ehrengard, his youngest daughter, had caught his eye. She had distinguished herself as a teacher at the Altenburg institute and then was brilliant in the role of a page in a theatrical performance in Trieglaff. Her name was Barbara Blank. She was a commoner and her mother was English.

Whether because the elderly Adolf had wearied somewhat of politics by this time, or because the social activity of his dynamic daughter Elisabeth became too much for him, it is certain that he brought the conferences to an abrupt end at that point and forced Elisabeth out of the house. The grandmother commented:

> I trust God will help Elisabeth to victory. She fights bravely and doesn't spare herself. May her choice of profession be the right one! I wouldn't care to see her plunge into politics. That could take place at cost to her inner self.[111]

The second event, Reinold's engagement, which followed shortly thereafter, promised to affect the family at least as much. In terms of social backgrounds it could not have been more contrary, for it not only brought Pomerania a daughter of the world of south Germany but also opened the door to the world of high nobility. Baroness Elisabeth von Thüngen came from an old family of Frankish imperial barons; her mother was a Princess von Ysenburg and Büdingen from Hesse.[112]

Once again it was the grandmother who had the proper instinct and sure sense of propriety to resolve complicated conditions. She wrote personally to the mother of her future daughter-in-law Elisabeth:

> In several days I will … see you, dear baroness, face to beloved face, when we will be able to share together what moves our hearts. May the time that is given to us for that not be too brief! It is burdened with various obstacles to which we must accommodate ourselves. You, dear baroness, will scarcely understand it, and will have to trust us blindly that we are unable to change it.[113]

What, in detail, were the obstacles that had to be dealt with? Marie spoke empathetically about her son Adolf and concrete possibilities for solutions.

My dear son, who otherwise is so easily susceptible to loving influence, is, in this belated romance into which he has fallen, being unyielding in keeping to his plans—he intends to abide by the date set for his wedding, the 25th of September.[114]

Besides, a *Volksfest* was to take place on 24 September as a preliminary celebration. This date very nearly collided with Reinold's intended celebration of his own engagement in Trieglaff, which was supposed to take place on a grand scale. For that reason Marie requested that the family members traveling from Franconia stay two days longer, to allow time for "a practical and heartfelt exchange," that had to become "capital" for the future.[115]

It was, in fact, possible then to arrange both celebrations successively to eliminate this friction. But in its stead, there began a conflict that could hardly have been avoided with the founding of two new families. It concerned partition of the inheritance. This would not have been Trieglaff if the dispute had not been attended by profuse deployment of counsel from highly placed personalities. And so people turned to an old friend of the family, the former Imperial Chancellor Georg Michaelis, with a plea for advice.

What, concretely, was at issue? From a letter by Grandmother Marie to Michaelis, we learn that Adolf was considering a division of the estates and wanted the smaller estate Vahnerow to pass, in the end, to an "anticipated" son from his second marriage. In Marie's opinion, though, this was "a great danger" for the family property, as wartime had brought with it an enormous loss of wealth. Holding on to Trieglaff had become "uncertain."[116]

An exact description of the economic situation of both estates followed. In Vahnerow holdings in cattle had sunk significantly, with the result that the farm had become "short on manure." Sheep had already been eliminated, so hardly any livestock was kept there anymore. Trieglaff, on the other hand, did not have enough wood and thus could "not be maintained" without deliveries of wood from Vahnerow. "If Vahnerow is to be pledged to the new son," Marie wrote, "it will limit all freedom of movement for Trieglaff and put the entire holdings of the family into uncertainty."[117]

Michaelis answered by return mail without frills or flourishes.

The course to follow has to be found by both sides. Adolf has to recognize that he has injured his children grossly with his action, and that he has to make up for it to the extent it is within his power. Part of that is that he does not diminish family property for the children from his first wife, insofar as that is not an imperative flowing from the rights of the wife and children of the second marriage. But the children from the first family, too, must recognize God's direction in it such that, in general, they genuinely seek to make themselves independent, so that they do not claim the paternal or maternal property as a peaceful resting place for a comfortable private life, but that they free themselves from it, so that they have it as though they did not have it.[118]

Such was the behavioral codex applicable to property dealings in post-feudal times. One does, indeed, still sense the lingering ethos of a class-structured world in the saying that people see in the family dwelling only the place of the blessings that pious ancestors caused to be at home there for their benefit. But now, after the close of the ancien régime, all that remained was the duty as a Christian to understand property as something given against a pledge and to handle it for the benefit and welfare of all concerned.

So in the end a compromise came about. The main estate Trieglaff remained initially in the hands of the father Adolf and his new family, while adjacent Vahnerow went to the son Reinold and his likewise newly established family, though within the perspective of an exchange of estates after some years. Both operations had to concern themselves with shedding debt and had to assist each other in doing so. And Grandmother Marie retained the right to live at Vahnerow to the end of her life, which she arrived at, serene and fulfilled at eighty-eight years of age, in March 1922.[119]

Notes

1. Translations based on text: Theodor Fontane, *Effi Briest*, ed. Helmuth Nürnberger, 3rd ed. (Munich, 1998), 769.
2. Letter of 13 October 1912 by Marie to Hildegard von Thadden, in the carton for Marie von Thadden, FA.
3. Werner Hühne, *Thadden-Trieglaff, Ein Leben unter uns* (Stuttgart, 1959), 46. On issues relating to the duel cf. Ute Frevert, *Ehrenmänner: das Duell in der bürgerlichen Gesellschaft* (Munich, 1991), 89ff., 133ff., 234ff.
4. Letter of 13 October 1912 by Marie to Hildegard von Thadden, in the carton for Marie von Thadden, FA.
5. Dorow was an estate belonging to the von Oertzens in the adjacent District of Regenwalde.
6. See above, chapter 4.
7. Letter of 19 October 1912 by Marie to Hildegard von Thadden, in the carton for Marie von Thadden, FA.
8. Letters of 26 and 13 October 1912 by Marie to Hildegard von Thadden, in the carton for Marie von Thadden, FA.

9. Rudolf von Valentini, *Kaiser und Kabinettschef,* ed. Bernhard Schwertfeger (Oldenburg i. O., 1931), 94ff.; Rudolf Morsey, "Georg Michaelis," in *NDB,* vol. 17 (Berlin, 1994): 432ff.

10. Letter of 26 October 1912 by Marie to Hildegard von Thadden, in the carton for Marie von Thadden, FA.

11. The wife Gertrud was a daughter from the second marriage of the old Trieglaff patriarch Adolph von Thadden. See above, chapter 3.

12. Bodo Scheurig, "E. von Kleist-Schmenzin," in *NDB,* vol. 12 (Berlin, 1980): 29f.

13. Letter of 19 October 1912 by Marie to Hildegard von Thadden, in the carton for Marie von Thadden, FA.

14. Reuß, *Adolf von Thadden,* 282f.

15. Ibid., 283f.

16. Born in 1891 in Mohrungen, East Prussia.

17. Hühne, *Thadden-Trieglaff,* 49.

18. Cf. W. Mommsen, *Bürgerstolz und Weltmachtstreben,* 7/2: 564ff.

19. Letter of 17 January 1914 by Reinold von Thadden from Gnesen to his Aunt Hildegard in Altenburg, in the carton for Reinold von Thadden, *Briefe aus dem Ersten Weltkrieg,* FA.

20. Letter of 19 October 1914 by Reinold von Thadden, in the carton for Reinold von Thadden, *Briefe aus dem Ersten Weltkrieg,* FA.

21. Letter of 11 November 1914 by Reinold von Thadden to his mother, Marie, in the carton for Reinold von Thadden, *Briefe aus dem Ersten Weltkrieg,* FA.

22. Postcard of 8 December 1914, by Reinold von Thadden while in service, to his Aunt Hildegard, in the carton for Reinold von Thadden, *Briefe aus dem Ersten Weltkrieg,* FA.

23. Letter of 22 December 1914 by Marie to her brothers Leopold and Max Witte, in carton for Marie Witte, *Briefe an Leopold Witte,* FA.

24. Ibid.

25. Ibid.

26. Ibid. This statement lends a foretaste of the conflict between the later imperial chancellor Georg Michaelis and the highest military leadership.

27. Letter of 21 January 1915 by Marie to Leopold Witte, in carton for Marie Witte, *Briefe an Leopold Witte,* FA.

28. Letter of 22 January 1915 by the head of the military cabinet, Baron von Lyncker, to Landrat Adolf von Thadden-Trieglaff, in the carton for Reinold von Thadden, *Briefe aus dem Ersten Weltkrieg,* FA.

29. On the vocational hopes of the sons, see the comments in the letter of 13 September 1905 by Otto Lange to his great-aunt Ulrike Wangerin, in the carton for U.S. letters, FA.

30. A memorial to the fallen was dedicated 13 August 1922. A report is in the family album, FA.

31. Wehrmann, *Geschichte von Pommern,* 2: 324ff. Further, W. Mommsen, "Die zunehmende Überforderung der Landwirtschaft," in *Bürgerstolz,* 682ff.

32. Cf. W. Mommsen, "Die alliierte Blockade, der U-Boot-Krieg und die Vereinigten Staaten von Amerika," in *Bürgerstolz,* 646ff.

33. Letter of 6 March 1915 by Elisabeth von Thadden to her uncle Johannes Ritter, in the carton for Elisabeth von Thadden, FA.

34. Ibid.

35. On the concept of a *Volksgemeinschaft* from a conservative point of view, see Max Hildebert Boehm, *Das eigenständige Volk. Volkstheoretische Grundlagen der Ethnopolitik und Geisteswissenschaften* (Göttingen, 1932).

36. Letter of 6 March 1915 by Elisabeth von Thadden to J. Ritter, in the carton for Elisabeth von Thadden, FA.

37. Letter of 27 March 1915 by Elisabeth von Thadden to J. Ritter, in the carton for Elisabeth von Thadden, FA.

38. Letter of 3 November 1915 by Elisabeth von Thadden to J. Ritter, in the carton for Elisabeth von Thadden, FA.

39. Letter of 23 October 1915 by Elisabeth von Thadden to J. Ritter, in the carton for Elisabeth von Thadden, FA. On Anton Fendrich cf. the article in Wilhelm Heinz Schröder, *Sozialdemokratische Parlamentarier in den deutschen Reichs- und Landtagen 1867–1933. Ein Handbuch* (Düsseldorf, 1995), 436.

40. Theodor Heuss, "Friedrich Naumann," in *NDB*, vol. 18 (Berlin, 1997), 767ff. The mentioned work, *Mitteleuropa*, appeared in Berlin in 1915.

41. Letter of 11 December 1915 by Elisabeth von Thadden to J. Ritter, in the carton for Elisabeth von Thadden, FA.

42. Cf. the more recent work by Stefan Grotefeld, *Friedrich Siegmund-Schultze. Ein deutscher Ökumeniker und christlicher Pazifist* (Gütersloh, 1995), 63ff.

43. Cf. Hermann Delfs, "Der Weg der ökumenischen Freundschaftsarbeit," in *Lebendige Ökumene, Festschrift für Friedrich Siegmund-Schultze zum 80. Geburtstag,* ed. Heinrich Foth (Witten, 1965), 45ff.

44. Cf. Irmgard von der Lühe, *Elisabeth von Thadden. Ein Schicksal unserer Zeit* (Düsseldorf and Cologne, 1966), 29ff.

45. Letter of 4 October 1916 by Elisabeth von Thadden to Siegmund-Schultze, cited from von der Lühe, *Elisabeth von Thadden*, 33.

46. Cf. W. Mommsen, *Bürgerstolz*, 754f.

47. For critical discussion of this, ibid., 755ff. The letter, from early November 1917, by Elisabeth von Thadden to Siegmund-Schultze, is cited from von der Lühe, *Elisabeth von Thadden*, 40.

48. Von der Lühe, *Elisabeth von Thadden*, 40.

49. Extended presentation in Rudolf von Thadden, "Herkunftswelt und Prägungen Elisabeth von Thaddens," in *Elisabeth von Thadden*, ed. Matthias Riemenschneider and Jörg Thierfelder (Karlsruhe, 2002), 32ff.

50. Letter of 2 March 1918 by Elisabeth von Thadden to Siegmund-Schultze, in Bestand [holdings] 51/S IIb 6, Evangelisches Zentralarchiv (EZA) Berlin. Also in FA. The three members of the Reichstag under consideration were Messrs. Peus, Kalliske, and Schulz. On this, see Schröder, *Sozialdemokratische Parlamentarier*, 142.

51. Conference program, reprinted in *Akademisch-Soziale Monatsschrift*, cited from von der Lühe, *Elisabeth von Thadden*, 51.

52. Cf. Jens Wietschorke, "Defensiver Paternalismus. Ostelbischer Landadel im Dialog mit der 'Sozialen Arbeitsgemeinschaft Berlin-Ost' (1918–1922)," in *Histo-*

rische Anthropologie 14, no. 2 (2006): 232ff., particularly the conclusion, which discusses failed Trieglaff Conferences in oversimplified form, p. 267.

53. In Pomerania at the time, there were also many attempted explanations for these happenings. Thus the *Greifenberger Kreisblatt* of 2 February 1919 published — according to a declaration of Landrat von Thadden — the following attempt at an explanation: "If Germany bore any fault for the World War in 1914, then it was our far-too-optimistic estimation of the world situation that animated us. We knew who our enemies were, but apart from these counted upon numerous good friends. That was a delusion."

54. On the workers' and soldiers' councils cf., throughout, Eberhard Kolb, *Die Arbeiterräte in der deutschen Innenpolitik 1918–1919* (Düsseldorf, 1962), 90, 99f., 371ff.

55. On this, Kyra Inachin, "Die Entwicklung Pommerns im Deutschen Reich," in Buchholz, *Pommern*, 471.

56. Ibid.

57. Georg Michaelis, *Für Volk und Staat* (Berlin, 1922), 400.

58. Ibid.

59. Ibid., 403.

60. Ibid., 403f.

61. *Greifenberger Kreisblatt* of 4 January 1919.

62. *Akten des Landratsamts Greifenberg* [Files of the administrator's office, District of Greifenberg], Abt. 16, Rep. 66, in Gazinski et al., *Staatsarchiv Stettin — Wegweiser*, 96ff.

63. Cf. on this Hans Mommsen, *Die verspielte Freiheit. Der Weg der Republik von Weimar in den Untergang 1918 bis 1933* (Berlin, 1989), 49.

64. Ibid., 50f.

65. Figures in Dietmar Lucht, "Die Provinz in Daten und Fakten," in Buchholz, *Pommern*, 443.

66. Figures per *Greifenberger Kreisblatt* of 25 January 1919.

67. Cf. Wolfram Pyta, *Dorfgemeinschaft und Parteipolitik 1918–1933* (Düsseldorf, 1996), 94f.

68. In the *Greifenberger Kreisblatt*, notices consistent with this are to be found in the days prior to elections to the National Assembly.

69. Figures in the *Greifenberger Kreisblatt* of 25 Janaury 1919.

70. Cf. Horst Möller, "Preußen von 1918–1947," in *Handbuch der Preußischen Geschichte*, ed. Wolfgang Neugebauer (Berlin, 2001), 3: 312f.

71. Address of 13 March 1919, in Paul Hirsch, *Der Weg der Sozialdemokratie zur Macht in Preußen* (Berlin, 1929), 229.

72. Envelopes from the years 1900–1909, in the carton for U.S. letters, FA.

73. Original in family album, FA.

74. Rudolf von Thadden, "Herkunftswelt," 34.

75. Von der Lühe, *Elisabeth von Thadden*, 50f.

76. Conference program; photocopy in the carton for Elisabeth von Thadden, FA.

77. Von der Lühe, *Elisabeth von Thadden*, 53.

78. He spent the end of the war on the eastern front in Estonia and became acquainted there with an influential Dorpat minister, Traugott Hahn, whom the Bolsheviks shot in early 1919. Letter of 4 February 1919 by Reinold to his Aunt Hildegard, in the carton for Reinold von Thadden, FA.

79. Reinold von Thadden, *Völkerrecht und Völkerbund. Eine Studie zur Rechts-natur zwischenstaatlicher Beziehungen,* vol. 8 of *Monographien zum Völkerbund,* ed. Deutsche Liga für Völkerbund (Berlin, 1920).

80. Ibid., 18, 15. Of Walther Schücking's writings he mentions above all *Die völk-errechtliche Lehre des Weltkrieges* (Leipzig, 1918), and *Der Staatenverband der Haager Konferenzen,* (Munich and Leipzig, 1912).

81. Reinold von Thadden, "Völkerrecht und Völkerbund," 15, 22.

82. Ibid., 24.

83. Ibid., 24f. U.S. call to action, spring 1918.

84. Ibid., 27f.

85. Ibid., 27.

86. Hermann Kutter, *Die Revolution des Christentums* (Zurich, 1912). About this book, Reinold wrote to his grandmother Marie, "I do not deny that I am at the moment, while held enchanted by the simultaneous suggestive charm of the atmosphere of the big city, stirred considerably by the ideas of this Swiss social-democratic Pastor." Letter of 11 January 1920, in the carton for Reinold von Thadden, FA.

87. Reinold von Thadden, "Völkerrecht und Völkerbund," 62.

88. Ibid., 59. References to 1776 and 1789 are to be found on p. 22.

89. Cf. on this H. Mommsen, *Die verspielte Freiheit,* 93ff.

90. Ibid., 94.

91. Letter of 14–15 March 1920 by Reinold to his father Adolf, in the carton for Reinold von Thadden, FA.

92. Ibid.

93. Ibid.

94. Ibid.

95. Ibid.

96. Hildegard von Blanckenburg, *Meine Erinnerungen an Zimmerhausen* (private printing, 1982), 26f., FA. The author was a granddaughter of the well-known historian Leopold von Ranke.

97. Ibid., 26f.

98. Ibid., 26f.

99. "Nachrichten aus der Provinz," in *Greifenberger Kreisblatt,* 20 March 1920.

100. Letter of 13 September 1905 by Otto Lange to his great-aunt Ulrike Wangerin in the United States, in the carton for U.S. letters, FA. Further, verbal statement by her relative Siegfried Lange.

101. Cf. H. Mommsen, *Die verspielte Freiheit,* 99.

102. Elections to the Reichstag on 6 June 1920, in *Die Statistik des Deutschen Reichs,* N.F. [new series], vol. 291, passim.

103. Ibid. Entries for Plathe in the District of Regenwalde there also.

104. Entries in the *Greifenberger Kreisblatt* of 12 June 1920.

105. See above, chapter 4.

106. Cf. on this Rudolf von Thadden, "Herkunftswelt," 34ff.

107. Letter of 27 April 1920 by Elisabeth to Siegmund-Schultze, photocopy in the carton for Elisabeth von Thadden, FA.

108. Letter of 14 July 1920 by Marie to Siegmund-Schultze and his wife, in the carton for Marie von Thadden, FA.

109. As found in the record of the conference of 1920, quoted from Wietschorke, "Defensiver Paternalismus," 253.

110. Letter of 14 July 1920 by Marie to Siegmund-Schultze and his wife, in carton for Marie von Thadden, FA.

111. Letter of 21 November 1920 by Marie to Siegmund-Schultze and his wife, in the carton for Marie von Thadden, FA.

112. Rudolf Freiherr von Thüngen, *Das reichsritterliche Geschlecht der Freiherren von Thüngen* (Würzburg, 1926), 2: 546, 560ff.

113. Letter of 8 September 1920 by Marie to Elisabeth Baroness von Thüngen, in carton for Reinold von Thadden, FA.

114. Ibid.

115. Ibid.

116. Letter of 2 April 1921 by Marie to Georg Michaelis, in the carton for Reinold von Thadden, FA.

117. Ibid.

118. Letter of 8 April 1921 from Georg Michaelis to Marie von Thadden, in the carton for Reinold von Thadden, FA.

119. Sermon at the burial service of Frau Marie von Thadden née Witte on 23 March 1922 in Trieglaff, in the carton for Reinhold von Thadden, FA.

Chapter 6

The Generation of the World Wars, 1923–1945

Into the Abyss

A s the Weimar Republic fell into its initial profound economic crisis and steered toward unimaginably high inflation, partition of the Thadden family holdings came to completion. In Trieglaff, Adolf's second family expanded to, in the end, six children, and in Vahnerow the progeny of his son Reinold ultimately numbered five. Available cash permitted no great leaps forward under such circumstances.[1]

Just how large were the estates Trieglaff and Vahnerow at this time? What did the livestock number? How extensive was the acreage that underlay the businesses? According to the *Landwirtschaftliches Güter-Adreßbuch* (Agricultural directory of properties) of 1939,[2] which presents precise data on estates and larger farming operations up to World War II, there had been substantial growth since the previous survey in the nineteenth century.[3] An additional amount of new farmland had been gained via drainage of marshes.

The Trieglaff estate had at its disposal 2,834 acres (1,147 hectares). Of that, 2,078.2 acres were arable, 182.9 meadow, 180.4 pasture, 224.9 wooded, 81.5 lake-covered, and 210 non-arable. Livestock comprised 80 horses, 270 head of cattle, 180 hogs, and 1,500 sheep. In addition to ten medium and smaller independent farmers, one large farmer had 61.8 acres (25 hectares), including 49.4 arable, 7.4 meadow, 2.5 pasture, and 2.5 untillable. He owned 2 horses, 15 head of cattle, and 15 hogs.

The estate of Trieglaff also had two outlying properties, Gruchow and Idashof. The larger, Gruchow, had—as subpart of the estate as a whole—645 acres of pasture and meadow, with a small adjoining woodlot. What gave the place its agricultural significance, however, was its sizable sheep breeding operation, with a flock of more than 400 head of breeding stock. Renowned throughout the District of Greifenberg, it had been tended through several generations by the shepherd family Lange. The family was part of the kinship network of the Trieglaff Langes who maintained correspondence with the Americans. There were no independent farmers in Gruchow.[4]

Vahnerow had no farmers either, only estate property. It was listed as having 1,067.5 acres, of which 741.3 acres were arable, 84 were meadow, 37 pasture, 185.4 wooded, and 19.8 non-arable. Livestock included 32 horses, 100 head of cattle, 180 hogs, and—from the 1930s on—170 sheep. So Trieglaff was by far the largest operation.

These figures say something about how the two estates ranked in size, but they offer no insight into the condition in which they were found following their partition between the heirs. For this, a sketch drawn up by the husband of Ehrengard von Thadden, old Adolf's first wife's namesake and youngest daughter, provides information. It was occasioned by an issue concerning the actual disposition of inheritance in 1928. The husband was Percy Ernst Schramm,[5] a historian at Heidelberg and later at Göttingen. According to the sketch, Vahnerow in particular found itself in a serious crisis.

Schramm reported that his brother-in-law Reinold painted a bleak picture to him about this secondary estate, which had at first been promised to him [Reinold]. "It was actually nothing but a pile of rubble, which, before anything else, he had again made into an estate with new buildings and self-sacrificing work." Vahnerow was now once more profitable, "though, indeed, a sizeable portion of the current debt would have to be cancelled."[6]

Whence the debt? Reinold Thadden said, according to Schramm, that it "came into being of necessity because Vahnerow was completely run down." The estate was burdened with debt amounting to half of its taxable worth.[7] But other reasons could probably be added. It was true that all agricultural operations during the 1920s were still suffering the consequences of World War I. More than anything, shortages of chemical fertilizer due to the Allied naval blockade had reduced crop yields significantly, so that afterward means were insufficient to modernize operations.[8]

To that were added the effects of inflation. It helped agriculture rid itself of some part of the debt it had taken on earlier in good money, so that debt could now be paid off cheaply in bad money. But at the same time, it ate away all reserve and working funds so that later, a pressing shortage of capital made the necessary investments practically impossible. Businesses were forced to market their harvests immediately in order to raise cash.[9]

Reinold Thadden elaborated an even darker picture in 1928. In his opinion, a bad harvest meant that it would scarcely be possible to keep Vahnerow, and only if the wealthier principal Trieglaff estate assumed a portion of the debt. Eventually father and son agreed on what would be needed to hold Vahnerow. It came to half the amount of the new mortgage.[10]

This world, with all its worries and cares, was suddenly interrupted by an arrival from afar, one that affected workers' families more than it did the estate owners. It was the visit from the United States of a descendant of the Wangerin family of émigrés. Adolph, the youngest son of Albert and Ulrike Wangerin[11]—who had received his given name in remembrance of the "patriarch" Adolph von Thadden—hit upon the idea of looking up the old Pomeranian homeland and seeing what, in that world, might correspond with the stories he had heard at home as a child.[12]

By good fortune, Adolph Wangerin kept a diary of his travels in Europe in which he entered detailed notations on each stopover during his journey through Germany in 1929. According to the diary, he made his way first to Berlin-Charlottenburg, where he was given a "royal welcome" to his cousin Reinhold Ramthun's home. Then he traveled farther alone by train to Greifenberg, got off there at the—for him—"most primitive" Hotel Fuß near the station, and then went, together with his cousin Anna Lange, "per Auto" to Trieglaff to have a look, first of all, at the graves of his family and relatives in the cemetery there.[13]

Following that, on the basis of a quite stupendous knowledge of the place, he made his way to all the "spots loved by my mother." He remembered them by their German names: the *Herrenschloss* (manorial castle) beside the *Herrensee* (manorial lake), where he found the *Mädchenstube* (maids' quarters) "where Grossmama [his grandmother] lived and slept." A servant girl showed him everything there. From there he went into the old church, where his father and his mother had been baptized and confirmed. There he played the organ,[14] and set eyes upon the pulpit from which old Pastor Rudel had preached. Then he found the *Stellmacherei* (cartwright's shop) in which his father had worked, and lastly visited the *Altlutherische Kirche* (Old Lutheran church) that held a special place in the spiritual memories of so many emigrants.

But Adolph Wangerin's search for vestiges of the past in the old family homeland was not confined to Trieglaff. It led him to all the places in the Thadden family holdings, and everywhere aroused a lively echo among the current generation of village inhabitants: "Big excitement amongst all the people."[15] First he wandered farther to Vahnerow, where he visited the manor house, because his father had also worked there for a time. Then he sought out the *Wirtschaftshof* (workyard), where some of the workshops in which his father had worked still stood. At last he met an old woman who still remembered "Großpapa" (Grandpa). "Then along Dorfstrasse on which Grosspapa always walked to work."[16]

From there Adolph walked past sheds and barns with straw roofs and stork nests to Kardemin, where he espied the *Lehrerhaus* (teacher's house) from which his father used to leave to attend singing lessons in Trieglaff. At the nearby outlying farmstead of Gruchow he located the house where his father was born, "a big yard between sheep barns." He then made his way via Trieglaff to Batzwitz to visit relatives and stand at the grave of Gertrud Senfft von Pilsach née von Thadden, whom his mother had lovingly attended for many years as lady's maid.[17]

A brief but intensive itinerary it was, leaving a lasting impression upon Adolph Wangerin and his family in the United States. This can be sensed from a letter that his daughter, Lucy Ruedt—now turned 100—wrote a few years ago to Germany: "It was a very rewarding and never-to-be-forgotten day for him."[18] It helped that he still knew German, owing to the fact that his father, old Albert Wangerin, had spoken no English in the family. Thereby Adolph aroused such strong interest in the old homeland that Lucy, at the age of seventy-seven, decided to fly to Europe to visit the home village of the Wangerin family, now-Polish Trzygłów. A grateful memory remains.

It is striking to a reader of the diary that it makes no political observations. It holds neither reflections on the mounting nationalism in Europe nor a hint of the perils attending the impending world economic crisis. But these topics were the talk of Pomerania.

Beyond that, people were discussing statutory modification, considered overdue, of legal relationships between estate overlords and agrarian labor, specifically the dissolution of estates as quasi-independent jurisdictions.[19] Upon the November Revolution of 1918 these became essentially a decided issue. For the social democratic government of Prussia under Otto Braun it was a matter of course to finally do away with this last legal bastion of feudal class domination on the land and thus conclude the process of defeudalization introduced 120 years earlier. It no longer fit the political landscape that the person in possession of an estate was also automatically the head of local governance. In keeping with this, estates as civil units were eliminated on 1 October 1928 and attached administratively to their neighboring municipalities.[20]

It did take longer for the act to be incorporated also into the behavior of the population. The relationships of dependency were now, as before, too pronounced, and accustomed rights too strong, for legal provisions to become social reality immediately. But above all, estate owners commonly occupied a position that, owing to tradition and the esteem in which they were held, assured their long-term influence with the estate workers. If, in addition, the local clergyman and schoolteacher declined to challenge the old structures, "the estate" kept its foundations of authority.[21]

So it was only with difficulty that people in Triglaff and Vahnerow assented to elimination of the estate jurisdictions. Reinold von Thadden, especially, saw this as state encroachment upon old, historically developed institutions, inadequately taking into account tangential issues.[22] Admittedly, he was failing to give any thought to the political changes subsequent to November 1918.

In these years of expiration of the old feudal structures, Reinold von Thadden turned more toward other realities that had long since taken deep root in his life, issues of Christian renewal of human coexistence. While the majority of estate owners reacted to the termination of feudal legal conditions by withdrawing into private life or, amongst the younger generation, by tending toward political radicalization,[23] he concentrated on what he termed the realities of faith, bringing other priorities to the fore. The more his political world seemed to him a dead end, the more he set his hopes on a dimension of spiritual renewal, of the church as well as of society.

But where to begin, when living in Eastern Pomerania and chiefly engaged in agriculture? For Reinold von Thadden, ownership of his estates was not an end in itself but rather constituted a base for responsible activity beyond the borders of the country, consistent with the family tradition. In his memoirs, written after World War II, *Auf verlorenem Posten?* (A lost cause?) he gave expression to this attitude repeatedly.[24]

Yet in one way he went far outside the bounds of the usual voluntary and honorary involvement: he also sought and cultivated friendships abroad. Following the collapse of national models, this agriculturist, conscious of his origins in a province east of the Elbe, found in the Christian associations of the Anglo-Saxon countries and France the bit of world that he needed for his ideas about renewal. In those places lived personalities who thought beyond national borders and who were building international organizations that offered promising starts toward overcoming the nationalistic blind alleys of the World War I era.[25]

Especially in France—politically the enemy—he came upon the kind of friends he longed for in defeated, humiliated Germany. They held out their hands to him and were prepared to unite in thinking about the causes and consequences of nationalistic policies of expansion. Taking the lead in this, and winning his trust, was Pierre Maury, president at the time of the French "Fédération" of Christian student organizations and later president of the Reformed Church in France. As a retrospective assessment expressed it:

> Both had experienced the war of 1914–1918, one on the Marne and at Verdun, the other on the Russian front. From 1917 on, convinced that the world was changing and that the worst of all evils is nationalism, of an ultimately diabolical nature, they had through many years, thinking above all of their students, discussed their task, the one as a pastor, the other as jurist, duty bound jointly to the "genuine" Gospel.[26]

For the French Protestants, it meant a lot that both were diligent readers of Karl Barth's writings: "They interpreted the events as a call to a return to the deep roots of the Christian faith, as the power that alone was in a position to counter the political chaos, the tyranny, and the crime."[27]

The common understanding between these two nationals of hostile countries was deep. In building bridges to the French Protestants, Reinold von Thadden was undoubtedly helped by his fluent mastery of their language. Thus the later chair of the French Christian student association, Suzanne de Dietrich, spoke very positively of Thadden's "captivation by French culture" and called him a "born European."[28] But the Anglo-Saxons and the Americans too welcomed his ecumenical ways of thinking, which accorded with their own intellectual traditions. In addition to the Scot Robert C. Mackie and the American Francis Pickens Miller, who was president of the World Student Christian Federation (WSCF), it was the towering personality of the U.S. Nobel Prize recipient John R. Mott who attracted him and led him permanently into associations with Protestant international organizations. Not to be forgotten in this circle is the influential Hollander Willem A. Visser't Hooft, who later became general secretary of the World Council of Churches in Geneva.[29]

So as the Weimar Republic finally collapsed, the Eastern Pomeranian estate owner Reinold von Thadden maintained connections with an ecumenical circle of friends. They would remain faithful to him through the imminent dark years, until the period after World War II.[30] But how did these contacts, so important to his life, come about? It is striking that the various relationships essentially emerged out of a single involvement, namely, Thadden's personal bond with the German Christian Students Association (Deutsche Christliche Studentenvereinigung, DCSV), anchored in the institutions of higher education.

Here, too, contact was first established in the house of the former Imperial Chancellor Michaelis, president of the DCSV after 1912. A Freiburg clergyman close to Michaelis, Hermann Weber, who began serving as general secretary of the student association in 1923, persuaded Thadden to join the new board. In 1928 it elected him president, not entirely without opposition.[31]

That opened doors to the related student associations in France, England, and above all the United States. As nationalistic inflexibility mounted from month to month in Germany, ties to the neighboring associations gained ever more strength, so that in the end they resulted in visits to Trieglaff, too. The wide world encountered a diminutive universe in the east of Pomerania.[32]

The later theme of Reinold von Thadden's life soon played a substantial role in discussions. This was the question of participation of lay people on church boards and committees.[33] It was merely consistent with the views he held, therefore, for Thadden to permit his own election to the Pomeranian provincial synod and then, in 1929, to the Prussian general synod. It seemed imperative that his various engagements had to come together in an institution tied to the land — whether travel from Trieglaff to Berlin remained tedious or not.[34]

The question poses itself all the more insistently, then, how estates like Vahnerow or Trieglaff endured the frequent absence of their owners. In Thadden's own judgment, his estate Inspektor and later administrator, Wilhelm Engelke, merited maximum credit.[35] He was in charge of the whole operation, but also assigned the workers tasks and supervised their activities. As much as possible, he discussed the work program of the following day with the estate's master.[36]

On larger operations the Inspektor, for the most part, had at his side a second "official" (*Beamter*) who took care of the housing of livestock and the storage and shipment of crops. Special responsibilities were borne, finally, by the overseer (*Hofmeister*), the "*Schweizer*" (dairyman, lit. "Swiss") responsible for the cows, the shepherd, and craftsmen like the smith, cartwright, and gardener, who worked with greater freedom to make decisions. To be sure, only the "officials" were addressed as *Herr*.[37]

So structured, these operations worked pretty decently, as a rule. Management functioned, and the hierarchy within the working class remained uncontested. But it did not solve the problem of succession with regard to those who bore district-wide responsibilities. Where were people to be found to represent the interests of the rural areas in officialdom? In a detailed letter to a friend, Reinold von Thadden expressed this concern with a grave earnestness:

> Quite soon we will no longer have the people of character and business ability among us who are absolutely indispensable for occupying even lesser positions, as superintendents (*Amtsvorsteher*), members of the district council, members of the supervisory council for dairies, precinct supervisors (*Gemeindevorsteher*).[38]

Thadden did not drop the matter with a description of the situation. Given the discussions current at the time about partition of large estates, so as to settle more farmers on the land,[39] he regarded it as necessary to undertake a more fundamental analysis of the background:

> A historical guilt may be present for the trans-Elbe aristocracy because it did not understand in the past how to raise up, model for, and gradually empower the mid and lower strata of its world as sub-leadership.[40]

It would become difficult at this point to make up for all that in a short time.

Reinold von Thadden's eye for these problems was sharpened also because, per agreement, he had in the meantime taken charge of the larger estate, Trieglaff, and handed over the smaller, Vahnerow, to his elderly father and the family from his second marriage. From 1 July 1930 on Reinold was the master of Trieglaff, with all the responsibilities—public also—that hinged upon that. His father Adolf died two years later as a highly regarded former Landrat in the District of Greifenberg.[41]

The years of this move from Vahnerow to Trieglaff were simultaneously years of momentous changes in the Reich. They led to not only a new worldwide depression of undreamed proportions, but also a political crisis that ended the Weimar Republic unexpectedly rapidly and entailed an end as yet unforeseeable.

Nothing appeared unsettling at first. The Reichstag elections of 20 May 1928 strengthened the socialist SPD and also the communist KPD (28.7 percent and 10.6 percent). The DNVP, the party most congenial to landed interests, was weakened in comparison with the previous election (14.2 percent), while the liberal parties, notwithstanding losses (DVP 8.7 percent and DDP 4.9 percent), remained capable of governing. The radically nationalistic NSDAP did not yet play a role (2.6 percent), but the new "business party" (Wirtschaftspartei) of the German middle class certainly did (4.5 percent).[42]

Nor did election results in the District of Greifenberg evince any hints of the approaching storm. The traditional dominance of the conservative DNVP (53.1 percent) continued, even though the SPD made some gains (23.5 percent). Both liberal parties (DVP and DDP) held at under 5 percent, and the NSDAP obtained a mere 3.9 percent. Noteworthy beyond that was only the addition of the new Wirtschaftspartei, appealing to the middle class (with ca 10 percent).[43]

So election results as a whole presented no reason for a mood of crisis. Yet within the DNVP, important to the estate holders, program differences then taking shape would lead to a factional split the next year. At issue was the vital question whether they should, in the long term, place their bets on positive cooperation within a parliamentary state or on a role in radical opposition.[44]

The moving force of the radicals was Alfred Hugenberg, an industrial leader originally from Hanover who had built an influential publishing empire and was close to the nationalistic Alldeutscher Verband (Pan-German League). Following the resignation, not wholly voluntary, of Count Westarp, who inclined toward compromise, Hugenberg seized the DNVP chairmanship in 1928 and introduced thereafter a policy of marching in step with the NSDAP. This prepared the path to power for Hitler in January 1933.[45]

This intra-party strife reached as far as to Pomerania and into the world of Vahnerow and Trieglaff. For several years, the DNVP for this eastern agricultural province was headed by one of Hugenberg's fiercest opponents, the estate owner Schlange-Schöningen. Early on he had warned about radicalization of the DNVP and decided, first, to lay down the chairmanship of the Pomeranian Landesverband (a regional confederation), and in the end to leave the party two years later. He formulated his justification for it as follows:

> I saw no hope anymore. The German National Party's basic premise for conservative government had sunk to a state-destroying radicalism which, rather than resisting, sought vainly to trump the mounting National Socialism ... with powerful slogans.[46]

Numerous members left the DNVP's Reichstag faction together with Schlange-Schöningen, among them Count Westarp and the later founder of a popular conservative association, Gottfried Treviranus. Others were the historian of Eastern Europe Otto Hoetzsch and the long-time government minister Walter von Keudell. They rejected nationalistic stoking of the discord over the so-called Young Plan for revising German reparations payments[47] and denied allegiance to Hugenberg in an open vote of the Reichstag.

This breakup of the party moved Reinold von Thadden to write a letter to his friend, the erstwhile imperial chancellor Michaelis, to solicit advice and his stance. "There is no doubt," he said,

> that at this hour, when the battle for and against the current shape of the German National People's Party (DNVP) has flared up, altogether in the public eye, a weighty responsibility falls to us. To which side our rudder is to be turned I will not risk deciding. In any case, we don't dare to allow it ever to go so far that the most highly valued, and substantively most nearly allied, portions of the old German National People's Party establish new foundations for their activity and we remain with a Hugenberg-led rump party whose governing spirit is opposed to ours in all ways, and

whose dominant individuals will never consider giving a place in their ranks to the influence of Christian-conservative thinking.[48]

With concern, Thadden observed the disputes with Christian groups on the fringes of the DNVP. He sensed that it was becoming difficult to confront the arguments of the "Christian-social people" and the south German Christian People's Service, groups that feared the DNVP's estrangement from the traditions of Christian thought.

> Once we have been completely pushed away from the people around Keudell we will not succeed whatsoever anymore in keeping the Christian groups together with the national right. Then we'll be sitting hopelessly between 2 chairs and have no cards left to play against our opponents on the right and on the left.[49]

No letter of response from Michaelis is to be found in the possession of the von Thadden family. But Reinold von Thadden made a declaration of his own position in a letter to the brother of his friend Hermann Weber. In it he backed up his personal decision: He was unable to bring himself to opt for leaving the DNVP. Why? To answer, it is necessary to inquire of a complicated foregoing history.

Thadden identified essentially three points that shaped his decision. The first was his "conviction, anchored in faith, that Christians do not belong in a 'Christian' party, but in a 'secular one.'" A "Protestant center" comparable to the Catholic Zentrum was out of the question. Next was "the tragic fate of German democracy and social democracy, which, since the days of the French revolution and the Enlightenment, have anchored their politics, ideologically, in self-centered individualism, whereas the right, in its ideals at least, held fast to the old evangelical Protestant features of fear of God and social bondedness." Third, his "concrete Pomeranian agricultural situation" would allow him no political effectiveness except with the German National People's Party. "With any other decision I would, during this time of dire need for agriculture, simply be stabbing my colleagues and the Pomeranian union of landowners [Deutschnationaler Landbund] in the back."[50]

Quite obviously it was the third reason that tipped the scales. His ties to the political forces of his eastern Pomeranian world kept Reinold von Thadden from exiting the trusted DNVP, even though his scruples grew from month to month. So he wrote Hermann Weber in the summer of 1931, that is, at the time of the disastrous "Harzburg Front" of the DNVP and NSDAP: "Maybe I'm not saying too much if I state my opinion that I care least for that party to which I myself belong."[51]

The District of Greifenberg also remained loyal to the DNVP in its way. In the Reichstag elections on 14 September 1930 it still got 40 percent, whereas the NSDAP was already managing 26.8 percent of the vote. Compared with the average for the Reich (7.0 percent), the DNVP came out significantly better here, as always, but to offset this, the share of the votes for the NSDAP was 8 percent higher in the District of Greifenberg than in the Reich (18.3 percent). Comparison of voting results for the two workers' parties at district and Reich levels did not change the picture either: in this little-industrialized district, the SPD (15.8 percent to 24.5 percent) and KPD (5.8 percent to 13.1 percent) stood no chance of holding their own against the two parties on the right. And both liberal parties, as well as the business party, could be dismissed throughout Germany by this time.[52]

In Trieglaff and Vahnerow, too, the DNVP, well-disposed toward estate ownership as it was, asserted itself in this election as the strongest party. In the earlier local and district council elections on 17 November 1929 it received in the two villages together more than 70 percent of the votes: in Trieglaff 159 out of 214, in the composite rural precinct Batzwitz/ Vahnerow 149 of 217 votes. Among those were to be found 13 and 3 votes respectively for the German Farmers' Party (Deutsche Bauernpartei), which in 1930 presumably went to the NSDAP. But now there must have been farm workers, too, who voted for the radical nationalistic party.[53]

According to later accounts by contemporaries and from scholarly investigations, two things especially made the National Socialists attractive for the majority of the farmers, as well as increasingly for some groups of rural workers. Firstly, from 1928 on the great agricultural crisis drove an ever larger portion of the increasingly insecure rural population into the arms of Hitler's party, which aroused cheap hopes with its animus-laden promises. But secondly, the National Socialists found considerable support because they presented themselves as advocates of a seductive "united folk community"—the Volksgemeinschaft—opposed to ideas that were disturbing village life promulgating class warfare. They acted as if they wanted to overcome class egoisms.[54]

Indeed, there were counterforces. By no means did farm workers always feel themselves conjoined with the farmers in a community of common interests, for they were often employed by them and had negative experiences in the everyday world of work. The estate owners, who maintained a distance from the farmers socially in any case, clung in the majority to "their" party, the DNVP. Its authority rested upon older foundations than did any possessed by the less-wealthy farmers.[55]

So stronger integrative forces would have been necessary to keep the sense of community in the villages from becoming endangered during the agricultural crisis—the more so as the preceding programs for rural people (*Landvolkprogramme*) were unable to address the paramount economic power, the industrial society of the cities. As a result, the world of agriculture was isolated still further. What could seem more plausible, then, than for the forces of nationalism, prevalent in any case, to be mobilized, and for all strata of the population, however varied in character, to be brought together under the one roof of an ethnically united nation? The National Socialists achieved success with this program.[56]

But in the field of forces present in villages, a further factor played a role, with meaning for Trieglaff particularly, namely the church. Here it even presented itself in two forms. Ever since the Old Lutherans had split off in the middle of the nineteenth century, the united Protestant established church no longer included all the village's inhabitants.[57] Only about two-thirds of Trieglaffers still retained membership in it.[58]

Accordingly, two pastors held pulpits in the place. They could certainly differ thoroughly in their opinions. But what had affected only confessional membership up to this point now also garnered notice politically as the National Socialist Party grew. The NSDAP pushed into the ecclesiastical realm with a "faith movement" of its own, the so-called German Christians (Deutsche Christen), and anticipated taking over congregational governance and, at higher levels, the synods.[59] Thus a new front joined the old in the church.

It is not surprising that within the village population, this constellation was unhelpful to a quest for orientation and increasingly so, as conflicts throughout the whole country were coming to a twofold head. In November of 1932, elections to the Reichstag took place again, as did elections to congregational councils. If the German Christians succeeded in consolidating their position of power noticeably in the ecclesiastical bodies, that would have its effect also in political elections, and vice versa.[60]

The outcome of the church elections was alarming. In Pomerania the German Christians took nearly 50 percent of the seats.[61] Yet this was not the case in Trieglaff, where effects of the traditions of the nineteenth-century awakening movement lingered.[62] Especially the manor house, with its influence upon the congregational council—the estate holder, as patron, had a seat on this body—developed into a hub for the gathering of Christians loyal to the faith. With Reinold von Thadden, who was, moreover, a member of the Pomeranian provincial synod and the Prussian general synod, it became in the end a place of resistance to the neo-heathen German Christians.[63]

Yet where was the point of departure to be found for formation of a counterweight to the uninvited guests from the ranks of the brownshirts—"browns"—alien to the church? Already some months prior to the congregational council elections slated for November 1932, a number of Greifswald higher clergy recognized that the tactical lineup of the German Christians could only be met by some impressive large-scale religious event.[64] So the provincial church council sent out invitations to a "Pomeranian Protestant Kirchentag" (Pommerscher evangelischer Kirchentag, a convocation or rally) at Stettin, which assembled 20,000 participants from every district in the province for two days.[65]

At this Kirchentag Reinold von Thadden gave the main speech, in which he laid out the situation and the task of the Protestant Church against the background of the "inner bewilderment of modern humanity":

> It is as though a foot no longer finds solid ground upon which it can tread, not in thought, not in moral judgment, and therefore not in modes of acting either anymore. For that, perhaps nothing can be taken as so characteristic as the wavering back and forth of the voting masses between the political parties that we have been observing for a long time.[66]

Thadden saw the real danger to society in the people's lack of orientation. He observed with concern that they often sought refuge in dubious leaders, and demanded

> [n]o moral preaching and no erasure of boundaries between the obligations of church and state, but a message from God, the Lord, who tolerates no other authority besides Himself—not the authority of human Führer-personalities either—and meets every attempt to rob Him of His claim to majesty with the regal command: "I am the Lord your God, you shall have no other gods besides me."[67]

To pinpoint the spiritual locus of the actual confrontation even more precisely, Thadden directed attention to another aspect of the debate: the discussion with the atheistic leftists. Here he warned against mistaken perspectives:

> We have become godless, not because Moscow determined that it would oppose belief in God through a campaign of extermination, and not because amongst us there is an organized movement of godlessness here on German soil, but because, one and all, we have so often effectively stricken God from the lexicon of our everyday, and of our Sundays, too.[68]

His self-critical coming to terms with a personal tradition of self-righteous insulation against external enemies of faith ultimately led to a call to reflect upon the inner forces of regeneration:

> What is needed for that, more than anything, is the Christian congregation, of all classes and levels of the people, making sure that the message of the church does not remain an empty platitude or an uplifting phrase.[69]

In retrospect, the Stettin Kirchentag seemed to Reinold von Thadden to be "the pinnacle of our missionary activity."[70] Certainly it played—and not just as a historic memory—a role in the establishment of the German Protestant Kirchentag (Deutscher Evangelischer Kirchentag) in 1949, intended similarly, past and present, as a place of Christian witness in a world in need of orientation. The very concept "Kirchentag" was given potent meaning by the gathering in Stettin.[71]

Four months after the Stettin Kirchentag, Hitler was in power. Indeed, at first he had no part in the German Christians' incessant actions, so disruptive to church peace. Nevertheless, he bypassed no opportunity to garnish official acts with church services and thus give the impression that the new government attached importance to maintaining religious institutions. With his pseudo-religious language he wanted to appear as guarantor of a decisive advance against the "atheism" of the Marxists, as a counterforce against the "dechristianization" that the people sensed as a threat.[72]

In Pomerania, too, this policy gained currency as something that was not at all revolutionary. In the village of Trieglaff, people were mesmerized more by entrancing public displays anyway than by the substance of political pronouncements. And whenever possible, they went to the district seat of Greifenberg to watch, with others, a big parade that brought all the national organizations together.[73]

It was no different in the neighboring villages. In Vahnerow people probably looked more in the direction of less-distant Plathe than to Greifenberg. And in the manor house, thought was being given to where things were headed, particularly as the proprietress, Barbara von Thadden, had some Jewish friends in Berlin who were experiencing anxiety.[74] In the Blanckenburg manor house in Zimmerhausen, Hitler was regarded at first as

> a phenomenon of the times, like other politicians before who'd come and gone.... But relatively soon, strengthened by the opinion of Reinold von Thadden and other friends … we realized that with Adolf Hitler it was something new and dangerous, something that went contrary to everything that was dear and sacred to us. Notwithstanding all the big talk and all the promises, we knew that it was moving toward war against the church and toward bending the law, never mind that this was intermixed in uncanny fashion with all kinds of apparent good.[75]

Beyond that, people waited. "Our village population," the above report continues,

> stood back silently, with but few exceptions. The biggest adherents of the NSDAP were, as virtually everywhere, the teachers. They left the church and influenced their pupils, as much as they could, to not only follow the Führer, but to love him.[76]

Trieglaff did not have such a village teacher. "Herr Kopelmann," who acted simultaneously as registrar in the village (*Standesbeamter*), deliberately stayed with the Prussian established church and functioned as reader at church services when the pastor was absent. True, he was a pro forma member of the NSDAP, but he made no visible use of it and did nothing that could injure the oppositionally aligned manor house. As teacher he discussed in depth the sections in the Pomeranian primer (*Pommernfibel*), which—until 1938—contained Christian reading material, such as the section on Christmas, which, because the word utilized the infrequent capital C, included Christkind (Christ child) and therefore was not so easily replaced by other reading material.[77]

Under these circumstances it is not too astonishing that the Nazi policy of "streamlining" independent institutions (Gleichschaltung), carried out during the following months, made the rural population less uneasy than it did the people who bore responsibility within the democratic parties. In any case, a politics centering upon representative bodies had played no large role in villages. It made no big difference there if the Bürgermeister was no longer elected, but simply appointed. And a Landrat's being placed in office instead of elected by the district council did not change the fact that he could hold office only with the endorsement of the government. Führer structures, present now also in higher education and in associations, hardly disturbed anyone.[78]

Within the context of the Protestant Church of Germany this had a somewhat different appearance. Here democracy in fact had no home either, as certain responsible bodies were not willing to give a voice to others. From local congregational councils through provincial synods all the way up to the Prussian General Synod in Berlin, the traditions of autonomous organization that had taken shape proffered starting points for an attitude of resistance to interference from outside, despite a permeating mode of state-oriented thinking.[79]

For Pomerania, hence for Trieglaff too, the provincial synod in Stettin was the most important church institution, apart from the consistory. It came together once a year and included both theologians and lay people, who were given nearly equal importance. In the first elections in Hitler's Third Reich, held simultaneously with elections to a "Nationalsynode" for the whole Reich on 23 July 1933,[80] the German Christians garnered slightly more than two-thirds of the seats. But the group of confessional adherents Evangelium und Kirche (Gospel and Church), to which Reinold von Thadden belonged, managed to get almost a third (76 to 31).[81]

Here streamlining came up against a borderline, albeit a slim one. The new president of the synod, Pastor Thom, made it unmistakably clear at its first sitting that the "parliamentarianism of the synods and the collegial system of church bureaucracy" no longer fit the times. Evangelium und Kirche was to learn right from the beginning that power relationships had changed. The elections set to take place at the synodal gathering ensued entirely on the basis of unanimously accepted nominations, and the matters to come before the group were directed, without discussion, to the provincial church council.[82]

The conflict came to a head quickly enough. When the German Christians at the level of the Prussian General Synod resolved to introduce the official state paragraph concerning Aryans also into the church, and thereby establish that persons "of non-Aryan descent" "could not be called as clergymen or as officials of the general church administration," a breach resulted with the church opposition faithful to the Protestant confessional stance. Those attendees who belonged to this opposition left the assembly hall as one.[83]

In the sequel, more than 2,000 pastors from the Reich joined a so-called Pfarrernotbund (fellowship of pastors in distress) formed around the brothers Wilhelm and Martin Niemöller,[84] which numbered 130 members in Pomerania alone, Greifenberg being one of its centers.[85] Trieglaff's own faithfulness to character can be explained only in light of the background of the historical family tradition of the Thaddens, for what emerged here was a "Laiennotbund," a fellowship of lay people in distress.[86]

Reinold von Thadden was clearly concerned that the church opposition to the regime of the German Christians could take on a clerical imbalance. At any rate, from January of 1934 on, he committed his energies fully to forming a Laiennotbund as complement to the Pfarrernotbund. A circular provides information about it. "The fellowship," it states,

Figure 16. Reinold von Thadden (1891–1976), president of the Pomeranian synod of the Confessing Church and later founder of the German Protestant Kirchentag

came into existence under the leadership of Dr. von Thadden following the fervent pleas of many laypeople, on the basis of a commitment corresponding to that of the Pfarrernotbund, to grow into the latter's developing fellowship for confession and engagement. It does not desire to become a mass movement, but wishes to form the bottommost level of a genuine community of Christ founded upon Word and Sacrament alone.[87]

For its organization and leadership, the Laiennotbund was given a leadership council (*Führerrat*) to which belonged, besides Thadden, three other persons from the Pomeranian confessional movement. They undersigned the "commitment" referred to with these words:

> 1. I desire as an evangelical Christian to live, act and confess in the spirit of Jesus Christ. 2. I desire to ward off, to the best of my ability, all infractions against the authority of Holy Scriptures of the Old and New Testaments and the Confessions of the church. 3. I desire, to the best of my capacities, to take the part of all who are persecuted on account of loyalty to their faith and their confession.[88]

It requires no special imagination to visualize how the next meeting of the synod proceeded, two months after this declaration.[89] At the beginning, the members of the synod were informed that "no clergyman who had read aloud the declaration against Reich's Bishop Müller," the man installed by the Nazi authorities, would come into consideration for election.[90] Upon that, the members of Evangelium und Kirche refused to participate in the deliberations of the synod. A rump synod remained, which settled for dissolving the provincial synod for good.

What happened next was, for Pomeranian circumstances, unusual. The members who had left the former synod decided to found an evangelical confessing synod in Pomerania, the Evangelische Bekenntnissynode in Pommern, and call it into session in Stettin as quickly as possible, that is, on 7 May 1934 already. Thereby they set out on the risky path of detachment from the state church, which had at its disposal all financial means and administrative instruments.[91]

What did the confessing group have control over? To the surprise of others besides the initiators, in addition to twenty-five synodal delegates, more than a hundred pastors and laypeople from the whole province accepted the invitation. Nor was it surprising that they unanimously elected Reinold von Thadden as president (Figure 16). At his side a Council of Brethren (Bruderrat) was placed, to which all notables in the oppositional minority belonged.[92]

The Evangelische Berkenntnissynode then went before the public with a foundational declaration:

The efforts of current church government to shape external order independently of the nature and proclamation of the church contradicts the spirit of Christ and thereby endangers its Biblical and confession-directed foundations. The consequence of that, also in Pomerania, is arbitrary rule by force. Without legal process, and in part without statement of cause, 11 superintendents in our province have been robbed of their supervisory office. Pastors are being withheld from their congregations, contrary to the latter's express will. So long as such a dominance of the German Christians, justified neither legally nor spiritually, continues, cooperation with them cannot create any true unity. And a joint struggle against those deliberately opposed to the church holds no promise of victory.[93]

At Trieglaff, scarcely anybody in the village took notice of these happenings. People talked about the numerous trips taken by the master of the estate and observed the frequent visits by highly placed persons "from the city." But knowledge of what it all was about was reserved to only three people close to the manor house: Inspektor Engelke; the secretary of the estate, Billerbeck; and the coachman Köpsel. The pastor of St. Elisabeth's was not included because he was regarded as vacillating between the German Christians and the confessionally loyal officeholders.[94]

Yet their stance should not be assessed too critically. It had been a hundred years since theological disputes like those in the Pomeranian provincial synod had taken place in Trieglaff. And even if it can be assumed that the awakening movement had left traces,[95] concrete memories of the confessional split in the nineteenth-century church had certainly faded for most residents of the village. One was, simply, either "Old Lutheran" or "Prussian established church." People saw the two churches side by side in the village but were oblivious of the earlier history of the actual trial endured in the breakup.

But the memory of the struggles of old Great-grandfather Adolph von Thadden could very well still play a role in the conduct of Reinold von Thadden. In a retrospective of the conflicts of the years 1933 and 1934, he wrote in his memoir, *Auf verlorenem Posten?*:

> Only a few people realize that what is coming ... had a precursor, not so entirely harmless at all, almost exactly 100 years ago, when the absolute state in Prussia, "restored" after 1815, put the Christian groups of the Pomeranian awakening movement under pressure.[96]

Now, whether an event with precursors or not, the establishment of an independent confessing synod in Pomerania had consequences. First, it set loose a force for mobilization in the province. Nuclei of local congregations formed in almost every district. As we would say today, these groups "wanted to be networked."[97] Next, though, the synod chanced into the path of a far greater oppositional force that would later gain historical importance, the famed Barmer Synode.[98] This assemblage, called into being on 29–31 May 1934 in a Rhine congregation with Reformed traditions, was, strictly speaking, the act founding the Confessing Church (Bekennende Kirche) in Germany. It united 138 emissaries from all the regionally established German churches (Landeskirchen) and passed a theological declaration (*Theologische Erklärung*) consisting of six theses that delineated the commission of the church vis-à-vis that of the state with uncompromising clarity.[99]

Reinold von Thadden was among the signers of the declaration. He had traveled with four members of the Pomeranian Council of Brethren to Barmen, where he was involved primarily on the committee for renewal of clergy and congregations.[100] Beyond that, he had participated in the forbidden publication of an edition of a newspaper for the Wuppertal congregations that was promptly seized by the Gestapo.[101]

The return to Pomerania turned out to be sobering. How was it going to be possible to mediate such high-flown thoughts as those of the theological declaration to a village like Trieglaff? In his memoir Thadden wrote retrospectively:

> It is just not the same thing, whether one has behind oneself closed, tightly knit congregations and religious bodies of a good character, as in the Rhineland, or whether one must find support essentially in a circle of loyal pastors and loose, legally scarcely definable groups of confessing people who often afterward were not even capable of judging the implications of their decisions.[102]

Notwithstanding that, or perhaps precisely because of it, the Council of Brethren of the confessing synod of Pomerania decided to publish several circulars reporting on Barmen in detail.[103] In addition it set up and maintained a bureau in Stettin for filling out forms to join the confessing community. In Pomerania, the cards for that were green.[104]

But the German Christians were not inactive either. As a retort to Barmen, they conducted a great public demonstration in Stettin in early June, at which Reichsbischof Müller made an appearance. He emphasized that he intended to "build the German Protestant Church ... only through the German Christians," and publicly lauded their anti-Jewish theology. Rebuilding the church needed to begin with "the people" — the ethnic *Volk*.[105]

The Confessing Church, in turn, responded to this announcement with several events. The first came close to Trieglaff. The suspended superintendent of local area clergy, Buth, issued a summons to a demonstration for 7 June at Greifenberg. It drew an audience of six to seven hundred. Martin Niemöller was secured as principal speaker and reported at length on the Barmen synod.[106] What might the number of people from Trieglaff and Vahnerow have been, perhaps, who listened to him there?

Given such resonance, the question who else from the Thadden family belonged to the Confessing Church was sure to arise. Those at Vahnerow were not considered especially religious.[107] But then, there were other relatives in the country who no longer lived in Trieglaff. Of these, venerable Aunt Hildegard in Doberan ranked foremost. As provost at the Altenburg institute, she had earned for herself a high regard.[108] How did she comport herself in this precarious situation?

An exchange of letters with Reinold, of which unfortunately only half are extant,[109] shows clearly how intensively the two shared thoughts with each other. In this correspondence Reinold informed his aunt that he had in the meantime been ordered to silence, and so could not give a lecture planned for a congregation at Rostock.[110] A year later he enumerated for her all the pending meetings he was to attend of the Councils of Brethren at Prussian and Reich levels.[111] Finally, on 4 August 1936, he wrote to her, "Your letter, laden with worries in view of the present political situation of the church, elicits from me an echo more pronounced than you might perhaps think."[112]

Provost Hildegard's affiliation with the Confessing Church is quite apparent in a remark written after her brief arrest in 1938. In it she commented that, together with her sister Marie, she "had been accustomed for some time to 'be at home' in Doberan one evening a week for a circle of friends from Doberan's Confessing Church. People exchange news and writings about the church and close with song and prayer."[113]

She had been arrested for reproducing and distributing an open letter from East Prussian farmers to the general command in Königsberg, in which the writers had requested "that the release from confinement of some 50 to 60 arrested pastors might be effected from the highest level." Because the provost was unwilling to divulge to the Gestapo the name of the person who had reproduced the material, she was brought before a judge—who did, however, set her free again after two days of investigative detention.[114]

Naturally, this incident was discussed in Trieglaff. Likely even more important for the family was the news that someone from the younger generation had also resolved to join the Confessing Church—namely, Reinold's older sister Elisabeth (Figure 17), who had achieved wide renown as founder of the girls' school at Wieblingen near Heidelberg (Mädchenschule Wieblingen).[115] According to a membership card, she joined the "confessing community of the German Protestant Church in Baden" on 1 November 1934 and supported in particular the church's opposition to the German Christians.[116]

The program of purging the Bible of Jews (Entjudung der Bibel) was unacceptable to Elisabeth. It had already driven her brother into the resistance in 1933,[117] and was in deepest disagreement with her fundamental convictions. Another factor may have been her numerous Jewish friends, male and female, who felt increasingly excluded and persecuted. Thus Alice Salomon, a longtime acquaintance and the founder of Social Work by Women in Germany (Sozialarbeit von Frauen in Deutschland), could no longer work in the school Elisabeth had founded.[118] The social politician Marie Baum, also Elisabeth's friend, lost her commission to teach at the University of Heidelberg on racist grounds.[119]

Figure 17. Elisabeth von Thadden (1890–1944), founder of the Protestant boarding school for girls at Wieblingen, executed by the Nazi government in 1944

It goes without saying that people in the village of Trieglaff talked about Jews too, although differently than in Wieblingen. People there mainly knew Jewish businesspeople in the district seat of Greifenberg, who for the most part had had to give up their stores since 1933/1934. Many of them were on the point of emigrating. But the synagogue on Wallstraße remained, and it was still included by name in the directory of the town of Greifenberg for the year 1936.[120]

A memorandum to Hitler by the provisional administration of the German Protestant Church, written in May 1936 and co-drafted and signed by Reinold von Thadden, best thematized treatment of Jews.[121] Article V, which dealt with National Socialist ideology, stated clearly:

> Whenever Aryans are glorified, God's Word testifies to the sinfulness of all people; whenever anti-Semitism is forced upon Christians within the framework of the National Socialist conception of the world, obligating to hatred of Jews, the Christian command of love for one's neighbor negates it.[122]

With this memorandum the last barriers went down. Nevertheless, the Nazi leadership took its time answering. During the year of the Olympics in Berlin, it obviously did not want to risk conflict with the churches and therefore settled for lesser "measures" against disfavored troublemakers. Controls were put on their correspondence and, not least, their travel activity was monitored and sometimes prevented. To hinder trips abroad, it was possible to withhold passports.[123]

The Confessing Church was most vulnerable in its educational establishments. It suffered a heavy blow when the seminary at Finkenwalde near Stettin, influential far beyond Pomerania, had to shut its doors. It was led by Dietrich Bonhoeffer,[124] by that time a highly regarded theologian, who had cultivated close contacts with the Christian families of the Pomeranian landed aristocracy and thereby secured the seminary financially. To this end Reinold von Thadden had managed to open many a door for him, some not insignificantly through invitations to Trieglaff, which lay only 80 kilometers distant from Finkenwalde.[125]

In early summer 1937, the time had come to snatch somebody at Trieglaff, too. On the afternoon of 18 June, two figures in civilian clothes who identified themselves as Gestapo agents appeared and demanded to speak with the proprietor of the estate. However, at the time he was not on the manor grounds but in a field, where the gendarme of the village, who was well-disposed toward him, found Thadden and warned him. After a brief consultation with Inspektor Engelke, Thadden decided to present himself, rather than evade his probable arrest.[126]

What followed took place rapidly. Thadden was given an opportunity to pack his things and sign several business-related papers. Then he got into the car and was taken as directly as possible to the jail in Stettin. Only after two days was he relocated to a normal interrogation prison.[127]

The charges cited "resistance to state authority," "malice," and "attempted treason." Yet the grounds for indictment proved to have so little merit that the examining judge decided to release Thadden. This meant little, for again a Gestapo car was waiting outside the door to bring him to the jail at the Alexanderplatz in Berlin. The officers informed him in unmistakable terms that any attempt to escape would be prevented with weapons.[128]

We have information about the details of the Gestapo detention from a report by Reinold's younger sister, Helene—called Leni—a social aide,[129] who dared to visit her brother in Berlin to find out what might be brought up against him. With the assistance of President Kurt Scharf, who played an important role in the Confessing Church, she managed to push her way through to the outer office of the Gestapo official heading up the interrogation, where she witnessed an exchange of words that had grave consequences. "Then I hear," she wrote,

> Reinold, through the half open door of the office, as he is saying: "I am a Prussian aristocrat and not a Schweinehund [swine, SOB]." Unfortunately, he cannot tell me now what that had reference to. He was just in the process of signing the record and told the police inspector, altogether calmly, why laypersons are concerned with religious matters and that the battle against Christianity constituted undermining of the state.[130]

Later, Leni was given an opportunity to speak to her brother in person, though under observation. "He fearlessly described to me his treatment before and at the Alexanderplatz. It was really beneath human dignity."[131] In a second letter she described details of the detainment.

> During the 5 nights that he was there he never closed an eye, because with onset of darkness the bedbugs tormented him so badly that he got all swollen up. During the day it was forbidden for him even to sit down on the bed, much less lie down on it. The cell was 1½ m wide and 3 m long.

And about the food, she added, "At noon there was a thin cabbage soup in a rusted bowl such as you see sometimes in a kennel, and in the evening there was watery soup with farina."[132]

Leni wrote that a second interrogation conducted afterward was significantly more unpleasant than the first. "They suddenly presented a piece of writing to him for which he is, indeed, responsible. It had to do with a call to students to be part of the forbidden theological college in Berlin."[133] Thadden indeed had, in the name of the provisional administration of the German Protestant Church, encouraged three Berlin students to persist in attending courses by the Confessing Church and not to allow themselves to be discouraged by the threat of expulsion from the school of theology at the University of Berlin.[134] According to Leni's report, it then occurred to her brother

> to speak to the infamous head of the religious bureau of the Gestapo, Chantré, himself. When this was refused to him, he simply went to him in his office. In three-quarters of an hour he succeeded in getting the initially opposed and cynical man to change his mind. He listened earnestly as he spoke about his Christianity. Success was such that the new charge was immediately dropped.[135]

One day later Reinold von Thadden was released. In his memoir he described his subsequent return to Trieglaff in thoughtful words. Notwithstanding a joyful reception at home, the echo from the rural population was divided.

Yes, those estate workers and farmers with Christian inclinations who adhere to the Confessing Church share deeply in our joy. But the majority can't, in arriving at their judgment, quite yet extract themselves from the old long-traditional Prussian ideas of order, according to which it seems evident that imprisonment has a criminal character and must, somehow, have been imposed and carried out "justly" "by the state."[136]

Then too there were the people who raised the question, "And why is he messing with things that don't concern him!"

The "church struggles" between Nazism and the churches got little understanding from Elisabeth, Reinold von Thadden's wife, too, at first. She came from a Frankish family of simple religiosity that held monarchical national convictions. Critical confrontations with the state were foreign to that mentality. Hence she earned herself all the more approval when she stood behind her husband without reservation and faced the Gestapo courageously when it arrested him, an "innocent" person, repeatedly. Her sister-in-law Leni, who was sparing with praise, evaluated this comportment with the words, "Liesi is doing a lot more than she has ever done in her life."[137]

Peace and quiet were not forthcoming for this world that was experiencing continuous overtaxation of its capacities after the surge of arrests in summer 1937. Quite the opposite, for now internal conflicts broke out within the Confessing Church. Should people conform more to the political givens? Or should they hew all the more closely to a course of steadfast opposition?

The question took concrete form on a particularly sensitive point: Could a strategy be maintained whereby the Confessing Church accepted only those candidates for pastoral office who had passed their second theological examination before its own committees? Up to that point there had also been the traditional route, by way of examination before the established church's consistory in Stettin, where, to be sure, German Christians now participated and decided.

Reinold von Thadden, together with the Council of Brethren, endeavored to bring about "legalization" of the "illegal" candidates and vicars of the Confessing Church by agreement with the consistory, via recognition of the Confessing Church's examinations. But in this he was unsuccessful because the consistory insisted upon a follow-up examination of candidates by the book and threatened not to accept them into service in the Landeskirche otherwise.[138]

Inevitably, the Council of Brethren had to withstand a test of cohesiveness. On one side stood those who were unprepared to accept any compromise; on the other, those who shied from conflict with the boards at the head of the church, preferring to conform. In the end, bare numbers were decisive: of the originally 300-plus pastors who had signed a commitment to the Confessing Church, only 60 continued to support the governing church rules of the Council of Brethren.[139] Accordingly, important members left the council.

Trieglaff marched to its own tune. The village continued to be divided into the united church—the Landeskirche—and the free-church Old Lutheran congregation. That left little tolerance for new divisions.[140] But once again, an encounter with the nineteenth century materialized out of the blue. The great-great-grandson of the shepherd Friedrich Wangerin, himself not forgotten by families on either side of the Atlantic, came from the United States to visit relatives in Pomerania, aware that a hundred years earlier, Reinold's great-grandfather Adolph von Thadden had presented the elder Wangerin with a gold watch for his loyalty during the disastrous "fire wedding."[141]

Rudolph A. Wangerin had come to Europe with his brother Arnold, not to seek explanations of the present, but traces of the past. And he found them. In reading the work by Hermann Petrich published in 1931, *Adolf und Henriette von Thadden und ihr Trieglaffer Kreis* (their Trieglaff circle),[142] he came upon the story of the legendary gold watch and the German relatives who were, perhaps, still in possession of this watch. In Pomerania he found both: "In 1938 Arnold and I saw and examined this watch in the home of Gerhard Wangerin in Cammin, and ... it was the story of this watch which ... provided the 'break-through' in establishing positive relationships."[143]

A watch, and the memory of it, as key to a world of relatives who had nearly been lost sight of—what a symbol of biographical linkages spanning generations and continents! Royal Natzke regarded this event as so meaningful that he gave it special mention, in a footnote of its own, in *The Nobleman Among the Brothers*, the English translation of a book about the first Trieglaff Thadden.[144] But apart from this nothing is known about the conversations the Americans held with their German relatives. What might they have noted regarding Hitler's Germany?

Because of the surveillance of postal traffic, such gaps could hardly be filled through the exchange of letters. "What another person wants to know," Reinold von Thadden remarked in a letter to relatives, "one can't write, and what one can write is hardly worth knowing."[145] This observation became more valid yet after the structures of communication were destroyed, as occurred with the forced dissolution of the DCSV in July 1938.[146] Not only were gatherings forbidden, but all the property of the student association was "secured," as it was worded in the language of the Nazi regime.

Prompted by this, Thadden, as chair of the DCSV, wrote a circular to all its members in which he recalled its many years of collaboration with the World Student Christian Federation. "The DCSV found respect for its work in the WSCF and could, at the same time, perform an important political service for its own nation."[147] Everything would now become more difficult, but that would not touch solidarity in the faith.

These were the words of a man who on the one hand was at the end of his rope as far as church politics was concerned, but on the other clung to his Christian faith as absolute. It was plain to all that the ground beneath the Confessing Church was disappearing at an increasing rate. But there were also traditional practices and religious customs enough, in rural areas especially, to require maintenance of normal services. And everywhere the church owned buildings that, independently of the theological orientation of pastors, had to be maintained. A church affirmed by the people—a Volkskirche, grown up organically—does not take its departure overnight.[148]

* * * * *

Half a year after these dissolution proceedings, World War II broke out. It affected Trieglaff and Vahnerow in the same way it affected all other places in Germany, but here it exhibited several peculiarities. First, this Pomeranian region was one of the border areas through which military movements took place. Weeks before 1 September 1939, troops were in evidence along with their equipment and field kitchens, and attracted the notice of the population. Next, agriculture suffered harsh requisitioning that significantly diminished private businesses' latitude to calculate how they were doing, since they no longer had freedom to dispose of surpluses at will.[149]

And finally, the frequent call-ups to military service hit agricultural operations particularly hard because agriculture was already hurting from a shortage of labor. A farmer who forfeited his only worker felt the missing slice more keenly than did a large industrial operation that could more easily make up for shortfalls. But labor shortages affected the estates too, because mechanization of work processes had not yet advanced far enough to cushion them (Figures 18 and 19).[150]

The extent to which readjustments impeded estate operations in Trieglaff early in the war can be read from a letter by Reinold von Thadden to a friend and coworker of many years in the DCSV:

At the end of August a good part of my horses and a very high percentage of my workers of good working age were conscripted. At the same time the prospect was held forth by the Nazis' district farmers' organization that by mid-September, at the latest, 50 Polish prisoners of war would be made available as compensation. By the middle of October not a single Pole had yet appeared, though at considerable expense we had weeks earlier made accommodations ready, as prescribed, in my present barn for coach horses, with its adjunct spaces, including a kitchen and beds for prisoners.[151]

Further on, he describes how the POWs fared when they at last arrived for late deployment in harvesting and had to work in 48-degree (9° C) weather:

The Polish POWs are badly off, wholly inadequately clothed and often with just rags on their backs. Tomorrow I want to go by car to the prisoner-of-war camp in Stargard and personally get some of the most important things for keeping warm, and footwear, so that those people can at least work outdoors.[152]

At this point, reports about the plight of the Confessing Church recede perceptibly behind altogether different problems. One almost gets the impression that the war put an end to the church struggles—which corresponded to Hitler's desires.[153] Living through the first wartime Christmas illuminated an element of these changes that led to recognition of new realities. Reinold von Thadden described these vividly in a letter to his relatives in Doberan: "We are in a dining room in the front half of which ... our meals are to be taken, while the back part, totally in keeping with my tastes, is transformed into a cozy Christmas corner, with a short Christmas tree and modest crèche." The gift table reflected the restricted possibilities of this year. "I am most pleased with this accomplishment during our altered times. Actually, this is exactly how I have always quietly imagined Christmas to myself."[154]

Unusual in the new situation of war was that the Polish POWs were invited to the estate's Christmas celebration, not left out. Reinold reports that his wife Elisabeth was "a bit worn out from all the celebrating in church ... the village, and at home that includes guards and Polish POWs."[155] Beyond that, Pastor Haacke, on leave, had preached "so relevantly to the present and as intelligibly as never before to comrades in grey on leave, and to the congregation."[156] So the war was unable to sully Christmas.

Overall, though, the war did worsen the situation for the church. The numerous call-ups of pastors meant that many congregations lost their ministers, meaning that it was necessary to fill vacancies by burdening holders of pastorates elsewhere. In the province of East Prussia, almost half of all pastors were drafted.[157] Pastor Haacke at Trieglaff was no exception.

In a detailed report on the situation in the winter of 1939/1940 in the magazine *Pastoralblätter*, its editor, the church counselor Erich Stange, gave depth to his observations with a comparison. "Here it becomes factual," it reads, "that the Protestant pastorate is bearing arms in such proportions as affected only a few parts of the Empire in World War I."[158] After that, Stange addressed the generation-specific experiences of war: "It is not very easy for those among us who are older, who have already once tended wartime parishes, to liberate themselves from the memories of that to the extent that they grasp fully the present task in its own special uniqueness."[159] This task was being imposed far less extensively than earlier.

Reinold von Thadden saw the distinction between the situations of the two world wars similarly. After he, too, was recruited into the army in June 1940, he wrote from Brittany in France to his friend Eberhard Müller:

> This war assumes forms altogether different from the First and appears so far to be playing out less dreadfully. Its dangers for the inner life of the Christians in our military are for that reason not fewer, actually probably need to be addressed as more serious, as it is evident that fundamental mass secularization has grown immensely since 1918, and opportunities are far fewer to become mutually acquainted as Christians.[160]

In Trieglaff and Vahnerow, but also in Zimmerhausen, orders to report now gradually reached the very young generation born in the years from 1920 to 1924. Of the Thaddens, in Trieglaff Ernst-Dietrich and Leopold were drafted, soon also Franz-Lorenz; in Vahnerow the oldest son Adolf; also called were Günter and Peter von Blanckenburg in Zimmerhausen. In the villages the same was true for sons of farmers and farm workers. Life became quieter.

In agriculture, these losses were increasingly offset by POWs and then with forced laborers from occupied areas as well.[161] First, in 1940, came "the French," who were permitted to receive mail from their homeland and soon could also go about in civilian dress. Then, some fifty Russians arrived after the beginning of the "Russian campaign" in June 1941. An old cow barn along the lake was fixed up for them, and they were guarded by soldiers. Lastly Ukrainians, so-called eastern workers (*Ostarbeiter*), were provided lodgings in an old barracks for harvest crews in which the seasonal workers from Poland had previously been quartered.

Circumstances in Vahnerow were similar, yet with a meaningful difference: there were no Russian POWs. The Poles were followed in 1940 by twenty Frenchmen, whom the village inhabitants soon felt belonged. As was often the case, some of them worked in the garden, others in the farmyard, unguarded and in civilian clothes. At the end of the war, only nine of these individuals were left. A further group of foreign workers were the eighteen "eastern workers" from Ukraine, nine women and nine men,

Figure 18. Strawstack and elevator during harvest at Trieglaff in World War II

who arrived in 1942. They were far worse off than the French. They had to do fieldwork, and their state of health left much to be desired.[162]

For the POWs and deported "eastern workers," the estate Inspektor was as a rule the most important contact and reference person. Correspondingly, they considered him responsible for their treatment, too, sometimes viewed him with suspicion. Life together for so many involuntary and disparate laborers threw a general pall over everyday life in the village. Thus the way the manor house saw to the interests of the foreign workers, within the bounds set for it, had an effect on the atmosphere in the long term.

Over the course of the year 1943, so-called "evacuees" from the western areas elevated the number of people in the village. These refugees from the bombings of large cities in the Ruhr area were brought to regions of the German east that were regarded as still secure and protected. As Reinold von Thadden described things in a letter:

> In a short while we will be very limited in our use of empty rooms, insofar as we must make our house in large part available to refugees from the western German industrial region. I believe that in Trieglaff alone we are supposed to shelter 80 such people suffering from the bombings. Whether that can actually be done, in view of the circumscribed housing conditions in such a small village of estate workers and farmers, I'll venture to doubt. The attempt will in any case be made.[163]

Figure 19. Tractor and grain binder during harvest at Trieglaff in World War II

The attempt was successful. People nudged closer together and learned to share as best they could. The children of the refugee families were distributed into classes of their own in the schools in Greifenberg. At the Gymnasium, the students were taught in the afternoon by their own teachers. They met local students only in the German Youth Service (Deutsches Jungvolk, for ten- to fourteen-year-olds), or in the Hitler Youth (Hitler-Jugend, for fourteen- to eighteen-year-olds).

The numbers of fallen also rose in the wake of setbacks in the war against the Soviet Union, still commonly referred to as the "Russian campaign." In the Thadden family, first Ernst-Dietrich succumbed to a wound suffered in the winter battle near Moscow in 1941/1942. A year later Leopold fell in heavy fighting near Orel after writing his parents a moving letter about his experiences only a short time before.[164] And finally, the younger brother Bogislav also fell in the last weeks of war in Pomerania, so that of the five brothers, only two—Franz-Lorenz and Rudolf—survived the war.

In 1944 the family was also shaken by other, incomparably heart-wrenching news: that of the death of Reinold's oldest sister, Elisabeth von Thadden. From 1934 on she had been, as already mentioned, a member of the Confessing Church.[165] In the meantime she had lost the boarding school she founded at Wieblingen near Heidelberg because she fell into the crosshairs of the Gestapo. Now the family suddenly learned that she had been condemned to death and, after half a year of imprisonment in the concentration camp at Ravensbrück, executed. That was too much for the Trieglaff and Vahnerow village communities. Indeed, it was unimaginable, given the loyalty to the state that was so deeply inculcated from early on in Pomeranians.

In the fog of the untruths and half-truths of the Nazi regime, handling news reports was a survival skill, so it is hardly astonishing that rumors arose of something horrible having happened to Elisabeth von Thadden. But because there was no burial, and no notice in the *Greifenberger Kreisblatt* (newspaper) either, rumors were reformulated into suppositions that she had "gotten tangled up in" something that eluded precise knowledge. Only one thing was clear: you could talk about a soldier's death, but not about this mysterious one.[166]

Postal news, too, remained sparing. Her brother Reinold was caught up in the maelstrom of the western front as it fell apart—on the day of her execution, 8 September 1944, no less—and Franz-Lorenz was unreachable somewhere on the collapsing eastern front,[167] so communication in Trieglaff and Vahnerow remained limited to partial oral reports of the women of the family, who had received permission to visit Elisabeth only a few days prior. People were guarded when writing. Following reception of the news, Reinold von Thadden wrote to his friend Eberhard Müller without using names:

> In this case I am affected so deeply, and am so stricken in my soul, that I took in your comforting words like a thirsty person does the water from a fresh spring. Should we be permitted to see each other again one day— God grant it—then I will be able to tell you more, orally, about what has come to pass and what we experienced deep within ourselves.[168]

For the most part, it was only after the war that details of the shocking set of facts came to be known.[169] And even then, it was the circumstances in the foreground, more than deeper connections, that were of interest. People wanted to know just what had happened at that fateful tea party in September 1943, when Elisabeth von Thadden was betrayed by a Gestapo plant "for dangerous statements." Many relatives and friends asked what lay beneath the charge of subversion of the military (*Wehrkraftzersetzung*) that had been leveled against a woman who was, after all, utterly unmilitaristic. Did it constitute "resistance" merely to say that the war was lost and for that reason had to be ended as soon as possible?[170]

At any rate, by 1946 the reports and the attitudes[171] being communicated in West Germany did not reach the people in Trieglaff and Vahnerow. Under the conditions of the Soviet occupation and the Polish takeover of the country, complicated reports coming across the Oder-Neiße border were fragmented in any case. Besides, they were mostly overlaid by immediate cares of the everyday, so it amounted to a lot if someone even said in a conversation, "Well, after all, she was probably right when she was in favor of an early peace."[172]

But several months would elapse before the end of the war, which in Pomerania meant the arrival of the Red Army in early March 1945. These months were characterized above all by anxiety about the incalculability concerning the unfolding of events. Schools were closed from the beginning of the year. In February, a wave of refugees from East Prussia deluged Pomeranian villages. One particular *Treck* (group of refugees in flight) has dwelt in Trieglaffers' memory because accompanying it was a bit of unbroken "world of old," the Treck of Prince Dohna of Schlobitten.

For Pomeranian conditions, he seemed markedly lordly, as exhibited itself quite soon when the head forester's greeting of the prince, "Waidmannsheil Durchlaucht!" (salutation used by hunters, plus "Your Highness"), echoed over the manor area. The result was that the Trieglaff people standing around looked on, half respectfully, half unbelievingly. In his *Erinnerungen* (memoir), Alexander Dohna found words to acknowledge the adventure: "On our great Treck there was discipline such as that only because the order prevailing for a long time, namely, the relationship between superior and underling, had pretty much been preserved untouched."[173]

But this time-honored order remained an exception. It was visible from most Trecks during the following days and weeks that packing and departure through the vast land had taken place most hurriedly, so as to still make it across the Oder somehow. At Vahnerow a daughter, Barbara, described this world at the edge of the abyss:

Now we are getting, by turns, refugees from East and West Prussia, from the Warthegau and Danzig, and Treckers who want to sleep, stay, and be cared for. Vahnerow has lost its quiet tranquility! But we are still very lucky that we are so far off the main highway, and owing to that, I am very hopeful for our future as well.[174]

Would the highway from Plathe to Greifenberg be able to offer lasting protection? In the course of those days decisions were in any case made whether people wanted to stay or to trek. In Trieglaff and Vahnerow, the estate owners and those with them decided to stay. For the Trieglaff Thaddens, another reason to stay was that Reinold had, in the meantime, been discharged from the military on account of an injury, and had cause to fear arrest by the Gestapo at the bridge over the Oder. His final letter from Trieglaff closed: "May God have mercy upon us" (Gott sei uns gnädig!).[175]

Notes

1. On this, refer to the information in Ehrenkrook, "Die Familie von Thadden," 405f.

2. *Niekammer's Landwirtschaftliche Güter-Adreßbücher,* vol. 1, *Pommern* (Leipzig, 1939).

3. See above, chapter 2.

4. Ulrich, *Chronik des Kreises Greifenberg,* 301f., and reports by Siegfried and Werner Lange about their grandfather Albert Lange, in the carton *Trieglaffer Gutsarbeiter* [estate workers], FA.

5. Percy Ernst Schramm and Ehrengard von Thadden married on 5 March 1925 in Trieglaff.

6. Report by P. E. Schramm, September 1928, in the carton for Reinold von Thadden, FA.

7. Ibid.

8. Haushofer, *Die deutsche Landwirtschaft,* 226f.

9. Ibid., 257f.

10. Report by P. E. Schramm, September 1928, in the carton for Reinold von Thadden, FA.

11. See above, chapter 3.

12. Letter of 14 October 2006 by Lucy Ruedt to Rudolf von Thadden, in the carton *Amerikanische Briefe* [U.S. correspondence], FA.

13. Journal "My Travels," to Pommern 14–15 May 1929, in the carton *Amerikanische Briefe,* FA. The relatives were chiefly the families Ramthun and Lange.

14. Adolph Wangerin was an organ builder. In *Chronik der Familie Wangerin,* FA.

15. Wangerin's journal, FA.

16. Ibid.

17. Gertrud Senfft von Pilsach died in Batzwitz in 1921. She was more than seventy years old.

18. Letter of 14 October 2006 by Lucy Ruedt to Rudolf von Thadden, in the carton *Amerikanische Briefe,* FA.

19. For the prior history see above, chapter 4.

20. Cf. Pyta, *Dorfgemeinschaft und Parteipolitik,* 107.

21. Ibid.

22. Cf. Hühne, *Thadden-Trieglaff,* 80.

23. Cf. Wagner, *Bauern, Junker und Beamte,* 592.

24. Reinold von Thadden, *Auf verlorenem Posten?* 9.

25. Cf. regarding this Hühne, *Thadden-Trieglaff,* 103ff.

26. Françoise Smyth-Florentin, *Pierre Maury. Prédicateur d'Evangile* (Geneva, 2009), 116.

27. Ibid., 116. Unfortunately the correspondence between Pierre Maury and Reinold von Thadden has been almost completely lost. Only a few fragments are preserved in the holdings of the World Council of Churches in Geneva.

28. Suzanne de Diétrich, *Cinquante ans d'Histoire. La Fédération universelle des Associations Chrétiennes d'Etudiants* (Paris, 1948), 22.

29. Reinold von Thadden, *Auf verlorenem Posten?* 63ff.

30. See below, chapter 7.

31. Hühne, *Thadden-Trieglaff*, 85f.

32. Ibid., 94, for connections with the next general secretary of the DCSV, Hanns Lilje.

33. Cf. on this the exchange of letters with Hermann Weber, preserved in copied form in the Evangelisches Zentralarzhiv (EZA) Berlin, Akte [file] 34, Nr. [no.] 1, DCSV files; also cited in Hühne, *Thadden-Trieglaff*, 89. Cf. also Haejung Hong, *Die Deutsche Christliche Studenten-Vereinigung (DCSV) 1897–1938. Ein Beitrag zur Geschichte des protestantischen Bildungsbürgertums* (Marburg, 2001), 162.

34. Regarding this, Hühne, *Thadden-Trieglaff*, 123f. On the situation of the synods in Prussia cf. Rudolf von Thadden, "Die Geschichte der Kirchen und Konfessionen," 639f.

35. Reinold von Thadden, *Auf verlorenem Posten?* 86.

36. Cf. Pyta, *Dorfgemeinschaft und Parteipolitik*, 104.

37. Ibid. In Pomerania the Inspektors too were called *Beamte*, "officials."

38. Letter of 31 December 1931 to his Swiss friend, Alfred de Quervain, in the carton for Reinold von Thadden, FA.

39. Cf. H. Mommsen, *Die verspielte Freiheit*, 383.

40. Letter of 31 December 1931 by Thadden, in the carton for Reinold von Thadden, FA.

41. Obituaries in the carton for Landrat Adolf von Thadden, FA.

42. Cf. H. Mommsen, *Die verspielte Freiheit*, 255f.

43. Elections to the Reichstag of 20 May 1928, in *Die Statistik des Deutschen Reichs*, N.F. [new series], vol. 372. Figures cannot be presented for Trieglaff and Vahnerow, as the *Greifenberger Kreisblatt* of 1928, with detailed information for the villages, is missing.

44. Cf. H. Mommsen, *Die verspielte Freiheit*, 261ff.

45. Cf. Anneliese Thimme, *Flucht in den Mythos. Die Deutschnationale Volkspartei und die Niederlage 1918* (Göttingen, 1969), 45ff., 50ff.

46. Hans Schlange-Schöningen, *Am Tage danach* (Hamburg, 1946), 41.

47. Cf. H. Mommsen, *Die verspielte Freiheit*, 279f. Hugenberg had originated a so-called *Volksbegehren* [initiative, "the wishes of the people"] on the Young Plan that laid the groundwork for a gathering of signatures for rejection. An all-Reich vote of at least 10 percent was needed to make this initiative possible. In Pomerania the vote went to 33.3 percent, in the District of Greifenberg 56 percent, in Trieglaff 87 percent, in Vahnerow/Batzwitz 86.5 percent. So the Hugenberg wing of the DNVP was gaining momentum in the province. Percentages based upon the *Greifenberger Kreisblatt* of 31 October 1929.

48. Letter of 16 December 1929 to Georg Michaelis, in the carton for Reinold von Thadden, FA.

49. Ibid.

50. Letter of January 1930 (no date) cited from Hühne, *Thadden-Trieglaff*, 116. This letter is not to be found in the collection of copies of the EZA Berlin, Akte 34, no. 1. But another letter is present in which Thadden expresses to Hermann Weber on 9 December 1931 a not unimportant political judgment: "I'm just not at

all able to see the Christian Social People's Service [Christlicher Volksdienst] folks positively, even though I have all kinds of respect for Brüning and his tough will. It's just that the flow of national developments is going right past him. At what speed the transformation is taking place here could be seen quite well in Danzig and Königsberg. There, actually all the students and almost all of the younger 'old friends' (*Altfreunde*) were National Socialists."

51. Hühne, *Thadden-Trieglaff*, 117.

52. Elections to the Reichstag of 14 September 1930, in *Die Statistik des Deutschen Reichs*, N.F., vol. 382.

53. The corresponding annual edition of the *Greifenberger Kreisblatt* with entries for local election results is missing for the year 1930. Thus the figures for the antecedent precinct and district council elections must serve to fill the hole, even though they do not tell anything exact about the ascent of the NSDAP. Still, they are linked with information that is illuminating for the following years also: The DNVP dispatched a farm worker (Franz Dittmer) to the district council as the first person on its list. Moreover, he came from Trieglaff. In the *Greifenberger Kreisblatt*, 17 November 1929.

54. Cf. Pyta, *Dorfgemeinschaft und Parteipolitik 1918–1933*, 325f.

55. Ibid., 336f., 231.

56. Ibid., 226ff.

57. See above, chapter 2.

58. Ulrich, *Chronik des Kreises Greifenberg*, 412ff.

59. Kurt Meier, *Die Deutschen Christen. Das Bild einer Bewegung im Kirchenkampf des Dritten Reichs*, 3rd ed. (Göttingen, 1967), 16, and Rudolf von Thadden, "Die Geschichte der Kirchen und Konfessionen," 654ff.

60. Rudolf von Thadden, "Die Geschichte der Kirchen und Konfessionen," 657.

61. Werner Klän, *Die Evangelische Kirche Pommerns in Republik und Diktatur* (Cologne and Weimar, 1995), 144f.

62. In Vahnerow election results can be less precisely determined because the place did not make up a parish of its own, but belonged to the Batzwitz parish.

63. Reinold von Thadden, *Auf verlorenem Posten?* 11.

64. Klän, *Die Evangelische Kirche Pommerns*, 131f.

65. Kirchentag of 25–26 September 1932.

66. From the church broadcast, "Zeugnisse vom ersten pommerschen evangelischen Kirchentag," 11, copy in the carton for Reinold von Thadden, FA.

67. Ibid., 14.

68. Ibid., 11.

69. Ibid., 15.

70. Reinold von Thadden, *Auf verlorenem Posten?* 61.

71. See below, chapter 7.

72. Cf. Klaus Scholder, *Die Kirchen und das Dritte Reich* (Frankfurt am Main, 1977), 1: 281ff., and Rudolf von Thadden, "Die Geschichte der Kirchen und Konfessionen," 658f.

73. On this, the typed recollections of the third son, Franz-Lorenz von Thadden, 4, in the carton *Söhne der Familie*, FA.

74. On this, daughter Barbara Fox, *Finding a Way Home* (private printing), 22, FA.

75. Hildegard von Blanckenburg, "Meine Erinnerungen an Zimmerhausen" (private printing, 1982), 51, FA.

76. Ibid.

77. Ferdinand Hirt, *Pommernfibel. Hirt's Schreibfibel* (Breslau, 1935), 77f. Hermann Kopelmann was vice chairman of the Trieglaff parish council from 1928 to 1945. He opposed a National Socialist mayor for Trieglaff in favor of having no Nazis on precinct representative bodies. Regarding this, his letter of 23 July 1947 from Wenningstedt on the island of Sylt to Reinold von Thadden, in the carton *Nachkriegszeit* [postwar period], FA.

78. Cf. Pyta, *Dorfgemeinschaft und Parteipolitik*, 472ff.

79. Rudolf von Thadden, "Die Geschichte der Kirchen und Konfessionen," 657f.

80. Ibid., 665.

81. Klän, *Die Evangelische Kirche Pommerns*, 181.

82. Ibid., 182ff.

83. Scholder, *Die Kirchen und das Dritte Reich*, 1: 599f. A statement by Reinold von Thadden has been transmitted, "A Bible without Jews is baloney."

84. Cf. Jürgen Schmidt, *Martin Niemöller im Kirchenkampf* (Hamburg, 1971), 123ff.

85. Klän, *Die Evangelische Kirche Pommerns*, 193f.

86. Ibid., 221f.

87. Circular of the Pfarrernotbund of 25 January 1934, in the files of Pastor Friedrich Schauer in the archives of the consistory of Greifswald, copy in FA.

88. Ibid. Stefanie von Mackensen, Eberhard Baumann, and Friedrich Schauer also belonged to the Führerrat.

89. The provincial synod was convened on 16 March 1934. Cf. Klän, *Die Evangelische Kirche Pommerns*, 239ff.

90. References an announcement of 7 and 14 January 1934 from the pulpit by the Pfarrernotbund.

91. Klän, *Die Evangelische Kirche Pommerns*, 247.

92. Ibid. Further, Kurt Meier, *Der evangelische Kirchenkampf*, vol. 1, *Der Kampf um die Reichskirche* (Göttingen, 1976), 296.

93. Cited from Klän, *Die Evangelische Kirche Pommerns*, 248.

94. Franz-Lorenz von Thadden, typed recollections, 14, FA.

95. See above, chapter 2.

96. Reinold von Thadden, *Auf verlorenem Posten?* 99.

97. Klän, *Die Evangelische Kirche Pommerns*, 249f.

98. For literature pertaining to this see above all Scholder, *Die Kirchen und das Dritte Reich*, vol. 2 (Berlin, 1985), 181ff., and Rudolf von Thadden, "Die Geschichte der Kirchen und Konfessionen," 669f.

99. Thesis 5 stated: "We repudiate this false teaching, as though the state were, beyond its own particular commission, to become the single and total order for human life, and therefore to fulfill also the commission of the church," in *Quellen zur Geschichte des deutschen Protestantismus 1871–1945*, ed. Karl Kupisch (Göttingen, 1960), 274.

100. Klän, *Die Evangelische Kirche Pommerns*, 252, and Scholder, *Die Kirchen und das Dritte Reich*, 2:189.

101. A special edition of the *Gemarker Bote* of 30 May 1934 contained a lengthy article about the Barmen synod.

102. Reinold von Thadden, *Auf verlorenem Posten?* 94.

103. The circulars are accessible in the library of Greifswald University.

104. Klän, *Die Evangelische Kirche Pommerns*, 254.

105. Ibid., 255.

106. Ibid., 257f.

107. Maria Wellershoff, *Von Ort zu Ort. Eine Jugend in Pommern* (Cologne, 2010), 124f.

108. See above, chapter 4.

109. Only Reinold's letters sent to Doberan have been preserved. Those sent in the other direction were presumably destroyed—for fear they were being monitored by the Gestapo.

110. Letter of 26 December 1934, in the carton for Reinold von Thadden, FA.

111. Letter of 26 December 1935, in the carton for Reinold von Thadden, FA.

112. Letter of 4 August 1936, in the carton for Reinold von Thadden, FA. It covers the resolution of confessional differences within the Confessing Church.

113. Notation from early March 1938, for attorney Kassow in Schwerin, in the carton for Reinold von Thadden, FA.

114. Ibid.

115. See above, chapter 5.

116. Cf. Thierfelder, "Von der Kooperation zur inneren Distanzierung," 107f. The membership card mentioned is to be found in the carton for Elisabeth von Thadden, FA.

117. See above, chapter 6.

118. See above, chapter 5.

119. Cf. Thierfelder, "Von der Kooperation zur inneren Distanzierung," 103.

120. *Einwohnerbuch der Stadt Greifenberg in Pommern* [Directory of the residents of the city of Greifenberg in Pomerania], 1936, p. 124f., FA.

121. "Denkschrift der Bekennenden Kirche an Hitler vom 27.5.1936," in *Studienbücher zur kirchlichen Zeitgeschichte*, ed. Martin Greschat, vol. 6, *Zwischen Widerspruch und Widerstand: Texte zur Denkschrift der Bekennenden Kirche an Hitler (1936)*, ed. Martin Greschat (Munich, 1987), 7f.

122. Ibid., 113f.

123. Cf. Hühne, *Thadden-Trieglaff*, 133f.

124. Cf. Eberhard Bethge, *Dietrich Bonhoeffer. Eine Biographie* (Munich, 1967), 652ff.

125. Ibid., 498f., 501f., 503f. See here an exact portrayal of the milieu of the landed aristocracy that Bonhoeffer first became acquainted with in Pomerania.

126. Reinold von Thadden, *Auf verlorenem Posten?* 106f.

127. Ibid., 108.

128. Ibid., 110.

129. See below, chapter 7.

130. Letter of 2 July 1937 by Helene von Thadden to her relatives in Doberan, in the carton for Reinold von Thadden, FA.

131. Ibid.

132. Letter of 7 July 1937, in the carton for Reinold von Thadden, FA.

133. Letter of 2 July 1937, in the carton for Reinold von Thadden, FA.

134. Memo of 9 June 1937 to the theology students of the German Protestant Church, their parents, and their teachers, in the carton for Reinold von Thadden, FA.

135. Letter of 2 July 1937 by Helene von Thadden, in the carton for Reinold von Thadden, FA. Chantré was of Huguenot extraction. Reinold von Thadden reminded him of that during the interrogation, in Reinold von Thadden, *Auf verlorenem Posten?* 112.

136. Reinold von Thadden, *Auf verlorenem Posten?* 115f.

137. Letter of 19 July 1937, in the carton for Reinold von Thadden, FA.

138. Cf. Klän, *Die Evangelische Kirche Pommerns*, 537.

139. Ibid., 541f. Further, Bethge, *Dietrich Bonhoeffer*, 691.

140. A press report of 23 June 1948 on the conferral upon Reinold of an honorary theological doctorate by Kiel University states: "Perhaps he owes this trait, a capacity for assembling, to the fact that from childhood on he saw Prussian Union and Lutheran free church bonded in a tight village community within the narrowest confines of his village home. And perhaps this experience was substantially instrumental in bringing about recognition that in the Protestant world, where no papal force constrains unity, unity can only flourish in freedom," in correspondence with E. Müller, in the carton *Zweiter Weltkrieg* [World War II], FA.

141. See above, chapter 1.

142. See above, chapter 1.

143. Wangerin, *The Family Wangerin*, FA.

144. Cf. the footnote by Royal Natzke in the U.S. translation of the book by Wolfgang Marzahn, *The Nobleman Among the Brothers*, 23. Also see above, chapter 1, note 9.

145. Letter of 7 November 1937 to Marie von Thadden in Doberan, in the carton for Reinold von Thadden, FA.

146. Enacted by Himmler on 22 July 1938.

147. Circular of February 1939, by Reinold von Thadden, in Reinold von Thadden, *Auf verlorenem Posten?* 198.

148. See Rudolf von Thadden, "Die Geschichte der Kirchen und Konfessionen," 485.

149. Cf. Haushofer, *Die deutsche Landwirtschaft*, 266f.

150. Ibid., 268f.

151. Letter of 24 November 1939 to E. Müller, in the carton *Zweiter Weltkrieg*, FA.

152. Ibid.

153. This is the sense of the decree of the Reich interior minister of 24 July 1940; cited in Bethge, *Dietrich Bonhoeffer*, 771.

154. Letter of 22 December 1939 to the aunts in Doberan, in the carton for Reinold von Thadden, FA.

155. Letter of 26 December 1939 to Provost Hildegard von Thadden in Doberan, in the carton for Reinold von Thadden, FA.

156. Ibid.

157. Exact numbers in Günter Brakelmann, ed., *Kirche im Krieg. Der deutsche Protestantismus am Beginn des Zweiten Weltkriegs* (Munich, 1979), 245.

158. See the reprinted contribution "Unser Dienst heute," ibid., p. 254.

159. Ibid.

160. Letter of 17 November 1940 by Reinold von Thadden to E. Müller, in the carton *Zweiter Weltkrieg*, FA.

161. Cf. on this mainly Ulrich Herbert, *Fremdarbeiter. Politik und Praxis des "Ausländer-Einsatzes" in der Kriegswirtschaft des Dritten Reiches* (Berlin and Bonn, 1985), 96ff., 154ff., 285ff.; Joachim Lehmann, "Zwangsarbeiter in der deutschen Landwirtschaft 1939 bis 1945," in *Europa und der "Reichseinsatz,"* ed. Ulrich Herbert (Essen, 1991), 127ff.

162. Cf. Fox, *Finding a Way Home*, 62, FA.

163. Letter of 18 July 1943 to E. Müller, in the carton *Zweiter Weltkrieg*, FA.

164. Letter of 16 March 1943 by Leopold, in the carton *Briefe der Brüder*, FA. He fell on 17 March 1943, Ernst-Dietrich died on 11 April 1942 in the military hospital at Stendal, and Bogislav fell on 13 February 1945 in the vicinity of Tempelburg in Pomerania.

165. See above, chapter 6. Cf. Thierfelder, "Von der Kooperation zur inneren Distanzierung," 118ff., 134ff.; von der Lühe, *Elisabeth von Thadden*, 157ff.

166. Personal recollection of Rudolf von Thadden, in the carton for Elisabeth von Thadden, FA.

167. The U.S. troops reached Louvain, Belgium, where Reinold von Thadden was district commandant, on 5 September 1944. In letters of 19 and 29 January 1943 by Adam von Trott zu Solz to his brother Heinrich that date from Thadden's time in Belgium, von Trott advised him to become acquainted with Reinold von Thadden; see Benigna von Krusenstjern, *"daß es Sinn hat zu sterben—gelebt zu haben." Adam von Trott zu Solz 1909–1944. Biographie*, 2nd ed. (Göttingen, 2009), 463. The original letter of 19/1/1943 stated in greater detail, "I'm hurrying, urging you to announce yourself at the next opportunity to captain Dr. von Thadden, commandant of the town of Louvain, someone in fact whom I became acquainted with only recently in Brussels, but whom you will find to be gentlemanly and reliable in every respect and also ready to be of assistance. Reference me and pass along heartfelt greetings," in Bundesarchiv Koblenz N 1416 (estate of Adam von Trott zu Solz).

168. Letter of 28 October 1944 by Reinold von Thadden to E. Müller, in the carton *Zweiter Weltkrieg*, FA.

169. In 1948, details about the last days of Elisabeth von Thadden were brought to light by a prison chaplain, August Ohm. Near the end, she dictated to him the following statements about her imprisonment and the time afterward in the Ravensbrück concentration camp:

> In January 1944, I was taken into custody in Meaux, France at 8 o'clock in the morning. I was brought by car from Meaux to Paris and interrogated there from 9 in the morning until 6 in the evening. Following a one-hour evening mealtime, the

interrogation continued throughout the night. During the course of the next day, they announced my arrest. Several times there were opportunities to get away. I deliberately did not make use of them, so as to avoid putting my brother in danger. Then I was brought to Berlin and interrogated once more all night; the severity of the inquisition was simply horrendous. They asked me about the Confessing Church and the [ecumenical movement] una sancta. I didn't let one single word slip that might have incriminated someone else. The Ravensbrück concentration camp was terrible. I had nothing to do with the assassination attempt of 20 July, don't know any of those people. I was too influential, my circle had become too important. We wanted to assist people in need, at a time when there was want of such help. That this moment had to arrive was evident. We wanted to be good Samaritans—not anything political though.

170. Reichsminister for justice, "Führerinformation" no. 181, in the carton for Elisabeth von Thadden, FA.

171. Foremost, Elly Heuss-Knapp, *Schmale Wege* (Tübingen and Stuttgart, 1946). She was the first author who traced the course of Elisabeth von Thadden's last days, witnessing to that other Germany "which can scarcely be believed by the world anymore," p. 1. Further, Ricarda Huch, "Elisabeth von Thadden," undated manuscript, in *In einem Gedenkbuch zu sammeln*, ed. Wolfgang M. Schwiedrzik (Leipzig, 1997), 127ff.

172. Personal recollection by Rudolf von Thadden, in the carton for Elisabeth von Thadden, FA.

173. Alexander Fürst zu Dohna-Schlobitten, *Erinnerungen eines alten Ostpreußen* (Berlin, 1989), 274, 281.

174. Letter of 22 February 1945 by Barbara von Thadden (now Fox), in the carton *Kriegsende und Nachkriegszeit*, FA.

175. Letter of 1 March 1945 to Franz-Lorenz von Thadden at Piding in Bavaria, reprinted in Hühne, *Thadden-Trieglaff*, 160f.

Chapter 7

The Last German Generation

Loss and Remembrance

In the spring of 1980, I was party to an encounter that caused a certain date that was historically meaningful for Trieglaff and its neighboring villages to be cast into a new light for me. It was the date on which the Red Army marched into Trieglaff—5 March 1945. As it happened, I was on a trip to Israel to take part in establishing a chair for German history at the Hebrew University in Jerusalem. In the evening I located a newsstand and asked, in English, for a German newspaper. From the seller came the reply, "We can speak German with each other, no problem." Before I could get out even half a sentence, she tacked on a question.

"So what part of Germany do you come from?"

"From a place nobody would be familiar with—from Pomerania," I stammered.

"That's intriguing," she answered. "Where in Pomerania, if I may ask?"

"From a place that is totally insignificant. It's called Trieglaff."

It was getting interesting. The seller's face took on a wistful look, and she said, "Yes, okay, that is not very far from Dummadel."

That kind of intimacy with the region took me by surprise. "How do you know about Dummadel?"

She evaded the question, asking, "Where were you in Pomerania at the end of the War?"

"In Trieglaff. Where else!" I said directly.

As if mistrustful, she inquired, "When did the Russians get to you in Trieglaff?"

Seeing that the conversation was getting serious, I said that, as I remembered it, as a nearly thirteen-year-old boy at the time, it was toward evening on the fifth of March that they showed up on the manor grounds. She said, "That's possible. They freed us in Dummadel at two o'clock in the afternoon."

A pause ensued. She had used the word "freed." I, by contrast, had not felt myself set free on 5 March, but conquered. So I asked hesitantly, "Did the Russians set you free from a German transport vehicle for prisoners?"

Her answer was a simple one: "Yes."

Following that, I came to know her story, the story of her life, next to which my experiences with and under the Russians paled by comparison. Born to a Jewish family from Lithuania, she had lost her parents when the German armed forces marched in during the summer of 1941. Her father had been a German teacher and felt an attachment to German culture "on account of Goethe and Kant." She had been in the concentration camp at Stutthof near Danzig. After that—the ending, March 1945, between Dummadel and Trieglaff. I was silent.

Contact between us continued. Two years later she visited us in Göttingen, and we wrote regularly. She complained that people were learning so little and, in Israel, were slipping into new entanglements. I wrote that the new postwar Germany had become very western German and had, thank God, indeed evolved into a democratic system, but that it no longer knew anything about eastern Germany. It was also for that reason that I wanted to write a book about Trieglaff.

Most German portrayals of the postwar period proceed from a clearly defined breakpoint—the end of the war on 8 May 1945. That is in keeping with the tradition of political history, which orients itself about the dates of the major political decisions and takes facts of governance to be the determining reality. Historical events find their footing in treaties and constitutions.[1]

In contrast to this, there are historians who have recently deviated from the use of these primarily political boundaries, giving preference to economic, social, or biographical connections. Thus, Martin Broszat has paved the way to an approach that in many respects relativizes the discontinuity of the year 1945 with a volume he published entitled *Von Stalingrad zur Währungsreform* (From Stalingrad to monetary reform).[2] Similarly, Hans-Ulrich Wehler did not set the beginning and end of the fourth volume of his broadly laid out *Deutsche Gesellschaftsgeschichte* (History of German society) at the start of World War I and end of World War II either, but closed it off with the year 1949, thus drawing in the postwar period.[3]

Such approaches are consequential for the history of those Germans living east of the border established by the Potsdam Conference in 1945. They did not belong politically to the world of the four zones of occupation but were dealt with as Germans by the victorious powers and their allies, the more so as they themselves regarded themselves as Germans. For many years they lived on together in their communities as people with diminished rights, used, of course, the German names for their localities, and as far as possible remained affiliated with German congregations. Anyone who came to Trieglaff in 1947 or 1948 took away an impression of having been in a fragment of an atrophied German world under conditions of Polish and Russian domination.[4]

But to understand this, one must be aware of the local history after German sovereignty ended and German administration was suspended. More than ever, it is essential to embed a "small" history of everyday life in the "large" history of political events and realignments, and to keep in mind while doing so that remembered history (memory) and what actually happened (history) are by no means always congruent.[5]

From 1 March on in 1945, it was known in Trieglaff and Vahnerow that it could only be a matter of a few days until the Red Army reached the District of Greifenberg. Word had gotten around that the Russians had broken through the thin Pomeranian front at Stargard and were on their way to the Baltic seacoast at Kolberg and Kammin.[6] So people sensed that they were soon to be enclosed in a pocket, and that the refugee Trecks had scarcely any chance to escape anymore.

Something still unknown was of no less consequence, namely, that in the wake of the Russian entry, eastern Pomerania was to be incorporated into the resurrected Polish state. Stettin a Polish city! That was unimaginable in Trieglaff and Vahnerow. It fit into no view of history. Correspondingly, people felt utterly disoriented and simply lived day to day.[7]

Dissolving of the old order was perceptible in a number of little things. For one, the "evacuees," the refugees from bombings in the Ruhr and Berlin, started out across the Oder River—"über die Oder," as it was expressed at the time—conspicuously quickly. For another, Russian prisoners of war were withdrawn precipitously, to prevent their falling into the hands of their "brothers."[8] And finally, from one day to the next the Nazis skulked out of the city of Greifenberg and the villages as well, and made for the hills.

When the Red Army arrived at Trieglaff, Vahnerow, and their neighboring villages, it therefore found a population made up of widely varied groups of "those who stayed behind." First, there were the established families of farmers and farm workers—minus their sons at the front. On top of these were the Ukrainian "eastern workers" who had not been transported out, and, significantly, the numerous German refugees from East and West Prussia who, stranded in flight, had not made it "über die Oder." In addition, there were still "old POWs" everywhere from the early years of the war, mainly Frenchmen and Poles, who preferred to await the conclusion of the war in the localities familiar to them. For that reason, Trieglaff and Vahnerow had a larger population at this time than before the war.[9]

Yet the day before the Russians arrived, Reinold von Thadden had taken measures that would prove exceptionally useful. He ordered Treck-wagens to be driven into the nearby woods loaded with provisions and blankets, so that people could outlast the cycle of the first days and nights a bit more securely if necessary. Apart from that, the word was to stay home and avoid anything that looked like resistance.[10]

But in fact things took a different course in many ways. The first Russians arrived at Vahnerow by afternoon and shot a drunk Ukrainian.[11] At Trieglaff, soldiers in unfamiliar uniforms who plainly were not Russians appeared on the grounds. As the linguistically adept mistress of the estate determined, they were Frenchmen—members of the "Charlemagne Division" collaborating with Germany—who wanted to push through to the mouth of the Oder.[12] Then things quieted down on the premises.

A short time later the first of the Soviet battle troops forcibly entered the castle and came upon the manor's master, who presented himself to them in the presence of two Russian prisoners of war identifying themselves as officers. These vouched, verbally and in writing, that he had exhibited an "antifascist attitude," and so saved his life.[13] As the search of the castle got underway, the others, primarily the women living in the house, fled through back doors into the woods, and in this way mostly escaped rape, otherwise so widespread.

I myself slept through the entry of the Red Army. Suddenly, just before five in the morning, a Russian soldier was standing in my room. He sat down on my bed and offered me a cigarette. He clearly was one of the many Russians who were friendly to children and knew how to show it. Two hours after that, the castle was a wasteland. The soldiers had had their fun stabbing through the numerous portraits of ancestors, and especially doing damage to the paintings of generals from the old Prussian era. It is likely that none of them knew anything about the brotherhood in arms of Prussia and Russia against Napoleon.

But the Trieglaff castle itself was not destroyed. Whereas manor houses in the vicinity were frequently burned down, nothing happened to Trieglaff's. It was destined for a higher purpose, as soon became evident when it was set up as the local headquarters (*Militärkommandantur*) of the Soviet military. Just three days after their entry, Red Army officers moved into the castle and demonstrated the victor's claim to power in a most Russian way: they ordered the large clock on the Inspektor's house opposite the courtyard to be reset to Moscow time, two hours later than the time in central Europe.

As chance would have it, I witnessed this event. A Russian soldier looking for the key to the estate's safe pressed me to hurry up and get it because I happened to be within his reach. I knew that it was in the custody of the secretary, who was hiding in the greenhouse, and I hurried to fetch it, my eye on the clock. At that moment the clock was reset. Simultaneously, I saw that other soldiers were leading Inspektor Engelke away. He managed to call out "God be with you" to me, and was shot soon after at the edge of the village. It was learned later that the Ukrainian "eastern workers" had denounced him for his allegedly overly strict conduct toward them.[14] If the estate's owner was going to be spared, at least his Inspektor would have to pay a price.[15]

From then on it was obvious to everyone that something fundamental had changed. The Russian military command was in charge, and clocks showed Moscow time. What did this mean for Trieglaff in comparison with other villages in the area? Anyone who contrasts the stories of people from Vahnerow and Barkow with those of the Trieglaffers can establish that following the horror of the first days, alike for all, substantive differences between the villages soon became evident. Strict military order held sway in Trieglaff. In the longer term, it manifested itself also in the fact that the Poles gradually streaming into the land had a harder time asserting themselves and enforcing their own claims to ownership. In Trieglaff the Russians held the reins for years.[16]

At first no one could foresee what the establishment of a local headquarters in Trieglaff would mean. What met the eye was the presence of numerous officers, including some of higher rank; veterinary facilities set up for horses; and a host of signs reading "Berlin" in Cyrillic letters. Clearly Trieglaff had some function in the area of the rearward front, for Berlin had not yet been captured.[17] However, the Red Army's interests extended even beyond concluding the war to holding military positions east of the Oder and Neiße (Neisse) Rivers. The postwar situation they were striving for was not, as yet, secured.

Such a military command post's major tasks consisted in maintaining military order and the productive capacities of its area. "The local commandant," —as stated in a Russian newspaper article from the first days of occupation of German territory at the start of the winter offensive—"is duty-bound to maintain exemplary order, suited to the front, in the town. He bears responsibility for preservation of the confiscated estate and things of value, and must bring about a rapid restoration of the normal life of the town."[18]

But, lest there arise any perception of the war situation as less than serious, the article continued in a concrete vein: "economically important booty left behind by the enemy in the town and its environs is to be registered." "The precise recording of these spoils will contribute to their proper utilization, and to shielding from barbaric squandering or from theft."[19]

Understandably, such instructions to local commandants only went so far in impressing a helpless populace such as Trieglaff's. Of more concern to them was the commandants' authority to afford protection against plunderers or marauding soldiers. People hoped a strong hand would be exercised, as in Köslin, for example. According to the report of a witness,

> Someone reported a robbery, by Russians or by Poles, to the Russian command. In the course of a forenoon, many such reports came in that were entered into the record. Toward noon, then, a truck drove this way and that through the whole city to every one of the places, with all the complainants, an interpreter, and a Russian officer, issuing orders that restored justice once more.[20]

But even the power of a military commandant had its limits. Two weeks after the Red Army came into Trieglaff, unknown officers appeared on the grounds. They turned out to be commandos of the NKVD (Soviet internal affairs/secret police), come to fetch Reinold von Thadden and, as was learned later, haul him away to Russia. They did this in the presence of the commandant, who stood by, powerless. What explains this incident?

Following the advance of Soviet troops onto German soil as of January 1945, the ill-reputed People's Commissar for Internal Affairs, Beria, had issued guidelines for tasks in the occupied areas. In four orders, he gave detailed directions "to enforce the necessary Tschekist [NKVD] measures upon the territory liberated from opposition troops in correlation with the advance of the army units of the Red Army." To that pertained "detecting and arresting spies and saboteurs from the German secret services, terrorists, members of various enemy organizations, and groups of bandits and insurrectionists ... without regard for their nationality and citizenship."[21]

The Germans, assembled into work battalions, constituted a special group, "to be recruited for utilization as labor in the service of Soviet institutions as promptly as possible, and regarded, after a fashion, as a kind of live contribution to reparations by the Soviet Union." On 17 April 1945, Beria was able to report to Stalin that the NKVD had taken 215,540 persons into custody, among them 138,200 Germans, 38,660 Poles, and ca. 28,000 Soviet citizens.[22]

Reinold von Thadden's captivity brought him as far as the Arctic Ocean in the vicinity of Arkhangelsk. Over the four-week journey, he was interrogated again and again, and was repeatedly hard put to make his position in Hitler's Germany understandable in translatable terms. To the commissar's question whether he was a priest, he replied, according to his own report, "No, I am not a theologian."

"Then what are you?" asked the commissar.

"I am the president of the confessing synod in Pomerania."

"Oh, good, I understand. Holy Synod! And you are bishop?"

"No, I am not a bishop, but only a layperson in the church who was commissioned with tasks of leadership."

"What is a layperson in the church? The interpreter must look in the dictionary right away. Quick, quick!"

"Lay people are quite ordinary Christians who want to serve their church just a little."

The commissar then concluded, "Enough, don't lie, I am seeing that now. You are patriarch!"[23]

This exchange is a typical example of what today is called "cultural misunderstanding." A recurrent part of dialogue between people of divergent cultures, it could decide between life and death. The content associated with terms such as synod and layperson differed between an NKVD commissar and a German Gestapo officer. Ecclesiastical traditions induce effects in wholly extra-ecclesiastical domains as well.[24]

It took four weeks to travel from Pomerania to the Arctic Ocean. What changed in Trieglaff during this time? Little at first. The military command had obviously been assigned the task of supplying horses to the front on the Oder and recruiting people—women especially—to accompany them.[25] Its next task was to arrange shipments of cattle to the Soviet Union and ready agricultural machines and equipment located in the village for shipment.[26] Also, the second track at the Batzwitz train station was taken up.

People in the village wondered why the Russians were in such a hurry to ship away the cattle and equipment. But the reason was soon obvious: the Russians knew that in the future the territory was to be handed over to Poland.[27] There were, to be sure, scarcely any Poles in the area up to March 1945. Aside from the liberated Polish prisoners of war, it was only members of those Polish units fighting alongside the Red Army who showed up as harbingers of the pending incorporation into Poland. But those in the know already sensed that the Poles intended to seize ownership of the business concerns before long.[28]

For the German population, "the Russians," as they were known in common parlance, continued as the dominant power. But people began to compare them with the Poles. There were Germans who preferred to work under the Russians, but at the same time not a few placed their hopes upon the Poles, on account of the continued raping. Only ten days after the Red Army's arrival, the wife of the deported estate owner from Barkow, Käthe von Normann, noted in her diary, "Everybody reassures us that the Poles are not as bad as the Russians. That actually appears to be so, but time will tell."[29]

It was advisable to wait and see in any case, for it would take several more weeks to determine the final conditions of sovereignty in Eastern Pomerania, an area claimed by the Poles. First the war had to be brought to an end—with the capitulation of the Third Reich on 8 May 1945—enabling resolution of the issue of the function the Soviet military command would serve east of the now firmly planned German-Polish border along the Oder and Neiße Rivers.

Groundwork for further developments was established by Soviet Marshall and Army Supreme Commander Rokossovsky's order to hand over civil administration to Polish officials in those districts that the Poles now called "West Pomerania" by 13 June 1945.[30] Of course that did not mean that a Polish administration would hold the reins of power at once; rather, it would remain highly dependent on local Soviet military headquarters, which, for the most part, showed no inclination to share their power with the Poles. Accordingly, the transfer of jurisdiction dragged on for several months. In some districts it did not take place until the end of 1946.[31]

But even then, the interrelationship between Russian and Polish realms of governance remained tense. Many conflicts arose over the transfer of agricultural properties and smaller businesses, as well as over food supply and disposition of housing. Similarly, differences arose in dealing with the German population.[32]

In Trieglaff the Soviet military command post remained in place for a long time yet, augmented by an agency for economics. The last Russians did not leave the place until 1948. Hence there developed a *Doppelherrschaft* (dual governance)[33] that had to be organized pragmatically as well. It took shape after June 1945, as the first larger groups of Polish settlers came into western Pomeranian areas laying claim to land and farms[34]—in a very Russian manner. The village was divided. The houses and acreages at the so-called farmers' end of the village, the "Bauernende," were assigned to arriving Poles. The Germans staying behind concentrated themselves in the "Gutsende," the estate end, which fell under Soviet authority.[35]

But how could this work, or even assume form in practice, if, for example, Polish people wishing to go to Greifenberg needed the village road across estate lands to do so? Frequently this was cause for conflict, particularly after the expulsion of German populations from villages under Polish rule began in the summer of 1945. Thus, a serious incident took place when a Treck of some 200 Germans from Barkow and its surrounding area demanded passage under Polish military escort.

> The whole Treck had to stop at the entrance to the village of Trieglaff. The Polish officer had to request authorization for passage through Trieglaff. This was not only denied, but an immediate turnaround was ordered. In support, Russian soldiers took up positions with their machine guns at the entrance to the village. Toward evening the whole Treck departed again in the direction of Batzwitz.[36]

This amazing event took place within the context of the so-called *Wilde Vertreibungen* (wild, chaotic expulsions of Germans) ahead of the Potsdam Conference between the three victorious powers from 17 July to 2 August 1945. The Poles clearly had an interest in creating faits accompli, and in driving the German population from the border districts along the Oder and Neiße as speedily as possible. Thereby they hoped to bolster an assertion that there were hardly any Germans in these areas anymore, and that consequently the establishment of Polish administration was urgently desirable.[37]

The Russians, on the other hand, had little interest in accelerating evacuation of the Germans, for a number of reasons. For one thing, they needed labor to harvest crops. For another, they wanted first to see resolution of the problem of Stettin's national affiliation, a matter of contention during the months of May, June, and July.[38] The Stettin region, lying west of the Oder, was of significance to the Red Army because it had a large harbor. So it did not fall administratively under the military mission in Poland, but under the army of occupation in Germany. Accordingly, upon its occupation by the Soviet armed forces in late April 1945, the city of Stettin had a German mayor, who gave way to a Polish successor only in early July. The Russians acceded to that because in the meantime they had settled the matter of their power over the harbor and wanted the situation to be clear before the opening of the Potsdam Conference.[39]

The Germans in Trieglaff were, of course, unacquainted with this larger-scale context. They only saw that the Russian military commandant declined to approve the Polish policy of expulsion and forbade further efforts as well. Wherever Germans were still working for Poles only, expulsion moved along more quickly.[40] The Russians, on the other hand, began to protect their German workers.

I myself recall a memorable event from the summer of 1945. To our surprise, a Polish man in civilian clothes appeared at our home in the older structure attached to the castle, which itself was occupied by the Russians. He introduced himself to my mother as "the new Bürgermeister and precinct supervisor of Trieglaff." He spoke fluent German and declared that, beginning immediately, all actions of administration had to pass through him. At that my mother asked him whether he had settled the matter with the Russian commandant. He gave no more than a hesitant reply, whereupon she urgently counseled him to do so as quickly as possible. He left empty-handed.[41]

At any rate, the Poles began posting notices and signs in Polish in their section of the village. There were none in the Russian section.[42] It was especially noticeable that Trieglaff was now named Trzygłów by the Poles, whereas in the Russian section place signs went on carrying the German name, only in Cyrillic lettering. The Russians obviously held to the designations as given on their military maps, which—why would it be otherwise?—had displayed the German names for places when the Red Army marched into the eastern German areas.

In the vicinity, Trieglaff was generally considered to be a Russian island. Thus the mistress of the neighboring estate at Rottnow had a clear memory of the order in the village as she made her way to her relatives in Zimmerhausen. "Trieglaff," she wrote,

> was a veterinary hospital for horses and a Russian command post. So everyone from the Thadden home had to work, but according to a set order, and they were provided with food. Many localities were tolerably intact at that time. But those many of them that the Russians did not need were declared beyond the protection of law.[43]

But positive situations also occurred in villages dominated by the Poles. On the neighboring estate of Zimmerhausen, which had belonged to the Blanckenburg family, only Polish people lived alongside the remaining Germans after the Russians' withdrawal in June 1945. Due to exceptionally favorable circumstances, they ensured not only order in the village, but also a functioning agriculture in which operational structures remained nearly identical to the old ones, allowing the Germans to do almost the same work as in the preceding period.

Word soon got around that the Pole in charge here meant the Germans well. He had been a gardener on the estate while a prisoner of war, and clearly had been given favorable treatment. In any case, he now assumed the place of estate manager and, by and large, permitted the Germans to continue to work under self-regulation, according to their proven system. As an East Prussian refugee woman who made it no further than Zimmerhausen reported, "He continues to head the estate seamlessly, according to manorial mode. Good instincts have led him to resist the temptation to live and work out of the castle. He does it living in the farm supervisor's house.[44]

The population of this village was made up of native Germans who stayed, refugees from East and West Prussia who got stuck there, bombing refugees evacuated earlier from Berlin and the Ruhr, and some Poles: "There are not many Polish families here yet, basically only those that were brought here as farm workers during the war, and all speak more or less good German. They have taken over the farms."[45]

Now it was necessary to organize work for this hodgepodge population.

> No matter how freighted by fate and consequences this year of 1945 is in political and human respects, from the everyday and farming perspectives, it is as uniform as the following years. Events and routines are so alike that most of them could just as well be happening in 1946 or 1947.[46]

Zimmerhausen appeared to be an island of peace. On the way into the place stood a sign that read "Mechowo/Cymerhauzen."

Compared to Zimmerhausen, Vahnerow drew the short straw. To be sure, the Russians had withdrawn from here, too, at the end of June, as from the surrounding villages except Trieglaff. But the Poles who now moved in were different from the ones in Zimmerhausen. Part of a detachment of Polish soldiers who understood little of farming, they had less interest in working well together with the Germans who remained. The officers took up quarters in the manor house, leaving two rooms in the upper story for the mistress of the estate and her daughter. They could converse sympathetically with the secretary, who wanted to have nothing to do with "the communists."[47]

Not long before this shift, the Vahnerow Thaddens had reached the end of their rope. Unlike the Trieglaffers, they were not protected by a Russian military post; unlike the Germans in Zimmerhausen, they had no prospects of future work. So the mother, Barbara von Thadden, who was able to send her despairing letter via someone who delivered it in person to a relative in Potsdam, wrote:

> Is there ever going to be peace? … You just don't know what to believe. Ach! We always knew that the SS monstrosities would be frightfully avenged. And yet it is hard to bear that those people without a conscience to whom we owe this will have or have had an easy death, in place of the hard life that we have.[48]

Apart from the feeling of having been totally sacrificed, what made life so difficult was a persisting deficiency of news. In contrast to the four occupation zones in Germany, as a rule the regions east of the Oder and Neiße in 1945 had no mail yet, no radio, and no newspapers in German. So people there learned about the end of the war against Japan, brought about by U.S. atomic bombs, only at the end of the year, and even then without elaboration of any kind. Equally grave was the absence of German-speaking schools in Pomerania. Because of this, school-age children of German families got no education until they were forced out in 1947/1948 and thus were short two or three years of school thereafter.[49]

A chapter very much its own in the history of the postwar period is that concerning the churches.[50] In Pomerania, aspects of denominational conflict added to national-level conflicts, aggravating difficulties. Almost without exception, the Poles were Catholic, while the Germans were just as uniformly Protestant. So the process of transformation to Polish culture that began in 1945 amounted to a corresponding Catholicization. This expressed itself in no small way in the Polish Catholic Church's systematic dispossession of the Protestant congregations and takeover of the church buildings, along with the grounds belonging to them.[51]

Not until September 1946 was a regulation enacted that—disregarding exceptions—awarded Protestant church property to the national treasury. Then a law of 4 July 1947 went further, stipulating that the Polish Lutheran Church had no claim to assume the assets of the earlier German church either. The state could, of course, leave it to various institutions for their use.[52]

Initially, conditions in Trieglaff were more favorable to a coexistence of faiths, for there had, after all, been two churches in the village since the nineteenth century.[53] The Old Lutheran church at the farmers' end of the village was at the disposal of the immigrating Poles, whereas at the estate end the Germans kept the old Elisabethkirche, affiliated with the Landeskirche and subordinate to the Soviet military command. German-language services could be held in this one. As the pastor was being held as a POW in France, it was either Elisabeth, the deported estate owner's wife, or his sister, Helene, who conducted worship services. The old Trieglaff tradition of lay Christianity practiced in devotional services proved useful here.

The Russian commandant had nothing against worship services, as long as they took place before the beginning of work at seven o'clock. Unavoidable for him, however, was regulation of orderly affairs concerning a sensitive matter of everyday village life: the growing number of burials. This required people with courage and authority who went to the homes of the dying and were capable of speaking words of comfort at the cemetery. All this was expressed emphatically in a later report by a Trieglaffer:

At a great many burials there was a person present with comforting words for the survivors who again and again found the way to give mourners new courage to face life. It was Fräulein Helene von Thadden, the angel of Trieglaff as she was called at the time. Although it was forbidden, she insisted on speaking a prayer with the mourners at the grave.[54]

Helene von Thadden is also owed gratitude for her preservation of some quite valuable source material, namely, an exhaustive list of the dead who were buried in Trieglaff in the years from 1945 to 1947. This list contains not only the names but also the ages and the places of origin of the dead, so that precise details can be known about these individuals, who were by no means only from Trieglaff.[55]

First, the list presents the exact number of burials: 205 in total. Of these, 182 fall in the year 1945. Next, it permits the observation that nearly a third of the dead—61—were children, mostly infants who died in 1945. And lastly, it can be said on the basis of the list that 67 of the 205 deceased came from East and West Prussia. In other words, they were stranded in Trieglaff while fleeing with their Trecks.[56]

A strikingly large number of the burials were in summer 1945, when a typhus epidemic swept the land.[57] From the data, it can be concluded that during the months in which a German doctor could still work there, most of the typhus victims were cared for in the Greifenberg district hospital.[58] But these people were buried in Trieglaff.

One more list is equally informative: it itemizes baptisms conducted in Trieglaff. There were twelve of them, all in the years 1946 and 1947. One of them merits special attention, as it is noted explicitly that the child's father was a Russian. Other than that, the parents were frequently from surrounding villages in which there obviously were no worship services.[59]

These activities and achievements almost always lay in the hands of women. Whether within the framework of the church, of work, or the everyday life of the refugees, women bore the burden of the difficult life to which the German population in the regions east of the Oder and Neiße was fated. Because men had been taken prisoner or been deported to Russia, or had died, there was nothing that the women could do but take the burden upon themselves. To phrase it in the words of the title of a later much-read book, "the hour of the women" had arrived.[60]

But it was not just German women who dealt with everyday matters during that time. After the war's end, there suddenly appeared in Trieglaff a number of young women whom no one anticipated anymore—a group of Ukrainians. On their way home from working as forced labor in the Ruhr during the war, they were detained by the Russian commandant to help with the harvest and in the military kitchen in the castle. These Ukrainians occupied a curious middle position between the Russians and the

Poles. But they were largely astonishingly friendly toward the Germans, which raised the question why they had not been accepted as allies into Hitler's "Greater German Reich" (Grossdeutsches Reich). Evidently the German occupiers had been so blinded during the war that they no longer perceived their own real interests.[61]

How, then, given the prevailing circumstances, can this coexistence of such varied worlds be concretely visualized? It is scarcely believable, but it functioned. In the newer portion of the castle, the Russian commandant took up quarters with his retinue; in the smaller "old house," the members of the estate owner's family—those remaining—lived with the staff from earlier as well as with several family refugees; and the Ukrainians occupied the surrounding farmsteads. To ensure distance, doors between the two parts of the castle were locked. Each party then had its own entrances.

Use of the castle kitchen posed a problem at first, as the German residents depended upon moderate use of the stove. A temporary solution was hammered out, giving several German women access to the Russian military kitchen staffed by Ukrainians. Such regulation of affairs was most uncommon in the conditions of the time and made Trieglaff seem, in the eyes of many, "an oasis in the desert." The extraordinarily adroit and competent housekeeper of many years in the Trieglaff castle, Luise Buuk, deserves much of the credit for this. To go by the firsthand report of a reliable apprentice in the house, she worked it out "that we were all able to lead an existence worthy of humans there."[62]

Toward the end of 1945 it began to be evident that the triangular relationship between Russians, Germans, and Poles was gradually shifting in favor of the Poles. In the neighboring villages, a consolidated Polish administration began to expel the German population, and in Trieglaff word went around that the Russian local command post would soon be cut back.[63] So the danger existed that especially the oldest people, who were no longer capable of working, would be driven from the country.

But first came news that overtaxed the family's powers of comprehension. The eldest son of the Vahnerow Thaddens had made it across the Oder into Pomerania and arrived in the neighboring district seat of Naugard. A route from east to west—*that* was understandable, in a Pomerania bleeding to death. But no one was able to comprehend the reverse. What had driven Adolf von Thadden from Göttingen to Vahnerow?

According to the letter he wrote after his adventurous journey angling through the Soviet zone, which he delivered to relatives in the west by way of a person making his way "over the Oder,"[64] his motive was unambiguous: he wanted to fetch his mother and his sister out of the chaos. Equally evident, however, was that his plan was utterly at odds with reality and had to go awry as a result. A dismissed German officer with English papers in a Pomerania torn back and forth between Russia and Poland—it could come to no good end.

The outcome was commensurate. The Poles in Naugard arrested the suspected adventurer. But after seven weeks' imprisonment, they recruited him for activity in the service of the new Polish administration. He still had the opportunity to see his mother in Naugard and get an idea of conditions in a Pomerania metamorphosing into Poland.[65] He even succeeded in getting to Vahnerow once. But by the end of 1946 he felt compelled to flee Pomerania and undertake the journey back to Göttingen.[66]

Regardless of whether or not it was this unanticipated visit by her son that made her suspect, Barbara von Thadden was in turn arrested by the Polish militia in early December 1945 and detained for several weeks in Greifenberg. Her daughter Barbara came to Trieglaff over Christmas to escape the chaos in Vahnerow. In the "old house" in Trieglaff, a modicum of safety still remained.[67]

But for how long? In early January, Fräulein Buuk, as we called her, felt constrained to speak to my mother and counsel her to get started across the Oder with me and an older friend of the family. Clearly the Russian military commandant himself had suggested this step to her, as he was no longer able to warrant a bearable future for people who could not be classified as laborers in the changing conditions.

The difficult decision was made on 5 January 1946. Fräulein Buuk had managed to persuade the Russian commandant to place at our disposal one of his one-horse Panjewagens, which took us to the nearest train station, in Plathe. Before that, he had allowed a statement to be drawn from him that for some time constituted, for me, a firm historical legend: The Russians did not want Pomerania to become Polish, but the Americans had decided it that way at the Potsdam Conference.[68]

The danger-filled two-day trip to Berlin took us through Stargard, Kreuz, and Küstrin. This route helped us avoid the dreaded border crossing at Stettin, rife with checkpoints, and meanwhile presented us with two experiences characteristic of the Russian-Polish dual governance. At the train station at Stargard we happened to be sitting beside an older Polish man who asked us where we were from and then told us he was being resettled in this selfsame District of Greifenberg. He added, "I'm sorry that politics wanted it that way." One day later we experienced a similarly conciliatory gesture on the part of a Russian soldier. As Polish train officials were about to block our way getting onto a train over the Oder, he assisted us with boarding and gave us a loaf of bread. Two farewells, two memories.[69]

Our arrival in Berlin was even less congruous with the schema of typical expulsion stories. Having betaken ourselves toward the home of Bishop Otto Dibelius, whose address was the only one in Berlin that we had available,[70] we heard him say in astonishment to my mother upon our arrival, "You're probably here to fetch your husband!" Equally astounded, she replied, "No, my husband has been deported to Russia." But Dibelius insisted, "No, he has been in Berlin for several days, in the hospital at Zehlendorf to be exact."[71]

Now surprises followed one after the other. First, in Zehlendorf we did indeed find our father Reinold, emaciated and visibly drawn but as animated and mentally alert as ever. Next we heard that Francis Pickens Miller, an old American friend from the World Student Christian Federation,[72] was on the staff of the U.S. military governor Lucius D. Clay and wished to take care of his friend Reinold. That meant not only urgently necessary additional food but also, and not least, reconnection with worldwide Christendom and the ecumenical movement. In the language of the pietistic tradition of old Trieglaff, this was declared "a dispensation of Providence."[73]

Thereafter, Trieglaff assumed a dual manifestation. In the one, the place abode in the many expellees' memories as a mental, spiritual, and intellectual heritage. In the other, the remains of the material legacy continued for two more years in the hands of the German population left over after all the departures. Eventually, the Polish people newly settling there also began to build up a relationship with what they were taking over. It did, in fact, require many more years before the various perceptions were brought together.

Soon after the overwhelming reunion in Berlin, it became evident that life's experiences are not soon reconciled and assimilated. Reinold von Thadden, who was dealing with the effects of nine months' imprisonment next to the Arctic Ocean, felt that his old friends from the time of the Confessing Church were in many ways living in another world. His wife and his youngest son had experienced how a place that is home can become, before their eyes, a place from which its denizens feel estranged. And Francis P. Miller faced the fact, rather uncomprehendingly, that the German reality he was seeing in Berlin in 1945 no longer had much to do with the reality he had become acquainted with fourteen years earlier in East Pomeranian Trieglaff.

And so the first letter by Reinold von Thadden to his relatives and friends after he returned from Russia is testimony beyond compare to the search for mental and political orientation in postwar Germany. At the turn of 1945/1946, he wrote:

If someone has lived in the boggy forests of Russia for three quarters of a year ... and has had to consider that he might never again return, he seems to himself like someone who has come back from the dead and is permitted to see the light once more, notwithstanding all the darkness in impoverished, fragmented, and starved Germany, and notwithstanding all the dark messages of mourning that gradually reach him in detail—almost all the people who belonged to him are no longer alive—and notwithstanding the painful fact that I cannot return to my Pomeranian homeland, which is probably lost forever.[74]

There is no bitterness in the letter and no arguing with fate. Instead, there are sentences that even show understanding for the Russians:

Looking back, I can only be grateful for the medical care by the Russians and for the humane treatment that we experienced in the concentration camp. As a German you would have had to expect something else entirely under the circumstances.[75]

From then on Reinold von Thadden faced more toward the future in his thoughts. He developed a far-reaching correspondence with old friends from the years of the church struggles—the Kirchenkampf—and sought possibilities for reaching understanding with them about fundamental issues for a future German course. He wrote from the Zehlendorf hospital to Martin Niemöller, after reading the transcript of a lecture by him, that it made him happy "to what high degree my own thoughts on the question of guilt in a New Testament sense, matured in Russia, are related to yours."[76] Upon this foundation one could contemplate an "enduring issue-centered cooperation."

And, of course, Thadden reestablished his close ties with Eberhard Müller, who had begun in the meantime to build up an Evangelische Akademie in Bad Boll in Württemberg.[77] Next, he took up contact with the family of his wife in south Germany, particularly because it was there that he had been released by the Russians. And he also got into contact with his son Franz-Lorenz, who had just begun the study of law in Freiburg in the French occupation zone and was, much to the surprise of his family, about to go over to the Catholic Church.[78] The Trieglaff tradition was going to be moving onto wider-gauge tracks.

The way west concluded with one further adventurous journey. Following the Thaddens' reunion in Berlin, and thanks to the intervention of the U.S. Colonel Francis P. Miller, a U.S. Army vehicle took the Thaddens through the Soviet-occupied zone, through Helmstedt and Göttingen, and to the south German/Franconian family property of Elisabeth Thadden, the mother of the family. But not even this trip was free of shadows. During a night's stay in Braunschweig, the vehicle was completely cleaned out, and the family arrived in longed-for West Germany without any belongings.[79]

The people who had stayed behind in Trieglaff knew nothing of all that. Only in early 1946 did mail traffic over the Oder slowly begin to flow, and the number of people crossing from west to east diminished continually. Communication with the people in the regions east of the Oder and Neiße was something altogether different from that between those living in the various zones of occupation in the rest of Germany.

What all of the Germans who had stayed behind in East Pomerania did soon experience were the systematic expulsions that began at this time. A "technical plan" of the Polish office for repatriation of 22 February 1946 stipulated that Germans not capable of working were to be expelled first. Next, workers in state factories and household workers were to leave the land in phases. "Specialists" who could not be replaced by Poles were to stay for the time being, the specially trained workers in the rural economy too, therefore.[80]

Of course, the Germans who worked for the local Soviet headquarters and in other positions had to be considered in these quotas too. Since the Polish officials did not yet have any say regarding them, exact total numbers remained quite indefinite. The demand for German labor was hard to plan.[81]

What could be planned, however, were the so-called collection points in the district seats, also termed transition camps. Schools, former barracks, and storehouses were used, having as yet found no other purpose. Reports out of Trieglaff make clear, however, that the waiting period for village residents intended for expatriation was unjustifiably long. Thus several families complained that they had been detained from four to six months in the transition camps in Greifenberg, that is, well into the year 1947. Purportedly, insufficient transportation capacity was available for use.[82]

This affected above all the Germans in the Polish section of the village. Those working in the Russian part were still shielded from expulsion but instead had to experience a replacement of the military commandant. This led to certain changes. The commandant brought with him, besides different soldiers, German prisoners of war to be used as agricultural labor. And he procured horses, which were needed everywhere after the great shipments of livestock in spring 1945. So economically, things appeared to be on the upswing under his command.[83]

Yet these developments, despite providing a degree of hope, did not alter the fact of soldiers' unabated plundering of houses. In one of the first postcards to reach West Germany (Figure 20), Helene von Thadden wrote that they had taken from her "all the warm clothes for the winter."

Figure 20. Postcard from Helene von Thadden to Hildegard von Thadden from Polish Trzygłów, formerly German Trieglaff

"Regardless of new commandants, it continues to be like that."[84] A few months later, this commandant too was rotated out and replaced by the one responsible for the village of Rütznow, not far away.[85] But this brought no substantive improvement either.

Still, a formal complaint met with some success. When repeated reporting of the ongoing "robberies" bore no fruit, the erstwhile housekeeper Luise Buuk—advanced to "superintendent of grounds"—handed in an official complaint that led to an

> immediate interview with the commandant this very evening at 11:30, at which I could lay everything out before him, and already the next morning 2 officers from Liegnitz were here who, in turn, called the commandant to account, and now we are left in peace by the robbers.[86]

So two years after the end of the war it was possible for Germans to file complaints in higher places. According to a later report, the commandant and his brigadier were, in the end, "sent to Siberia for 10 years, for his ongoing embezzlement."[87] But this did not lead to improvement of the material well-being of the German population. "Now anymore, provisions consist only of potatoes and flour.… 3 people earn and 10 eat, and supplies are running out."[88] It was understandable that the old Trieglaffers were now striving to get out of the Russian part of the village, too.

In Vahnerow, under its Polish command unit, this had long been the case. The onetime estate owner, Barbara von Thadden, with her daughter Barbara, had embarked on the trip "über die Oder" in March,[89] and most of the German inhabitants had likewise departed the village in 1946. Only the laborers from the outlying farmsteads, detained by the Russians, were absorbed at the farm the Russians operated at Rütznow.[90]

Zimmerhausen once again constituted a positive exception. Owing to the pro-German attitude of the Polish manager, oriented toward the productive capabilities of the operation, the German workforce was granted tolerable living conditions until the end of 1947. According to the report of an East Prussian refugee woman, the workday scarcely differed from what it had been during the German era:

> There is, besides, the Polish way of life, which is still traditional, a mixture of feudal and middle class, but in any case Catholic. Until now there is no socialism, no norms … but in place of that a whole bunch of church holidays, and we Germans benefit equally from their amenities.[91]

In Zimmerhausen up to this point—1946—there were no great difficulties of language either. The people moving in were largely Polish families that had known forced labor in western and southern Germany during the war and were now returning to Poland, so all the villagers could communicate in German. German remained the "everyday language" for a long time. If there were problems of language at all, they were between East Prussian refugees and the locals, who commonly used Plattdeutsch, the local Low German dialect, amongst themselves.[92]

Nevertheless, feelings of hopelessness grew in Zimmerhausen too. "It isn't the individual miseries that afflict us so, and not the deprivations in total," it says in the report, "it is the endlessness that gets to us, the endlessness and having no way out and no hope."[93] With every month it became clearer that the Germans had no real prospects for the future. Eventually only the hope of an early and bearable expulsion remained.

At the beginning of 1947, a change in the Germans' attitude to departure from their villages and towns set in. Whereas before then a hope of being able to stay in their old homeland had persisted for most of them, now the wish to leave a Pomerania that had become Polish and reach one of the four zones of occupation west of the Oder-Neiße border gained the upper hand.[94] Their discontent was aggravated by an especially cold winter. In Trieglaff, the impulse was intensified by a grave shortage of fuel for heating that resulted in entire barns being torn down and the old trees on the castle grounds being felled for fuel. Even more, it did not halt at the old, tradition-rich village church. People used the pews as well as the organ paneling for fuel. At last they went at the wooden exterior of the steeple, too. The result was that soon there was nothing more left of the church.[95]

Helene von Thadden described this process in a letter filled with sorrow. In it she gave expression to the utter bleakness of the situation:

> The sheds here have been demolished without exception for use in heating. Now they are sawing up the timbers from the barns and house floors. Some eight days ago they fetched the organ paneling from our church to make crates for butter out of it.

She then concluded, "It is good that Reinold is not here."[96]

Indeed, this news left its mark on her brother Reinold. Thanks to Visser't Hooft, he had found a position with the ecumenical World Council of Churches in Geneva, where he had occasion to discuss the condition of the church in east central Europe.[97] In this case, though, he was affected personally. "What a crazy world," he said in my presence: "In pious Trieglaff the old church, which harbors so many memories, is destroyed, and the castle, far less significant, is preserved."[98]

Thus, while the Trieglaffers staying behind in Pomerania experienced their ancient home literally breaking to pieces, those who had left the village thought about the deeper reasons for the loss of that home. At this time Reinold von Thadden wrote, to a young theology student with German nationalist tendencies who had returned from the war a bewildered officer,

> We're facing the most difficult topic of our conversation. It is the share contributed by our Christian-conservative, our patriotic classes ... to the political conceptions and the monstrous repercussions of the brown regime, down to our militaristic thinking and acting, in a word, a share in the actual guilt of our people.

He continued more pointedly:

> People could have expected something altogether different from us. And therefore, our past has been one long chain of unpardonable offense consisting in our utter failure before the war, our considerable complicity in the war, our unreflecting transfer of concepts of patriotism that have, for the longest time already, been devoid of genuine value for the conditions of a much-changed present. More than anything, we have, while swearing solemn oaths, incessantly played fast and loose, in relation to the "Führer," with moral fundamentals such as "loyalty," "honor," "dedication," "sacrifice," in nothing short of an irresponsible manner.[99]

The Poles in Trieglaff had no such thoughts. Amongst them, another culture of memories that soon took shape pertained, above all, to the role of the church in the development of a new village society. They could hardly imagine that Poles, too, might have participated in the destruction of a church. For that reason, they fostered a narrative in which the Russians were "of course" chiefly responsible, especially since this church was in their part of the village. The German role in this appalling process thus remained obscured.[100]

The difficult complex of the local mode of dealing with the churches must be seen within this context as well. According to Helene von Thadden, the Polish militia, unlike the open-minded superintendent, balked at the conduct of German-language worship services. "'Why pray?' it was often asked. My answer then was that it is done throughout the world every Sunday, why not here?" The response of the Polish militia made clear that "devotions in a home qualify as gatherings, which are even less permissible." A denominational element obviously played a role in this, for it was known that the Polish Protestant Church did not want devotions to be obstructed. "A few months ago a report from our congregation here had to be sent there."[101]

Some weeks later, at Easter, a German Protestant service was again permitted. But difficulties persisted.[102] One can only assume that the destruction of the old village church, prompted by conditions, contributed to the conflict. Now there was only the Old Lutheran church at the farmers' end of the village, which, since fall 1945, had belonged to the Polish Catholic Church. The Protestant congregation of the Germans no longer had a building at their disposal.

But there was no longer any room for the German people who had occupied the castle up to this point, either. In the summer of 1946 they were compelled to leave their lodgings in the "old house," and move into the housing for farm workers, where they then crowded together into a small space:[103] "We Germans are crushed together in the poorer dwellings of the workers. It is just good that no really bad places to live exist at all."[104]

Then the balance of things in the village shifted quite definitely:

We who work for the Russian command post are worse off, in material terms, than those who work for the Poles. In spite of our strenuous work, we have not received a zloty in pay for months, and only one pound of flour and some salt each day, no other food whatsoever. There is no fat of any kind. So we're selling the last of our things that we can do without at prices that are laughable.[105]

Against this backdrop, it becomes understandable that by now, even the closest circle of faithful Trieglaffers had overcome their hesitation about leaving their old homeland and were preparing for departure across the Oder. Thus, Luise Buuk wrote to Elisabeth von Thadden in Geneva that I too have had my mind made up for several weeks now to give up the position into which I was placed. I am saddened only by the thought that our holding out here has been so totally without use to your family.[106]

With this parting thought, leaving took on a further dimension for the Trieglaffers who belonged with the estate. For them it was not just a matter of property but also one of heritage. For that reason Reinold von Thadden took up this central point in his last letter from Geneva to Luise Buuk in Trieglaff:

> It must not burden and disappoint you that you probably did not succeed and will not succeed in preserving for us the earthly possessions that you would so gladly have saved. Many thousand times more valuable than these material possessions is what, in a way, stood behind it in human terms, and you can take along with you into your later life and into the new tasks that it assigns to you a proud consciousness that you played out to the end a piece of German history in the East with dignity.[107]

A few weeks later the Trieglaffers set out across the Oder. They left behind a place that remained vivid in their memories and at the same time gave them hope for a brighter future. But that did not at all alter the fact that their integration into the societies of the western zones of occupation, which had remained German, was difficult.[108]

The story of the Trieglaffers associated with the estate did not quite end with the departure of the group around Helene von Thadden, however. Because the Russians still needed expertise where they had jurisdiction, 142 Germans stayed behind, among them 67 farm workers.[109] They would be permitted to leave only after the Russians had left Trieglaff once and for all. But this dragged on, since first the previous staff in the castle had to be repositioned near Treptow. Only an economic detail remained behind. And the Trieglaff castle stood empty.[110]

On 1 December 1948, the last remaining elements of the once-mighty local Soviet military *Kommandantur* left Trieglaff.[111] Whoever no longer had any chance of crossing the Oder using transportation provided for expatriates was taken to Kummerow in the District of Regenwalde, to Polish military agricultural property. There the Germans were, in fact, markedly better off than under the Russians.[112] To offset that, though, the exit to Germany was delayed by a full eight years.[113] The last Trieglaffer, Wilhelm Dittmer, departed Pomerania, now become Polish, on 1 February 1957, as a "late émigré."[114]

By this time a new history of postwar Germany had long since begun. In 1949 the Bundesrepublik Deutschland (BRD, Federal Republic of Germany) and in the east the Deutsche Demokratische Republik (DDR, German Democratic Republic) were founded, creating new conditions for living and new modes of orientation, especially for expellees from the former eastern regions. After that, the Trieglaff world with its way of life, one having a German character, continued to exist only in memory.

But what were the roads leading out of that tiny universe? How would they fan out, given the new circumstances? Most of the Trieglaff and Vahnerow village inhabitants ended up in rural parts of the DDR, but also in urban ones, while the smaller part became assimilated in the northern area of the Federal Republic—in the British zone, in other words. In both instances the expellees were seldom able to find work in their previous occupations.[115]

As for the members of the Thadden family who survived the war, their paths forked in a great variety of ways. The Trieglaffers' older son, Franz-Lorenz, moved to Freiburg in the French zone and there took a step that many at the time saw as a break with the Prussian-Protestant world: he went over to the Catholic church.[116] It was hardly surprising, then, that he found his political home in the newly founded CDU and became a Christian Democratic Union member of the German Bundestag.

The oldest Vahnerow son, Adolf, however, entered upon an exasperating political path. Nationalistic ways of thinking had so fixed themselves in his mind that he affiliated with the German Reichspartei (DRP, German Empire Party), and represented it for several years in the Bundestag. Later he became chairman of the radically right NPD (National Democratic Party of Germany) for awhile, and thereby excited considerable tension within the family.[117]

Conversely, his sisters' life choices led away from exclusively German ties. Three of them married into foreign countries in Europe or across the sea and founded families, opening new language horizons along the way.[118]

In the 1950s Ehrengard Schramm, the youngest sister of Elisabeth and Reinold von Thadden, took an extraordinary step in the family tradition. She decided to join the SPD, the Socialist Party of Germany, and took a seat representing this party's electoral district of Göttingen in the Landtag of Lower Saxony. At the same time, showing exemplary energy, she contributed to reconciliatory work in Greece, at Kalavrita, a place destroyed by German military forces.[119]

It was the last owner of Trieglaff, Reinold von Thadden, whose step into the new world had the most far-reaching consequences: he founded the German Protestant Kirchentag. In doing so, he broke the path that bore the spiritual hereditary capital of an earlier feudal era into the new democratic social order by activating laypeople in those halls of tradition occupied by the ecclesiastical bureaucracy of the Protestant Church. So it was only consistent that from then on he always went by the name Reinold von Thadden-Trieglaff.[120]

Notes

1. Heinrich A. Winkler, *Der lange Weg nach Westen* (Munich, 2000), 2: 116ff., gets closest to the question of 1945 as caesura in his approach to it.

2. Martin Broszat, Klaus-Dietmar Henke, and Hans Woller, eds., *Von Stalingrad zur Währungsreform. Zur Sozialgeschichte des Umbruchs in Deutschland* (Munich, 1988), xxvf.

3. Hans-Ulrich Wehler, *Deutsche Gesellschaftsgeschichte*, vol. 4, *Vom Beginn des Ersten Weltkriegs bis zur Gründung der beiden deutschen Staaten 1914–1949* (Munich, 2003), above all 941f.

4. Cf. Rudolf von Thadden, "Aus der Wirklichkeit gefallen," 137ff.

5. On this, Rudolf von Thadden, "Die Gebiete östlich der Oder-Neiße in den Übergangsjahren 1945–1949. Eine Vorstudie," in *Flüchtlinge und Vertriebene in der westdeutschen Nachkriegsgeschichte*, ed. Rainer Schulze, Doris von der Brelie-Lewien, and Helga Grebing (Hildesheim, 1987), 117ff.

6. Cf. Rolf-Dieter Müller, ed., *Das Deutsche Reich und der Zweite Weltkrieg* (Stuttgart, 2008), 10/1: 550ff.

7. Cf. Hans-Jürgen Bömelburg, Renata Stößinger, and Robert Traba, eds., *Vertreibung aus dem Osten. Deutsche und Polen erinnern sich* (Olsztyn, 2000), above all the introduction in re remembering and the culture of memories, 7ff.

8. Cf. Antony Beevor, *The Fall of Berlin 1945* (New York, 2002), 117ff.

9. The record does not show officially attested figures, but it does present questionnaires filled out by people who lived in Trieglaff between 1945 and 1947. In the carton *Nachkriegszeit* [postwar period], FA.

10. Report of experiences by the last of those who were friends at the Trieglaff school: "Trieglaff, mit Gruchow und Idashof. Schicksalsjahre eines Dorfes, aufgezeichnet zwischen 1993 u. 1995" [Trieglaff, together with Gruchow and Idashof. Critical years for a village, compiled between 1993 and 1995], in the carton *Nachkriegszeit*, FA.

11. Barbara Fox, "Finding a Way Home," (Private printing), 79f., FA.

12. Cf. Erich Murawski, *Die Eroberung Pommerns durch die Rote Armee* (Boppard, 1969), 217.

13. On this, cf. the informative report of 25 December 1945 by Ursula Wasmund to Franz-Lorenz von Thadden in Freiburg im Breisgau, 1f.: "Your father had one of these Russians, who identified himself as an officer, write out a certification in Russian that presented him as an antifascist, and that saved him very often in the following weeks." In the carton *Nachkriegszeit*, FA. Cf. Hühne, *Thadden-Trieglaff*, 163, who writes only about Reinold von Thadden's "humane deportment" (*menschliche Haltung*).

14. Some years later (in 1951), I wrote a report on this incident titled *Tempora mutantur et nos in illis* (Times are different, and we along with them) for the Pomeranian *Heimat-Brief* (homeland letter). The original is no longer available in FA, but strangely, an English version of the article was recovered from the United States, specifically in a history of the Kiekhäfer family, which emigrated from Trieglaff in the middle of the nineteenth century, *The Kiekhaefer Family Register* (Private printing, 1979), Appendix, 33f., FA. Apparently German relatives saw to it that the report got across the Atlantic.

15. The Inspektor in Vahnerow was also murdered by the Russians, while in Batzwitz the owner of the estate, Gerhard Baron Senfft von Pilsach, was found shot. On this, see Fox, "Finding a Way Home," 82, FA. The neighbor Walter von der Marwitz from Rütznow was shot as well upon entry of the Red Army in early March, and the neighbor Philipp von Normann from Barkow lost his life after he was carried off at the beginning of April.

16. Cf. the reports of experiences by Fox, ibid., and Käthe von Normann, *Tagebuch aus Pommern 1945/46*, series dtv dokumente (Munich, 1962). Particularly revealing is the report of 25 December 1945 by Ursula Wasmund to Franz-Lorenz von Thadden in Freiburg im Breisgau, 3: "The Russian commandant was well disposed toward your father and appointed him at once as civil commandant. This Kapitano always protected us and was even reprimanded by his superiors on account of it." In the carton *Nachkriegszeit*, FA.

17. The major attack on Berlin took place 16 April 1945.

18. Article of 28 January 1945 in *Krasnaja Zvezda*, quoted in Müller, *Das Deutsche Reich und der Zweite Weltkrieg*, 10/1: 742.

19. Ibid., 743.

20. Theodor Schieder, ed., *Die Vertreibung der deutschen Bevölkerung aus den Gebieten östlich der Oder-Neiße*, vol. 2 (Munich, 1954, repr. 1984), doc. 209, p. 278.

21. Quoted from Müller, *Das Deutsche Reich und der Zweite Weltkrieg*, 10/1: 749.

22. Ibid., 750ff.

23. Thus verbatim in Reinold von Thadden, *Auf verlorenem Posten?* 84f.

24. Doris Bachmann-Medick, "Kulturelle Texte und interkulturelles (Miß-)verstehen," in *Perspektiven und Verfahren interkultureller Germanistik*, ed. Alois Wierlacher (Munich 1987), 653ff.

25. Fox, "Finding a Way Home," 86, FA; I. Gloor-Radüntz, "Mein Leben," 26f., manuscript in the carton *Nachkriegszeit*, FA.

26. Report of experiences by Henning Köpsel and H. Wegner in "Trieglaff, mit Gruchow und Idashof," in the carton *Nachkriegszeit*, FA.

27. This follows from the reports of experiences, "Trieglaff, mit Gruchow und Idashof," in the carton *Nachkriegszeit*, FA.

28. In her introduction to the selection of sources for the Stettin Voivodeship, Katrin Steffen points to the dearth of sources for the months of March and April 1945, in *Die Deutschen östlich von Oder und Neiße 1945–1950. Dokumente aus polnischen Archiven*, ed. Wlodzimierz Borodziej and Hans Lemberg (Marburg, 2004), 3: 279f.

29. Von Normann, *Tagebuch*, 28.

30. Cf. Steffen, Introduction, 281.

31. Ibid., 282.

32. Ibid.

33. The term *Doppelherrschaft* is widespread in modern scholarly literature, ibid., 276.

34. Cf. Bernadetta Nitschke, *Vertreibung und Aussiedlung der deutschen Bevölkerung aus Polen 1945 bis 1949*, [German translation from Polish (Munich, 2004)], 89ff.

35. See the report by H. Köpsel in "Trieglaff, mit Gruchow und Idashof," in the carton *Nachkriegszeit*, FA.

36. Report by H. Wegner, ibid. Cf. the concordant presentation of the event in von Normann, *Tagebuch*, 130. Resembling it as well, a report from Küssin in the District of Greifenberg that gives information about Russian commandants' hindrance of Polish efforts at expulsion in July 1945, in Schieder, *Die Vertreibung*, 767f.

37. Cf. Steffen, Introduction, 304f.

38. Ibid., 277, 287ff.

39. Cf. Clemens Heitmann, "Die Stettin-Frage. Die KPD, die Sowjetunion und die deutsch-polnische Grenze 1945," *Zeitschrift für Ostmitteleuropa-Forschung* 51 (2002): 25ff.

40. Report by Wegner, in the carton *Nachkriegszeit*, FA.

41. Personal memories, Rudolf von Thadden, in the carton *Nachkriegszeit*, FA.

42. In Vahnerow too, signs were now put into Polish. Cf. Fox, "Finding a Way Home," 92.

43. Christa von Blanckenburg, "50 Jahre meines Lebens," 297, manuscript, in the carton *Nachkriegszeit*, FA.

44. Eva-Maria Mallasch, *Erinnerungen an Zimmerhausen*, ed. Peter von Blanckenburg and Doris Mallasch (Greifswald, 2009), 14.

45. Ibid., 13.

46. Ibid., 15.

47. Fox, "Finding a Way Home," 92f.

48. Letter of 3 June 1945 by Barbara von Thadden to Lena von Woedtke in Potsdam, in the carton *Nachkriegszeit*, FA.

49. Steffen, Introduction, 284, emphasizes that some Russian commandants, particularly in the eastern districts of Pomerania, bypassed the Polish administration and opened schools.

50. Works pertinent to church history in the postwar period in Pomerania are lacking. No documents are reprinted in Steffen's volume of sources from the Polish archives, either.

51. Nitschke, *Vertreibung*, 160f.

52. Ibid., 164.

53. See above, chapter 2.

54. Report by G. Hoffmüller in "Trieglaff, mit Gruchow und Idashof," in the carton *Nachkriegszeit*, FA.

55. "Liste der Toten, …" [list of the dead who were buried in Trieglaff during the period from 5 March 1945 to 8 March 1947], in the carton *Nachkriegszeit*, FA.

56. Ibid.

57. Cf. Steffen, Introduction, 290ff.

58. Von Normann, *Tagebuch*, 157.

59. "Liste der Taufen," in the carton *Nachkriegszeit*, FA.

60. Christian Graf von Krockow, *Die Stunde der Frauen. Bericht aus Pommern 1944–47* (Stuttgart, 1988), above all 88ff.

61. Cf. Herbert, *Fremdarbeiter*, 154ff., 278ff.

62. Letter of 25 December 1945 by Ursula Wasmund to Franz-Lorenz von Thadden in Freiburg im Breisgau, p. 6, in the carton *Nachkriegszeit*, FA. Also there is the personal judgment, "I also believe that it stands as an isolated instance in Pomera-

nia that the owner is living in his house with all the house personnel and the people remain loyal to their employer." Further, personal recollections of Rudolf von Thadden, in the carton *Nachkriegszeit*, FA.

63. Report by H. Wegner, ibid.

64. Letter of 14 November 1945 by Adolf von Thadden to Ruth Schramm, copy in the carton *Nachkriegszeit*, FA.

65. Typewritten report of January 1947 by Adolf von Thadden, "Über die Lage...," [on the situation of the Germans as well as on the economic situation in onetime German East Pomerania], in the carton *Nachkriegszeit*, FA.

66. Adolf had in the meantime learned that his brother Gerhard was shot by poachers in the forest near Hann. Münden at the beginning of October. This news, and his experiences in a Pomerania that had become Polish, don't adequately explain, though, why he took a political turn following his return to the British occupation zone at the end of 1946, a turn that led him into the German Bundestag as representative of the radically right German Empire Party—Deutsche Reichspartei—in 1949 and into the extreme right National Democratic Party of Germany—NPD—in the sixties.

67. Fox, "Finding a Way Home," 99.

68. Personal recollections of Rudolf von Thadden, in the carton *Nachkriegszeit*, FA.

69. Ibid.

70. Otto Dibelius was an acquaintance from the years of the church struggles.

71. Personal recollections of Rudolf von Thadden, in the carton *Nachkriegszeit*, FA. The event is portrayed somewhat differently in Hühne, *Thadden-Trieglaff*, 183ff.

72. See above, chapter 6.

73. Hühne, *Thadden-Trieglaff*, 184.

74. An addendum is attached to this letter of 30 December 1945 with the names of those close to Reinold von Thadden who had lost their lives in the previous year. In the carton *Kriegs- und Nachkriegsbriefe Reinold von Thaddens* [war and postwar correspondence], FA.

75. Ibid.

76. Letter of 20 February 1945 as answer to a Niemöller letter of 6 February 1945 not present in FA, in the carton *Kriegs- und Nachkriegsbriefe Reinold von Thaddens*, FA.

77. Exchange of letters with E. Müller, ibid.

78. Exchange of letters with Franz-Lorenz von Thadden, ibid.

79. Exchange of letters with F. P. Miller, ibid.

80. Cf. Steffen, Introduction, 311.

81. Ibid.

82. Report of experiences by E. Brockhaus and G. Hoffmüller, in "Trieglaff, mit Gruchow und Idashof," in the carton *Nachkriegszeit*, FA.

83. Report by H. Wegner, ibid.

84. Postcard of 26 September 1946 to Rudolf von Thadden in Switzerland, in the carton *Nachkriegszeit*, FA.

85. Postcard of 15 December 1946 to Rudolf von Thadden, ibid.

86. Letter of 18 January 1947 by Luise Buuk to Reinold von Thadden in Geneva, ibid. Main headquarters of the Soviet military in central Europe, with jurisdiction over Pomerania, were located in Liegnitz in Silesia.

87. Later letter of 7 December 1947 by Buuk to Frau Elisabeth von Thadden in Geneva, ibid.

88. Letter of 18 January 1947 by Buuk, ibid.

89. They made an interim stop in Zimmerhausen with Brigitte von Woedtke, née von Blanckenburg, and then spent a long time in a transit camp in Stettin-Scheune. Cf. Fox, "Finding a Way Home," 104.

90. Gloor-Radüntz, "Mein Leben," 31, 33f., manuscript in the carton *Nachkriegszeit,* FA.

91. Mallasch, *Erinnerungen,* 29.

92. Ibid., 28, 29f.

93. Ibid., 37.

94. Cf. Steffen, Introduction, 326.

95. Letter of 23 March 1948 by Wilhelm Dittmer to Reinold von Thadden, in the carton *Nachkriegszeit,* FA.

96. Letter of 24 April 1947 by Helene von Thadden to her sister Ehrengard Schramm in Göttingen, in the carton *Nachkriegszeit,* FA.

97. The Hollander Visser't Hooft was general secretary of the World Council of Churches at the time.

98. Personal recollections of Rudolf von Thadden, who was at this time attending a school near Geneva, in the carton *Nachkriegszeit,* FA.

99. Letter of 8 January 1947 to Peter Köhler, in the carton *Kriegs- und Nachkriegsbriefe Reinold von Thaddens,* FA.

100. Report for the writer by the later Catholic priest in Greifenberg, Joachim Fenski.

101. Letter of 6 February 1947 by Helene von Thadden to her brother Reinold in Geneva, in the carton *Nachkriegszeit,* FA.

102. Postcard of 16 April 1947 by Helene von Thadden to her aunt, Provost Hildegard von Thadden, in Doberan, ibid.

103. Postcard of 22 October 1946 by Helene von Thadden to Hildegard von Thadden, ibid.

104. Letter of 12 March 1947 by Helene von Thadden to her sister Ehrengard Schramm, ibid.

105. Ibid.

106. Letter of 18 January 1947 by Buuk to Elisabeth von Thadden in Geneva, ibid.

107. Letter of 15 May 1947 by Reinold von Thadden to Buuk, ibid.

108. Conveying this, a letter of 18 June 1946 from Schleswig-Holstein by Lisbeth Müller to Rudolf von Thadden, ibid. Cf. Andreas Kossert, *Kalte Heimat. Die Geschichte der deutschen Vertriebenen nach 1945* (Munich, 2008), 14f., 87ff.

109. Letter of 10 December 1947 by Wilhelm Dittmer to Helene von Thadden in Doberan, in the carton *Nachkriegszeit,* FA. The names of the most important families are listed there also.

110. Letter of 23 March 1948 by Dittmer to Reinold von Thadden, ibid.

111. Report by Dittmer on a filled-out questionnaire about the postwar history of Trieglaff, written 1975, ibid.

112. Letter of 1 January 1949 by Dittmer to Helene von Thadden, ibid.

113. Cf. Steffen, Introduction, 304f.

114. Letter of 31 January 1975 by Dittmer to Elisabeth von Thadden in Fulda, in the carton *Nachkriegszeit*, FA.

115. Cf. Kossert, *Kalte Heimat*, 90ff., 98ff.

116. Franz-Lorenz von Thadden expressed this in a letter in May of 1946, in the carton for Franz-Lorenz von Thadden, FA.

117. Cf. Werner Treß, "Adolf von Thadden," in *Handbuch des Antisemitismus*, ed. Wolfgang Benz (Berlin, 2009), 2/2: 822ff.

118. Refer to the genealogical diagram of the von Thadden family in the front matter.

119. Cf. Helga-Maria Kühn, "Ehrengard Schramm, geborene von Thadden," in *"Des Kennenlernens werth." Bedeutende Frauen Göttingens*, ed. Traudel Weber-Reich, 4th ed. (Göttingen, 2002), 289ff.

120. On this, Rudolf von Thadden, "Vision und Wirklichkeit. Reinold von Thadden und der Kirchentag," in *Fest des Glaubens — Forum der Welt. 60 Jahre Deutscher Evangelischer Kirchentag*, ed. Rüdiger Runge and Ellen Ueberschär (Gütersloh, 2009), 12ff.

History Reconciled

Trieglaffers Old and New

Departure of the last Germans from their former home in Trieglaff was not to be the last word in the long history of this place and its wealth of traditions. Forty-five years later, in 2002, an act of reconciliation took place between the old and the new Trieglaffers that deserves to be told, for it, too, reverberated.

Not by accident the path to understanding opened in the 1970s, soon after treaties within the framework of Willy Brandt's eastern policy (*Ostpolitik*) went into effect. At that time, parties arrived step-by-step at measures for reduction of tensions and easing of travel restrictions between the Federal Republic of Germany and most eastern-bloc countries, with Poland holding a significant place among them. Borders became passable.[1]

But barriers between peoples had by no means fallen as a result. For too long, individuals were molded by what they had experienced and gone through, and too strongly prejudiced by the images of national history that they had lived with down through the generations. More than anything, each war generation, in Poland as in Germany, spoke of the war and its consequences in its own way. The Polish generation told of the discrimination and atrocities suffered under Nazi rule, the Germans by contrast of the experiences of war with the Soviet Union, and the U.S. and English bombing attacks on German cities. They knew next to nothing about each other.

Yet another obstacle came into play, however. When Germans discussed the new eastern treaties, their initial thought was for easing travel between the German Democratic Republic (East Germany) and the Federal Republic of Germany (West Germany). They thought next about the need for security versus the Soviet Union. Only after that did they think of Poland. Berlin and Moscow superseded Warsaw in significance.[2]

As face-to-face encounters gradually began taking place between Germans—mainly those from the old eastern regions—and Poles, then, it was of paramount importance that people listened to each other. If, in the end, one managed to learn something biographical about a conversational partner, a basis was created for greater understanding of life circumstances on both sides. Thus, I remember a conversation I had with an older Pole in 1978, when I had my first opportunity to return home to Trieglaff. He told me about his journey from eastern Poland to the now Polish western areas—by way of Siberia, Persia, and Italy! He could not return to his home in formerly Polish Pinsk because this city now belonged to the Soviet Union. Trieglaff was as foreign to him as Pinsk was foreign to me.[3]

Crucial for me in establishing a decent personal relationship with Trieglaff in its Polish manifestation as Trzygłów was an encounter with Leon Momot, then administrator of the agricultural operation on our family's onetime estate. He greeted my wife and me with much friendliness, and as he could also speak some German, he was able to inform us about the state of the local economy. I, for my part, told him about the Trieglaff of my childhood; my detailed acquaintance with the house and the whole complex won his confidence. A visit afterward to the old family cemetery convincingly established my Trieglaff roots.[4]

Repeat visits grew out of that first encounter. The trips always passed through East Germany, so that the German-Polish dialogue that was getting underway at the time underwent a peculiar refraction.[5] It was noticeable, to be sure, that the Trieglaff Poles had more contact with Germans in the East German state, which, lying nearer to them geographically, was therefore also more readily accessible. But one sensed, too, that their real interest was in the Germans in West Germany, who were not bound to the social system of the Soviet Union. Former German Trieglaffers lived in both parts of Germany.[6]

How did the Polish people of Trieglaff perceive the world of the Germans? What picture had they formed of them, two generations after the war's end? A young Polish woman who grew up in Trieglaff, the daughter of the administrator mentioned above, described her first encounters with Germans as follows:

> Germans were present in Trieglaff ever since my childhood. From the beginning of the eighties on, many earlier inhabitants of the village came to visit; it was nothing unusual. My first meeting with a German etched

itself particularly into my memory. At some time or other, I was maybe seven or eight years old, I repeatedly saw a strange man on a bench in the park in front of the castle. I asked my mother who it was. She said that it was a man from Germany who lived in this castle with his family until after the war. I asked more questions and she related more about the Second World War and its consequences. It was no problem for me to accept it that a German family had earlier made its home in my castle, and I was readily able to figure out why the man had come here again. He surely loved the castle at least as much as I did. I had the warmest feelings toward the unknown man. Unfortunately, I couldn't understand what he was saying to me at all.

At first, I was no more capable of understanding what was said in history classes. Those kindhearted people who had passed out ever so much candy were supposed to have divided Poland up and later killed millions of people? The picture of the neighbors that I knew from my home did not agree with the one in the history texts. There the Teutonic Order, partitioning of Poland, and the Second World War were reported on. The Germans were the aggressors who had always made life difficult for the Poles. So, in order to get to the very bottom of it all, I decided to learn German at the Gymnasium and privately. Ten years after the Berlin wall fell, I traveled to Germany to attend the university.[7]

The dialogue deepened after the Wall fell in 1989. It enabled visits by not only former Trieglaffers but also their friends and relatives, who otherwise would most likely never have found their way to Pomerania. They were just as interested in the landscape as in the people, and their questions brought entirely new emphases into the conversations between Germans and the Polish inhabitants of the village.

One day a French friend visited the castle and summed up her impressions with the final strophe of the beautiful poem "Schloss Boncourt" by Adelbert von Chamisso, who lost his home in Champagne during the French Revolution:

Be fertile, O precious soil,
My blessings, my tend'rest, I send,
With blessings redoubled for any
Whose plow o'er thee now its way wends.[8]

This kind of renunciation of thoughts of restoring the past was more difficult for many former German Trieglaffers. Differences showed between the East Germans and the West Germans. West Germans had had experiences with organizations of German expellees and with native-son groups that thought more about the past than about the future. East Germans knew only the speeches about orderly and systematic postwar resettlements that were the rule in East Germany. There was no room in those for memories of the early postwar years. Hence, there existed two ways of viewing things by people confronting their erstwhile home.[9]

Toward the end of the 1990s, East German Trieglaffers began to ask whether partners might not be found among the local Polish people for the placement of a remembrance and reconciliation plaque. They felt that the time was ripe and would permit approaches to individuals who were entirely unacquainted with Trieglaff's history or who knew only ideologically tinged accounts. The matter concerned the generations of young people on either side of the Oder-Neiße border too, after all.[10]

I picked up on the question and invited its initiator, Henning Köpsel, along with Magdalena Momot, now studying in Göttingen, to a planning discussion. Concluding that it was worthwhile to make the attempt, we decided to promote the idea among the various groups. People with responsibilities, in the village as well as in the congregation, were important contacts for us in Trzygłów, as were donors and craftsmen who were in a position to make up a larger-sized bronze plaque.

On the Polish side, the Momot family took charge of the matter and gained the support of Bürgermeister Szczygiel as well as the parish priest Fenski for preparing a major celebration in the community. On the German side, it proved possible to recruit a good third of former Trieglaff schoolmates who were ready to travel from all corners of Germany and

Figure 21. Bilingual reconciliation plaque fixed to the onetime Old Lutheran, today Catholic, church in 2002

take part in a celebration of reconciliation. Financing of the bronze tablet, cast in Poland, was arranged by members of the von Thadden family.

The celebration of the mounting of the memorial and reconciliation plaque took place on a warm late summer day, 8 September 2002—coincidentally the anniversary of Elisabeth von Thadden's execution at Plötzensee in 1944. It started in the formerly Old Lutheran, now Catholic church with an ecumenical worship service conducted bilingually. It concluded with an official unveiling of the plaque at the entrance to the church by the Bürgermeister and Rudolf von Thadden. A remarkable number of village people attended. The text of the plaque reads, in Polish and in German:

Pax vobis
(Peace to you.)
In memory of many generations
of German Trieglaffers who lived here
and knew happiness, and with good wishes
that things might go well for those
who make their home in Trieglaff today.[11]

The celebration at Trieglaff occasioned quite an echo in the Polish community, the political as well as the religious. A lengthy article in the newspaper *Tygodnik Powszechny* covered the event and sketched a detailed picture of the history of expulsions following the war.[12] On the German side, Federal President Johannes Rau quoted the text of the reconciliation plaque verbatim in his farewell address before the Sejm parliament in Warsaw on 30 April 2004, emphasizing that President Kwasniewski and he had composed their Danzig declaration (Danziger Erklärung) "in that spirit."[13]

Independently of the politically infused public attention that developed on its own,[14] a number of Trieglaffers even went a step beyond the reconciliation event of September 2002. The Thaddens pushed for restoration of the family cemetery, which lay devastated between the lakes. It held innumerable memories belonging to the history of the generations since the Napoleonic era. Buried there, among others, were Adolph von Thadden, the old patriarch and founder of the renewal movement in Pomerania, and his daughter Marie, friend of Otto von Bismarck.

The Polish partners assented readily and generously to this wish. The local community had the grounds arranged into a memorial site and saw to it that, besides the names of those once buried here, also names of family members left without a grave in the tumult of the foregoing era appeared on memorials (Figure 22). The arch at the entrance to the cemetery, inscribed with the Bible passage from the Gospel of John that had so characterized Trieglaff's Pietism, was also restored.[15]

The dedication ceremony on 11 September 2004, conducted by the Bürgermeister along with three pastors, was as dignified as the reconciliation ceremony two years before. Protestant Pastor Gaš from Stettin delivered the devotional address in German. There followed several German and Polish speeches dealing with the significance of the place and emphasizing its legacy for the European future. Remembrance of the dead transcended national borders.[16]

Lending a special accent to this day was the school's willingness to sponsor a conference devoted to the history of the locality and of the castle. At the center of it was Barbara Fox von Thadden's memorial address, dedicated to her half-sister Elisabeth von Thadden, who had been executed by the Nazis sixty years earlier. It was meant to secure a place for Elisabeth also in the memory of the Polish Trieglaffers. The Poles responded with impressive presentations by schoolchildren and with lectures on local history. Then, following a visit to Vahnerow, a reception was sponsored by the new tenant and present owner of the farm operation, Gerhard Bertram. He had moved from Germany to Pomerania, thus demonstrating that the border delineated by the Oder River had lost some of its significance.

Trieglaff—now it was a place of memories also in Poland.[17] Yet its impact would not remain confined to Pomerania. Soon after the acts of reconciliation, still other nearly forgotten former Trieglaffers spoke up, ex-

Figure 22. Memorial site placed at the location of the old von Thadden family cemetery in 2004

claiming that they, too, wished to belong to this remembering community. These were the descendants of the nineteenth-century Old Lutheran emigrants to the United States, eager to come to Europe to join German and Polish Trieglaffers in commemorating the varied history of this place.[18]

To everyone's astonishment, nearly sixty Americans, mostly from Wisconsin, crossed the ocean at their own expense, with Rev. Royal Natzke as their guide. They outnumbered the Germans and Poles together. Following a "pilgrimage" to Trieglaff, where they were most warmly received, they participated in a colloquium that took place the seventh and eighth of September, 2007, at Genshagen Castle near Berlin (Figure 23).[19] Devoted to a comparison of the cultures of memory in Germany, Poland, and the United States, it pursued answers to the questions "What endures?" and "In thinking about Trieglaff, what is worth remembering?"

What came to light was a remarkable diversity of cultures of memory. While Christian traditions dominated among the Americans, features of the everyday life and world of Trieglaff were conspicuous among the more secularized Germans. Among the Polish people, interest in the change of national identities understandably predominated. Thus the descendants of the Trieglaffers who had emigrated to the United States inquired a great deal about the religious development of the village, not least during the time of Hitler, whereas the Germans and the young Polish Trieglaffers

Figure 23. Group photo at the colloquium of American, German, and Polish Trieglaffers in Genshagen, 2007

were more interested in economic and social changes. Each had a unique image of Trieglaff.[20]

Common to all was the question of the powers of reconciliation hidden within Trieglaff traditions. How potent had these powers been during the periods of the great nationalistic wars, so rife with conflicts? And how much do they contribute today to the building of bridges within Europe and across the Atlantic? Historians must remain constantly mindful of the unwieldy reality of reconciled peoples' desire to have worlds that are also reconciled in their memory.

This raises the question of the connections between memory and history, holding particular importance for emigrants, refugees, and expelled and relocated persons. Whoever has abandoned or lost a home easily runs the risk of clinging to the realm of memory and overstraining historical memory. But a person can also mobilize real powers of reconciliation by taking the difference between remembered history and actual history seriously. That individual is then able to help "bring plural regions of memory together without mingling them."[21]

That applies to Trieglaff too.

Notes

1. Egon Bahr, *Zu meiner Zeit* (Munich, 1996), 338ff., describes the situation of Poland relative to the eastern policy: "Poland, Hitler's first victim, and divided between him and Stalin, emerged at the end of the war as loser among the victors. The treaty with our wounded and humbled neighbor meant more for Brandt than an agreement about a border that was not even one for the Federal Republic."

2. Cf. Rudolf von Thadden, "Sechzig Jahre danach. Zum 60. Jahrestag des Kriegsbeginns," in *Brückenwege nach Europa. Aufsätze und Essays* (Berlin, 2003), 300ff.

3. After Hitler invaded the Soviet Union in the summer of 1941, Stalin permitted a Polish army to be organized, the so-called Anders Army. Some parts were then removed to Iran and finally saw action in Monte Cassino in Italy.

4. An amateur film was made about this visit to Trieglaff, FA.

5. Cf Adam Krzeminski, *Polen im 20. Jahrhundert. Ein historischer Essay* (Munich, 1993), 147f., 176f.

6. After their expulsion and movement away, a majority of Trieglaffers ended up in the Soviet zone of occupation, roughly a third in the British, and the rest in the U.S. and French zones. Cf. Manfred Wille, "Die Vertriebenen und das politisch-staatliche System der SBZ/DDR," in *Vertriebene in Deutschland*, ed. Dirk Hoffmann, Marita Krauss, and Michael Schwartz (Munich, 2000), 203ff.

7. Magdalena Momot, born in 1978, later majored in German studies at Göttingen University and completed an MA there.

8. Brigitte Sauzay quoted this verse in *Retour à Berlin. Ein deutsches Tagebuch,* written following her journey to Trieglaff in April of 1996, 98ff. The verse by Chamisso reads:

Sei fruchtbar, o teurer Boden
Ich segne dich mild und gerührt
Und segne ihn zweifach, wer immer
Den Pflug nun über dich führt.

9. These differences, which came to light during the now yearly get-togethers of former Trieglaffers, were at times articulated in a most animated and controversial way.

10. This pertains to Henning Köpsel, who wrote a detailed report about his experiences during the years following the war, in "Trieglaff, mit Gruchow und Idashof," in the carton *Nachkriegszeit,* FA.

11. The plaque with the text is pictured above in Figure 21.

12. M. Kuzuminski, "Trieglaff der Geschichte zum Trotz," in *Tygodnik Powszechny,* 29 September 2002.

13. Johannes Rau, "Deutschland und Polen—unsere Zukunft in Europa," in *Reden und Interviews,* 5/2: 262; text of speech available at http://www.bundespraesident.de/SharedDocs/Reden/DE/Johannes-Rau/Reden/2004/04/20040430_Rede.html.

14. Foremost on this, Alfred Grosser, *Von Auschwitz nach Jerusalem. Über Deutschland und Israel* (Hamburg, 2009), 202.

15. John 11:25–26: "I am the resurrection and the life. He who believes in me will live, even though he dies; and whoever lives and believes in me will never die. Do you believe this?" (*New International Version,* 1984).

16. Talks presented by Rudolf von Thadden, Rev. Joachim Fenski, and Bürgermeister Andrzej Szczygiel.

17. Cf. Pierre Nora, ed., *Les Lieux de Mémoire,* vol. 1 (Paris, 1984), viiff.

18. On this, the letter exchange between Royal Natzke and Rudolf von Thadden, in the carton *Amerikanische Briefe,* FA.

19. Genshagen is headquarters of a foundation dedicated to German-French-Polish relationships. It continues the activity of the Berlin-Brandenburgisches Institut für deutsch-französische Zusammenarbeit [cooperation] in Europa, which Brigitte Sauzay and Rudolf von Thadden founded in 1993.

20. The talks presented under the auspices of the Genshagen colloquium, including one by Siegfried Lange, are to be found in the carton *Amerikanische Briefe,* FA.

21. Reinhart Koselleck, "Der 8. Mai zwischen Erinnerung und Geschichte," in *Erinnerung und Geschichte,* ed. Rudolf von Thadden and Steffen Kaudelka (Göttingen, 2006), 20.

Timeline and Modes of Transportation from Pomerania to Wisconsin

In his first letter written from Milwaukee in 1842 (quoted in chapter 2 of this volume), the shepherd boy Johann Carl W. Pritzlaff gave a rather detailed account of his travels from Trieglaff, Pomerania, to Milwaukee, WI, including a stopover in Buffalo, NY, to earn enough money to complete the rest of his trip to Wisconsin (see Appendix A Map):

> You know that I began my journey on May 16, 1839; I said farewell to you with many tears and a painful feeling of sadness as I began my emigration to America. Then, fourteen days after we had left home, we arrived safely in Hamburg, and waited there for a full month for the fellow countrymen and church members who had to stay in Stettin, as you undoubtedly know, because of the passports. The last day that we were in Hamburg, I wrote a letter to you which was done in great haste, but I don't know if you ever received it. On May 31, we (namely the Schwessow congregation) traveled on a steamship from Hamburg to England, and in 3 1/2 days landed in Newcastle. On the third day after our arrival there, we rode by train to Carlisle, and from there on a steamship to Liverpool. From here we boarded a large three-masted sailing ship, and on July 11 began our journey across the sea. After enduring many difficulties, and with God's gracious assistance, we landed on September 6th in New York in America. I was very ill the last 14 days of our ocean voyage and the first two weeks after our arrival in New York, but our gracious God, thanks be to His mercy, helped give me strength and endurance. After we left New York for Albany on a steamship, we went from there partly by train and partly by canal boats which were drawn by horses until we finally arrived in Buffalo. By this time the cash box was pretty well exhausted, and with so many people as there were in our group all coming at the same time, there wasn't enough work available; therefore, we had to part company. Those who could afford it, traveled another 1,100 miles by steamship to

Milwaukee and the surrounding area in the territory of Wisconsin, and the poorer ones found it necessary to look for work in and around Buffalo; many of us went 15 German miles from Buffalo to work on the canal. Here we had the same difficulty that so many immigrants encountered who were not familiar with the English language, and things didn't go too well. At the canal we earned enough money in a short time so that we could travel from one place to another, an activity to which I took a great fancy then, and still do.... [O]n the 29th of September, 1841, I moved too. I went part way by train, part way by canal boat to Buffalo, and from there, after a three-day layover, took a steamship (over Lakes Erie, Huron and Michigan) and arrived in Milwaukee, which is on the shores of the latter lake. This long journey of 1,300 English miles (or about 325 German miles) which cost me $20 (local money) I happily put behind me in nine days. My pleasure was very great at getting together again here with my countrymen and fellow churchmen, many of whom had already purchased land and had formed a German community. This past winter I worked for an American farmer and earned $9 a month. (Trans. Lucy Ruedt)

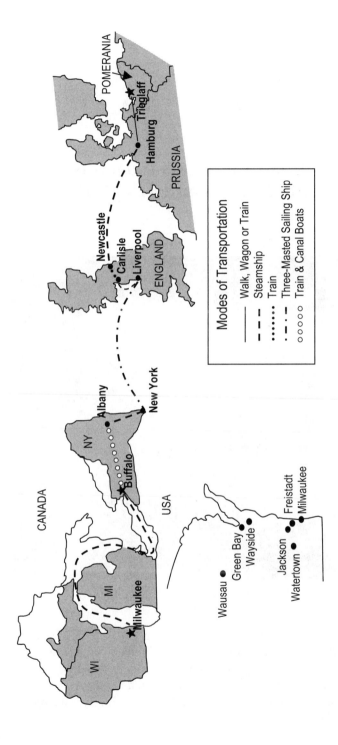

Route of travel of emigrants, Trieglaff to the United States. The map (not drawn to scale) is to illustrate the locations and the immigrants' modes of transportation from Trieglaff to Buffalo to Milwaukee as described in John Pritzlaff's letter of 1842. The first Pomeranian "Old Lutherans" settled in Buffalo, NY in 1837; from 1839 on, they settled either in Buffalo, or continued on to Milwaukee. Ever since the mid-1800's, Germans (many of whom came from Pomerania) have been the single largest ethnic group in Wisconsin. The descendants of the original Pomeranians spread from Milwaukee toward the west (Watertown), the north (Green Bay), and the northwest (Wausau). Map drawn by Martha Clapham.

Appendix B

Reestablishing Bonds Between the United States and Trieglaff

Lucy Ruedt gives Rudolf von Thadden the diary of Adoph Wangerin. (Photo: Royal Natzke)

In 2008 Rudolf von Thadden meets Lucy (Wangerin) Ruedt (100 years old), whose grandfather worked for the von Thaddens in Vahnerow. Lucy presented Rudolf with the diary her father, Adolph, kept while visiting Pomerania in 1929. Adolph was an organ and church furniture builder in Milwaukee, Wisconsin. Both Lucy and Rudolf were thrilled at this reconnecting of Trieglaff-Vahnerow families.

Rudolf von Thadden and Royal Natzke at the grave of Carl Kiekhaefer. (Photo: Royal Natzke)

On his trip to Wisconsin in 2008, Rudolf von Thadden's first stop was to visit the tombstone of a former Trieglaff resident, Carl Kiekhaefer, at St. John's Lutheran Cemetery on Mequon Road, in Mequon, WI. He shared this moment with Royal Natzke, great-great-grandson of Carl. A great-grandson of Carl's, by the same name, started Mercury Marine in Cedarburg, Wisconsin.

The Church in Germany

Each country has its own institutions with their unique terminologies. Terms relating to the church in Germany are not always congruent with those in use in the United States or Great Britain. To enable fuller understanding of terms used in the translation, explanations of those that play a significant role are provided here.

Staatskirche. State church; the church in its identity as public institution, tax-supported like other branches of government; an "official" church of a country. State churches contrast particularly with free churches (*Freikirchen*). Their clergy are civil servants. People pay church tax (*Kirchensteuer*). In the nineteenth century levy was universal. Citizenship and membership were linked, and people paid the tax irrespective of whether they attended. Since then only those who expressly desire membership pay it.

Freikirche. A free church, in contrast to a state church. It is "free" of the ties to government that characterize the latter. It becomes distinguishable especially where a *Staatskirche* is the norm. Financial support comes from its members; it is not tax-supported. For those accustomed to separation of church and state, a *Staatskirche* would be a public church and a *Freikirche* a private one, similar to the way public and private schools are distinguished. *Freikirche* can refer to a church body as a whole or to elements of it, or to a congregation.

Landeskirche. Regionally established or territorially defined church; a church adopted within a particular state, province, or similar political unit, a sort of regional *Staatskirche*. When monarchy prevailed, *Landeskirchen* found their respective bases in the various principalities. Upon establishment of republics (disappearance of monarchies), *Landeskirchen* ceased to be *Staatskirchen.*

Volkskirche. Literally "folk church," but without "down home" or "folksy" connotations; a church with which a given group generally identifies; a church that has the popular support of a majority of the people; a "majority church" as opposed to churches enjoying less than general (minority) support (*Minderheitskirchen*). The term came into use to replace *Staatskirche* when universal obligatory membership disappeared with the monarchies. The *Volkskirche* became a reservoir of general membership. Its meaning evolved from "church of the people" or "people's church," implying more personal identification, toward "church of the broad populace." The Nazis corrupted the term, transferring it to what was in essence a national church. Today it tends to be regarded as a "Kirche im Volk," a church (residing) *among* the people, more than a coherent "Volkskirche" (church *of* the people).

Amtskirche. Institutional church; the church as a bureaucratic, administrative entity, whether or not ties to government are a part. It is the "top down" church, vs. the "bottom up" dynamics characterizing the *Laienkirche* (lay church). The Church of England, the "established church," as it is known, could be termed an *Amtskirche*—as well as a *Staatskirche.*

Unionskirche, or Unierte Kirche. Union Church or Church of the Union. Created when King Frederick William III of Prussia combined the Lutheran and Reformed faiths into a single church in 1817, the Unionskirche stood opposite *Bekenntniskirchen* (confessional churches) like that of the Old Lutherans, who adhered to their confessional identity.

Altlutheraner. Old Lutherans. This body of strict Lutherans rejected the administrative Prussian Union with Calvinists (the Reformed Church) of 1817. Accordingly, they rejected the structure of a state church and organized themselves ultimately in free churches. Those who emigrated to the United States cultivated their confessional and liturgical traditions in their transplanted church. They settled heavily in western New York and southeastern Wisconsin.

Pastorenkirche. Clerical church, the church represented in and by the clergy, in contrast to the *Gemeindekirche* (represented in and by the congregation). Lay activity distinguishes the two. They must remain in balance in a healthy religious community. Fading of lay participation during the

Nazi era left the *Pastorenkirche* in deep crisis, deprived of its base of support. The term can be employed to belittle lay participation in church life.

Gemeindekirche. The church made up of congregations (*Gemeinden*); the "congregational church" that grows out of the commitment and active participation of lay people. Conceptually opposed particularly to *Pastorenkirche*. Without an active congregational membership, a church degrades to clergy fulfilling functions in somewhat of a vacuum.

Laienkirche. Lay church. The church regarded as the sum total of the ordinary people affiliated with it—its membership, versus the clergy and administrative personnel. The notable lay movement in Germany that originated at the end of the nineteenth century and continues today was not necessarily anticlerical; the German Protestant Kirchentag (convention)—a manifestation of the *Laienkirche*—is a joint endeavor with the clergy.

Bekennende Kirche. Confessing Church, not to be confused with *Bekenntniskirche*, a confessional (denominational) church. It arose during the Nazi era in opposition to the institutional church (*Amtskirche*), which the Nazis were using as an organ of politics and propaganda through their own religious arm, the German Christians (Deutsche Christen). The Confessing Church consciously promulgated religion based upon Bible teachings and confessional statements, advocating personal commitment that stood firm against Nazism after it seized control of the institutional church.

Bibliography

Archives

Von Thadden family archives (FA), Göttingen, held by Rudolf von Thadden
Bundesarchiv Koblenz. [Federal archives, Coblenz.]
Bestände des Konsistorialarchivs Greifswald. [Holdings of the Greifswald consistory archives.]
The *Greifenberger Kreisblatt*, in the holdings of Greifswald University Library.
Statistik des Deutschen Reichs, in the holdings of the Rostock University Library, prepared by Stefan Siebert.
Staatsarchiv Stettin — Wegweiser durch die Bestände bis zum Jahr 1945 [Stettin state archive: Guide to holdings up to the year 1945], prepared by Radoslav Gazinski et al. German edition, Munich, 2004.
Evangelisches Zentralarchiv (EZA) Berlin, Akten [records] der deutschen Christlichen Studenten-Vereinigung (DCSV).

Sources

Abel, Wilhelm. *Massenarmut und Hungerkrisen im vorindustriellen Europa*. Hamburg and Berlin, 1974.
Aldenhoff-Hübinger, Rita. *Agrarpolitik und Protektionismus. Deutschland und Frankreich im Vergleich 1879–1914*. Göttingen, 2002.
Allgemeine deutsche Biographie (ADB). 56 vols. Leipzig, 1894–1912. [Online, together with *NeueDeutscheBiographie (NDB)*, as *Deutsche Biographie*, http://www.deutsche-biographie .de/]
Bachmann-Medick, Doris. "Kulturelle Texte und interkulturelles (Miß-)verstehen." In *Perspektiven und Verfahren interkultureller Germanistik*, ed. Alois Wierlacher. Munich, 1987.
Bade, Klaus J. "Massenwanderung und Arbeitsmarkt im deutschen Nordosten von 1880 bis zum Ersten Weltkrieg. Überseeische Auswanderung, innere Abwanderung und kontinentale Zuwanderung." *Archiv für Sozialgeschichte* 20 (1980), 265–323.
Bahr, Egon. *Zu meiner Zeit*. Munich, 1996.
Bäumer, Wolfgang, and Siegfried Bufe. *Eisenbahnen in Pommern*. Egglham, 1988.
Beevor, Antony. *The Fall of Berlin 1945*. New York, 2002
Berner. "Adolf von Thadden-Trieglaff." In *Allgemeine deutsche Biographie (ADB)*, vol. 37. Leipzig, 1894. [http://www.deutsche-biographie.de/pnd131898973.html]
Bethge, Eberhard. *Dietrich Bonhoeffer. Eine Biographie*. Munich, 1967.
Beyreuther, Erich. "Die Erweckungsbewegung." In *Die Kirche in ihrer Geschichte*, vol. 4, ser. 1, ed. Bernd Moeller. Göttingen, 1972.
Bismarck, Otto von. "Erinnerung und Gedanke." In *GW*, vol. 15. Berlin, 1932.
———. *Gedanken und Erinnerungen*, Knaur edition (Munich, 1952).
———. *Otto von Bismarck. Die gesammelten Werke (GW)*. Vol. 14/1. Berlin, 1933.

Blanc, Louis. *L'organisation du travail*. Paris, 1839.

Bleich, Eduard, ed. *Der Erste Vereinigte Landtag in Berlin 1847*. Repr. Vaduz, 1977.

Boehm, Max Hildebert. *Das eigenständige Volk. Volkstheoretische Grundlagen der Ethnopolitik und Geisteswissenschaften*. Göttingen, 1932.

Bohnenkamp, Björn, Till Manning, and Eva-Maria Silies, eds. *Generation als Erzählung. Neue Perspektiven auf ein kulturelles Deutungsmuster*. Vol. 1 of *Göttinger Studien zur Generationsforschung*, ed. Bernd Weisbrod. Göttingen, 2009.

Bömelburg, Hans-Jürgen, Renata Stößinger, and Robert Traba, eds. *Vertreibung aus dem Osten. Deutsche und Polen erinnern sich*. Olsztyn, 2000.

Born, Karl Erich. "Epochen der preußischen Geschichte seit 1871." In *Handbuch der Preußischen Geschichte*, ed. Wolfgang Neugebauer, vol. 3. Berlin, 2001.

Brakelmann, Günter, ed. *Kirche im Krieg. Der deutsche Protestantismus am Beginn des Zweiten Weltkriegs*. Munich, 1979.

Brakelmann, Günter, Martin Greschat, and Werner Jochmann. *Protestantismus und Politik. Werk und Wirkung Adolf Stoeckers*. Hamburg, 1982.

Broszat, Martin, Klaus-Dietmar Henke, and Hans Woller, eds. *Von Stalingrad zur Währungsreform. Zur Sozialgeschichte des Umbruchs in Deutschland*. Munich, 1988.

Buchholz, Werner, ed. *Pommern*. In *Deutsche Geschichte im Osten Europas*, ed. Hartmut Boockmann et al. Berlin, 1999.

Buchsteiner, Ilona. *Großgrundbesitz in Pommern 1871–1914*. Berlin, 1993.

———. "Wirtschaftlicher und sozialer Wandel in ostdeutschen Gutswirtschaften vor 1914." *Archiv für Sozialgeschichte* 36 (1996), 85–109.

Bugenhagen, Johannes. *Pomerania*. Ed. Norbert Buske. Reproduction and translation [Latin/German] of 1517–18 manuscript. Schwerin, 2008.

Butzlaff, Heinz. *Geschichte des Friedrich-Wilhelms-Gymnasiums Greifenberg in Pommern*. Hamburg, 1984.

Capitaine, Reinhild von. *Unser liebes Stift. 267 Jahre Mädchenerziehung im Magdalenenstift in Altenburg/Thüringen*. Altenburg, 2005.

Clemens, Lieselotte. *Old Lutheran Emigration from Pomerania to the U.S.A.: History and Motivation, 1839–1843*. Kiel, 1976. [Translated from *Die Auswanderung der pommerschen Altlutheraner in die USA. Ablauf und Motivation 1839–1843*. Hamburg, 1976. Page citations from German edition.]

Cramer, Reinhold. *Geschichte der Lande Lauenburg und Bütow*. Vol. 1. Königsberg, 1858.

Delfs, Hermann. "Der Weg der ökumenischen Freundschaftsarbeit." In *Lebendige Ökumene, Festschrift für Friedrich Siegmund-Schultze zum 80. Geburtstag*, ed. Heinrich Foth. Witten, 1965.

Diétrich, Suzanne de. *Cinquante ans d'Histoire. La Fédération universelle des Associations Chrétiennes d'Etudiants*. Paris, 1948.

Diwald, Hellmut, ed. Ernst Ludwig von Gerlach papers: *Von der Revolution zum Norddeutschen Bund*. Part 2, *Briefe, Denkschriften, Aufzeichnungen*. Göttingen, 1970.

Dohna-Schlobitten, Alexander Fürst zu. *Erinnerungen eines alten Ostpreußen*. Berlin, 1989.

Ehrenkrook, Hans Friedrich von. "Die Familie von Thadden." *Genealogisches Handbuch des Adels*. Vol. 11. *Adlige Häuser*, A II. [Republished Limburg an der Lahn, C. A. Starke Verlag, 1955.]

Eifert, Christiane. *Paternalismus und Politik. Preußische Landräte im 19. Jahrhundert*. Münster, 2003.

Einwohnerbuch der Stadt Greifenberg i. Pom. für das Jahr 1936. Greifenberg, 1936. Reprint Hamburg, 2000.

Elias, Norbert. *Studien über die Deutschen. Machtkämpfe und Habitusentwicklung im 19. und 20. Jahrhundert*. Ed. Michael Schröter. Frankfurt am Main, 1989.

Engelberg, Ernst. *Bismarck. Urpreuße und Reichsgründer.* Berlin, 1985.

Engelberg, Waltraut. *Otto und Johanna von Bismarck.* Berlin, 1990.

Eschenburg, Theodor. "Tocquevilles Wirkung in Deutschland." In *Alexis de Tocqueville. Werke und Briefe,* vol. 1, ed. J. P. Mayer with Theodor Eschenburg and Hans Zbinden. Stuttgart, 1959.

Eyth, Max. *Hinter Pflug und Schraubstock.* Stuttgart, 1899.

Fontane, Theodor. *Before the Storm: A Novel of the Winter of 1812–13.* Trans. R. J. Hollingdale Oxford, 1985.

———. *Der Stechlin.* Ed. Helmuth Nürnberger. dtv (Deutscher Taschenbuch Verlag) ed. 3rd ed. Munich, 1998.

———. *Effi Briest.* Ed. Helmuth Nürnberger. 3rd ed. Munich, 1998

Frevert, Ute. *Ehrenmänner: das duell in der bürgerlichen Gesellschaft.* Munich, 1991.

Friedrich, Manfred. "Hugo Preuß." In *Neue Deutsche Biographie (NDB),* vol. 20. Berlin, 2001. [http://www.deutsche-biographie.de/pnd118596403.html]

Gall, Lothar. *Bismarck. Der weiße Revolutionär.* Frankfurt am Main, 1980.

Gehring, Paul. "Max Eyth." In *Neue Deutsche Biographie (NDB),* vol. 4. Berlin, 1959.

Geissler, Andreas. "Nutzung regionaler Handlungsspielräume für den Ausbau der Infrastruktur. Der Bau regionaler Bahnen in Pommern 1880–1914." In *Pommern im 19. Jahrhundert. Staatliche und gesellschaftliche Entwicklung in vergleichender Perspektive,* ed. Thomas Stamm-Kuhlmann. Cologne, 2007.

Gerlach, Jakob von, ed. *Ernst-Ludwig von Gerlach. Aufzeichnungen aus seinem Leben und Wirken 1795–1877.* Schwerin, 1903.

Gerlach, Leopold von. *Briefe des Generals Leopold von Gerlach an Otto von Bismarck,* ed. Horst Kohl. Stuttgart and Berlin, 1912.

Goff, Jacque Le. *Histoire et Mémoire.* Paris, 1988.

Greschat, Martin, ed. *Studienbücher zur kirchlichen Zeitgeschichte.* Vol. 6 of *Zwischen Widerspruch und Widerstand: Texte zur Denkschrift der Bekennenden Kirche an Hitler (1936),* ed. Martin Greschat. Munich, 1987.

Grosser, Alfred. *Von Auschwitz nach Jerusalem. Über Deutschland und Israel.* Hamburg, 2009.

Grotefeld, Stefan. *Friedrich Siegmund-Schultze. Ein deutscher Ökumeniker und christlicher Pazifist.* Gütersloh, 1995.

Hartmann, Julius von. "Leopold von Gerlach." In *Allgemeine deutsche Biographie (ADB),* vol. 9. Berlin, 1879. [http://www.deutsche-biographie.de/pnd118538705.html]

Haushofer, Heinz. *Die deutsche Agrargeschichte.* Vol. 5, *Die deutsche Landwirtschaft im technischen Zeitalter.* Stuttgart, 1963.

Heimpel, Hermann. "Friedrich Christoph Dahlmann." In *Die Großen Deutschen,* vol. 5. Berlin, 1957.

Heitmann, Clemens. "Die Stettin-Frage. Die KPD, die Sowjetunion und die deutsch-polnische Grenze 1945." *Zeitschrift für Ostmitteleuropa-Forschung* 51 (2002), 25ff.

Helbich, Wolfgang, et al., eds. *Briefe aus Amerika. Deutsche Auswanderer schreiben aus der neuen Welt. 1830–1930.* Munich, 1988.

Herbert, Ulrich. *Fremdarbeiter. Politik und Praxis des "Ausländer-Einsatzes" in der Kriegswirtschaft des Dritten Reiches.* Berlin and Bonn, 1985.

Herrlitz, Hans-Georg, Wulf Hopf, and Hartmut Titze. *Deutsche Schulgeschichte von 1800 bis zur Gegenwart.* 2nd ed. Weinheim and Munich, 1998.

Heuss, Theodor. "Friedrich Naumann." In *Neue Deutsche Biographie (NDB),* vol. 18. Berlin, 1997.

Heuss-Knapp, Elly. *Schmale Wege.* Tübingen and Stuttgart, 1946.

Heyden, Hellmuth. *Kirchengeschichte Pommerns.* Vol. 2. 2nd ed. Cologne, 1957.

Hirsch, Paul. *Der Weg der Sozialdemokratie zur Macht in Preußen.* Berlin, 1929.

Hirt, Ferdinand. *Pommernfibel. Hirt's Schreibfibel.* Breslau, 1935.

Hong, Haejung. *Die Deutsche Christliche Studenten-Vereinigung (DCSV) 1897–1938. Ein Beitrag zur Geschichte des protestantischen Bildungsbürgertums.* Marburg, 2001.

Huber, Ernst Rudolf. *Deutsche Verfassungsgeschichte seit 1789.* 2nd ed. Stuttgart, 1967.

———, ed. *Dokumente zur deutschen Verfassungsgeschichte.* Vol. 2. 3rd ed. Stuttgart, Berlin, and Cologne, 1986.

Huber, Ernst Rudolf, and Wolfgang Huber. *Staat und Kirche im 19. und 20. Jahrhundert: Dokumente zur Geschichte des deutschen Staatskirchenrechts.* Vol 1. *Staat und Kirche vom Ausgang des alten Reichs bis zum Vorabend der bürgerlichen Revolution.* Vol. 2. *Staat und Kirche im Zeitalter des Hochkonstitutionalismus und des Kulturkampfs 1848–1890.* 2nd ed. Berlin, 1990.

Huch, Ricarda. "Elisabeth von Thadden." Undated manuscript. In *In einem Gedenkbuch zu sammeln,* ed. Wolfgang M. Schwiedrzik. Leipzig, 1997.

Hühne, Werner. *A Man to Be Reckoned With: The Story of Reinold von Thadden-Trieglaff.* Edited by Mark Gibbs. London, 1962. [Translated by Robert W. Fenn from *Thadden-Trieglaff, Ein Leben unter uns.* Stuttgart, 1959.]

Inachin, Kyra. "Die Entwicklung Pommerns im Deutschen Reich." In *Pommern,* ed. Werner Buchholz. Berlin 1999.

Jureit, Ulrike. *Generationenforschung.* Göttingen, 2006.

Kamphoefner, Walter, Wolfgang Helbich, and Ulrike Sommer, eds. *News from the Land of Freedom. German Immigrants Write Home.* Translated by Susan Carter Vogel. Ithaca and London, 1988. [Translation and adaption from Helbich, et al, eds. See above.]

Klän, Werner. *Die Evangelische Kirche Pommerns in Republik und Diktatur.* Cologne and Weimar, 1995.

Klee, Wolfgang. *Preußische Eisenbahngeschichte.* Stuttgart, 1982.

Kocka, Jürgen, ed. *Verbürgerlichung, Recht und Politik,* vol. 3. Göttingen, 1995.

Kohl, Horst, ed. *Briefwechsel Leopold von Gerlach/Otto von Bismarck.* 2nd ed. Berlin, 1893.

Kolb, Eberhard. *Bismarck.* Munich, 2009.

———. *Die Arbeiterräte in der deutschen Innenpolitik 1918–1919.* Düsseldorf, 1962.

Koselleck, Reinhart. "Der 8. Mai zwischen Erinnerung und Geschichte." In *Erinnerung und Geschichte. 60 Jahre nach dem 8. Mai 1945,* ed. Rudolf von Thadden and Steffen Kaudelka. Göttingen, 2006.

———. *Preußen zwischen Reform und Revolution. Allgemeines Landrecht, Verwaltung und soziale Bewegung von 1791 bis 1848.* Stuttgart, 1967.

———. "Wie europäisch war die Revolution von 1848/49?" In *Europäische Umrisse deutscher Geschichte,* ed. Reinhart Koselleck. Heidelberg, 1999.

Kossert, Andreas. *Kalte Heimat. Die Geschichte der deutschen Vertriebenen nach 1945.* Munich, 2008.

Kostus, Wojciech. *Wladztwo Polski nad Leborkiem i Bytowem. Studium historycznoprawne.* [Polish rule in Lauenburg and Bütow. A historical study of law.] Wrocław, 1954.

Kraus, Hans-Christof. *Ernst-Ludwig von Gerlach. Politisches Denken und Handeln eines preußischen Altkonservativen.* Göttingen, 1994.

Krockow, Christian Graf von. *Die Reise nach Pommern.* Stuttgart, 1985.

———. *Die Stunde der Frauen. Bericht aus Pommern 1944–47.* Stuttgart, 1988.

Krusenstjern, Benigna von. *"daß es Sinn hat zu sterben—gelebt zu haben." Adam von Trott zu Solz 1909–1944. Biographie.* 2nd ed. Göttingen, 2009.

Krzeminski, Adam. *Polen im 20. Jahrhundert. Ein historischer Essay.* Munich, 1993.

Kühn, Helga-Maria. "Ehrengard Schramm, geborene von Thadden." In *"Des Kennenlernens werth." Bedeutende Frauen Göttingens,* ed. Traudel Weber-Reich. 4th ed. Göttingen, 2002.

Kupisch, Karl, ed. *Quellen zur Geschicht des deutschen Protestantismus 1871–1945.* Göttingen, 1960.

Kutter, Hermann. *Die Revolution des Christentums*. Zurich, 1912.

Kuzuminski, M. "Trieglaff der Geschichte zum Trotz." In *Tygodnik Powszechny*, 29 September 2002.

Laufs, Adolf. *Eduard Lasker. Ein Leben für den Rechtsstaat*. Göttingen, 1984.

Lehmann, Joachim. "Zwangsarbeiter in der deutschen Landwirtschaft 1939 bis 1945." In *Europa und der "Reichseinsatz*," ed. Ulrich Herbert. Essen, 1991.

Leisewitz, Carl. "Albrecht Daniel Thaer." In *Allgemeine deutsche Biographie (ADB)*, vol. 37. Leipzig, 1894.

Lorentz, Friedrich. *Geschichte der Kaschuben*. Berlin, 1926.

Lucht, Dietmar. "Die Provinz in Daten und Fakten." In *Pommern*, ed. Werner Buchholz. Berlin, 1999.

Lühe, Irmgard von der. *Elisabeth von Thadden. Ein Schicksal unserer Zeit*. Düsseldorf and Cologne, 1966.

Mallasch, Eve-Maria. *Erinnerungen an Zimmerhausen*. Ed. Peter von Blanckenburg and Doris Mallasch. Greifswald, 2009.

Marcks, Erich. *Bismarcks Jugend 1815–1848*. Stuttgart and Berlin, 1909.

Marzahn, Wolfgang. *The Nobleman Among the Brothers: The Life of the Pomeranian Farmer, Christian, and Statesman Adolph von Thadden-Trieglaff*, ed. Royal Natzke. Trans. Alma Ihlenfeldt. Bloomington, IN, 2006. [In German, *Der Edelmann unter den Brüdern*. Lahr-Dinglingen, 1978.]

Mayer, Arno J. *Adelsmacht und Bürgertum. Die Krise der europäischen Gesellschaft 1848–1914*. Munich, 1984.

Medick, Hans. *Weben und Überleben in Laichingen 1650–1900. Lokalgeschichte als Allgemeine Geschichte*. Göttingen, 1996.

Meier, Kurt. *Der evangelische Kirchenkampf*. Vol. 1, *Der Kampf um die Reichskirche*. Göttingen, 1976.

———. *Die Deutschen Christen. Das Bild einer Bewegung im Kirchenkampf des Dritten Reichs*. 3rd ed. Göttingen, 1967.

Meyer, Folkert. *Schule der Untertanen. Lehrer und Politik in Preußen 1848–1900*. Hamburg, 1976.

Michaelis, Georg. *Für Volk und Staat. Eine Lebensgeschichte*. Berlin, 1922.

Mickiewicz, Adam. *Pan Tadeusz*. Polish edition 1834; first German translation 1836. 2nd edition translated by Siegfried Lipiner under the title *Herr Thaddäus oder der letzte Einritt in Litauen*. Leipzig, 1882.

Möller, Horst. "Preußen von 1918–1947." In *Handbuch der Preußischen Geschichte*, ed. Wolfgang Neugebauer, vol. 3. Berlin, 2001.

Mommsen, Hans. *Die verspielte Freiheit. Der Weg der Republik von Weimar in den Untergang 1918 bis 1933*. Berlin, 1989.

Mommsen, Wolfgang J. *Bürgerstolz und Weltmachtstreben. Deutschland unter Wilhelm II. 1890–1918*. Vol. 7/2 of *Propyläen Geschichte Deutschlands*. Berlin, 1995.

———. *Das Ringen um den nationalen Staat. Die Gründung und der innere Ausbau des Deutschen Reiches unter Otto von Bismarck 1850 bis 1890*. Vol. 7/1 of *Propyläen Geschichte Deutschlands*. Berlin, 1993.

———. *1848. Die ungewollte Revolution. Die revolutionären Bewegungen in Europa 1830–1849*. Frankfurt am Main, 1998.

Morsey, Rudolf. "Georg Michaelis." In *Neue Deutsche Biographie (NDB)*, vol. 17. Berlin, 1994. [http://www.deutsche-biographie.de/pnd119059584.html]

Müller, Rolf-Dieter, ed. *Das Deutsche Reich und der Zweite Weltkrieg*. Vol. 10/1, *Das Ende des Dritten Reiches: Der Zusammenbruch des Deutschen Reiches 1945: Die militärische Niederwerfung der Wehrmacht*. Stuttgart: Deutsche Verlags-Anstalt, 2008. [Eng. trans. to be available ca. 2014. Search *Germany and the Second World War*.]

Murawski, Erich. *Die Eroberung Pommerns durch die Rote Armee.* Boppard, 1969.
Natzke, Royal. *The John George Natzke Family.* Private printing, 1979.
Natzke, Royal, ed. *The Nobleman Among the Brothers: The Life of the Pomeranian Farmer, Christian, and Statesman Adolph von Thadden-Trieglaff.* Trans. Alma Ihlenfeldt. Bloomington, IN, 2006. [In German, *Der Edelmann unter den Brüdern.* Lahr-Dinglingen, 1978.]
Naumann, Friedrich. *Mitteleuropa.* Berlin, 1915.
Neue Deutsche Biographe (NDB). Vols. 1–24 [others forthcoming]. Leipzig, 1953–. [Online, together with *Allgemeine deutsche Biographie (ADB)* as *Deutsche Biographie,* http://www.deutsche-biographie.de/]
Niekammer's Landwirtschaftliche Güter-Adreßbücher. Vol. 1, *Pommern.* Leipzig, 1939.
Nipperdey, Thomas. *Deutsche Geschichte 1866–1918.* Vol 1, *Arbeitswelt und Bürgergeist.* Munich, 1990 [In English, *Germany from Napoleon to Bismarck: 1800–1866.* Trans. Daniel Nolan. Princeton, 1996]. Vol. 2, *Machtstaat vor der Demokratie.* Munich, 1992.
Nitschke, Bernadetta. *Vertreibung und Aussiedlung der deutschen Bevölkerung aus Polen 1945 bis 1949.* Munich, 2004.
Nora, Pierre, ed. *Les Lieux de Mémoire.* Vol. 1. Paris, 1984.
Normann, Käthe von. *Tagebuch aus Pommern 1945/46.* Munich, 1962.
Oertzen, Elisabeth von. *Entenrike und andere pommersche Geschichten.* 1903, repr. Hamburg, 1956.
Petersdorff, Hermann von. "Heinreich (v.) Stephan." *Allgemeine Deutsche Biographie (ADB),* vol. 54. Leipzig, 1908.
Petrich, Hermann. *Adolf und Henriette von Thadden und ihr Trieglaffer Kreis. Bilder aus der Erweckungsbewegung in Pommern.* Stettin, 1931.
Preuß, Hugo. "Die Junkerfrage, 1897." In *Gesammelte Schriften.* Vol. 1, *Politik und Gesellschaft im Kaiserreich.* Ed. Lothar Albertin. Tübingen, 2007.
Priesner, Claus. "Justus Freiherr von Liebig." In *Neue Deutsche Biographie (NDB),* vol. 14, 497ff.. Berlin, 1985,
Puhle, Hans-Jürgen. *Agrarische Interessenpolitik und preußischer Konservatismus im wilhelminischen Reich (1893–1914).* 2d ed. Bonn, 1975.
Pyta, Wolfram. *Dorfgemeinschaft und Parteipolitik 1918–1933. Die Verschränkung von Milieu und Parteien in den protestantischen Landgebieten Deutschlands in der Weimarer Republik.* Düsseldorf, 1996.
Rabenhorst, Arthur L. *Family Lines.* Part 1: "Our German Roots." Private printing, 2008.
Rau, Johannes. "Deutschland und Polen—unsere Zukunft in Europa." In *Reden und Interviews,* 1 January–30 June 2004, vol. 5/2. [Speech by Bundespräsident Rau, Warsaw, 30 April 2004.]
Reif, Heinz. *Westfälischer Adel 1770–1860.* Göttingen, 1979.
Reuß, Elonore Fürstin. *Adolf von Thadden-Trieglaff. Ein Lebensbild.* 2nd ed. Berlin, 1894.
Ritter, Gerhard. *Die preußischen Konservativen und Bismarcks deutsche Politik 1858 bis 1876.* Heidelberg, 1913, repr. 1976.
Ritter, Gerhard, ed. "Altersbriefe Ludwig von Gerlachs. Ungedrückte Briefe des Präsidenten E. L. v. Gerlach an Adolf v. Thadden und Moritz v. Blanckenburg." *Deutsche Revue* 36, no. 1 (1911), 43-59.
Röhl, John C. G. *Wilhelm II. Der Aufbau der persönlichen Monarchie 1888–1900.* Munich, 2001.
Rothfels, Hans, ed. *Bismarck-Briefe.* Göttingen, 1955.
Sauzay, Brigitte. *Retour à Berlin. Ein deutsches Tagebuch.* Trans. with introduction by Richard von Weizsäcker. Berlin, 1999. [In French, *Retour a Berlin: Journal D'Allemagne 1997.* Paris, 1998.]
Scheurig, Bodo. "Ewald von Kleist-Schmenzin." In *Neue Deutsche Biographie (NDB),* vol. 12. Berlin, 1980. [http://www.deutsche-biographie.de/pnd119245469.html]

Schieder, Theodor, ed. *Die Vertreibung der deutschen Bevölkerung aus den Gebieten östlich der Oder-Neiße*. Vol 2. Munich, 1954, repr. 1984.

Schlange-Schöningen, Hans. *Am Tage danach*. Hamburg, 1946.

Schmidt, Jürgen. *Martin Niemöller im Kirchenkampf*. Hamburg, 1971.

Scholder, Klaus. *Die Kirchen und das Dritte Reich*. Vol. 1. Frankfurt am Main, 1977. Vol 2. Berlin, 1985.

Schoeps, Hans-Joachim. "Gerlach, Ernst Ludwig." In *Neue Deutsche Biographie (NDB)*, vol. 6. [http://www.deutsche-biographie.de/pnd118690787.html]

Schoeps, Hans-Joachim. "Gerlach, Ludwig Friedrich Leopold." In *Neue Deutsche Biographie (NDB)*, vol. 6. [http://www.deutsche-biographie.de/pnd118538705.html]

Schröder, Wilhelm Heinz. *Sozialdemokratische Parlamentarier in den deutschen Reichs- und Landtagen 1867–1933. Ein Handbuch*. Düsseldorf, 1995.

Schücking, Walther. *Der Staatenverband der Haager Konferenzen*. Munich and Leipzig, 1912.

———. *Die völkerrechtliche Lehre des Weltkrieges*. Leipzig, 1918.

Smyth-Florentin, Françoise. *Pierre Maury. Prédicateur d'Evangile*. Geneva, 2009.

Spenkuch, Hartwin. "Herrenhaus und Rittergut." *Geschichte und Gesellschaft*, 25 (1999), 3: 385ff.

Stamm-Kuhlmann, Thomas. "Pommern 1815–1875." In *Pommern*, ed. Werner Buchholz. Berlin, 1999.

Steffen, Katrin. Introduction. In *Die Deutschen östlich von Oder und Neiße 1945–1950. Dokumente aus polnischen Archiven*. Vol. 3. Ed. Wlodzimierz Borodziej and Hans Lemberg. Marburg, 2004.

Stephan, Heinrich. *Geschichte der Preußischen Post von ihrem Ursprunge bis auf die Gegenwart*. Berlin, 1859, repr. Heidelberg, 1987.

Stern, Fritz. *Gold und Eisen. Bismarck und sein Bankier Bleichröder*. 2nd ed. Hamburg, 2000.

Stüttgen, Dieter. Revision of *Grundriß zur deutschen Verwaltungsgeschichte 1815–1945*. Reihe [series] A, *Preußen*. Vol. 3, *Pommern*. Marburg an der Lahn, 1975.

Thadden, Adolph von. "Der Schacher mit den Rittergütern." In Elonore Fürstin Reuß, *Adolf von Thadden-Trieglaff. Ein Lebensbild*. 2nd ed. Berlin, 1894.

———. "Über Menschenschau unter Landwirthen." In Elonore Fürstin Reuß, *Adolf von Thadden-Trieglaff. Ein Lebensbild*. 2nd ed. Berlin, 1894.

Thadden, Hildegard von (pseud. H. Mellin). *Ikarus. Eine Reisenovelle*. Wolfenbüttel, 1896, fourth printing 1902.

Thadden, Reinold von. *Auf verlorenem Posten? Ein Laie erlebt den Kirchenkampf in Hitlerdeutschland*. Tübingen, 1948.

———. "Völkerrecht und Völkerbund. Eine Studie zur Rechtsnatur zwischenstaatlicher Beziehungen." In *Monographien zum Völkerbund*, ed. Deutsche Liga für Völkerbund. Vol. 8. Berlin, 1920.

Thadden-Trieglaff, Reinold von [variant form used by foregoing]. *Heinrich v. Oertzen auf Trieglaff. Ein Lebensbild nach seinen Briefen*. Greifenberg, 1932.

———. *War Bismarck Christ?* Hamburg, 1950.

Thadden, Rudolf von. "Aus der Wirklichkeit gefallen. Der 8. Mai 1945 jenseits von Oder und Neiße." In *Erinnerung und Geschichte. 60 Jahre nach dem 8. Mai 1945*, ed. Rudolf von Thadden and Steffen Kaudelka. Göttingen, 2006. Also appears as *Genshagener Gespräche*, vol. 9.

———. "Bismarck—ein Lutheraner?" In *Weltliche Kirchengeschichte. Ausgewählte Aufsätze*, ed. Rudolf von Thadden. Göttingen, 1989.

———. "Die Gebiete östlich der Oder-Neiße in den Übergangsjahren 1945–49. Eine Vorstudie." In *Flüchtlinge und Vertriebene in der westdeutschen Nachkriegsgeschichte*, ed. Rainer Schulze, Doris von der Brelie-Lewien, and Helga Grebing. Hildesheim, 1987.

————. "Die Geschichte der Kirchen und Konfessionen." In *Handbuch der Preußischen Geschichte*, ed. Wolfgang Neugebauer. Vol. 3. Berlin, 2001.

————. "Herkunftswelt und Prägungen Elisabeth von Thaddens." In *Elisabeth von Thadden. Gestalten. Widerstehen. Erleiden*, ed. Matthias Riemenschneider and Jörg Thierfelder. Karlsruhe, 2002.

————. "Mut zum Dissens. Dahlmann und Gervinus im Spannungsfeld von Geschichte und Politik." In *Weltliche Kirchengeschichte. Ausgewählte Aufsätze*, ed. Rudolf von Thadden. Göttingen, 1989.

————. *Prussia: The History of a Lost State*. Trans. Angi Rutter. Cambridge, 1987. [In German, *Fragen an Preußen. Zur Geschichte eines aufgehobenen Staates*. Munich, 1981.]

————. "Sechzig Jahre danach. Zum 60. Jahrestag des Kriegsbeginns." In Rudolf von Thadden, *Brückenwege nach Europa. Aufsätze und Essays*. Berlin, 2003.

————. "Umstrittene Erinnerung. Perspektiven und Grenzen eines europäischen Gedächtnisses." In *Der Streit um Erinnerung*, ed. Martin Sabrow. Leipzig, 2008.

————. "Vision und Wirklichkeit. Reinold von Thadden und der Kirchentag." In *Fest des Glaubens—Forum der Welt. 60 Jahre Deutscher Evangelischer Kirchentag*, ed. Rüdiger Runge and Ellen Ueberschär. Gütersloh, 2009.

Thierfelder, Jörg. "Von der Kooperation zur inneren Distanzierung." In *Elisabeth von Thadden. Gestalten. Widerstehen. Erleiden*, ed. Matthias Riemenschneider and Jörg Thierfelder. Karlsruhe, 2002.

Thimme, Anneliese. *Flucht in den Mythos. Die Deutschnationale Volkspartei und die Niederlage 1918*. Göttingen, 1969.

Thüngen, Rudolf Freiherr von. *Das reichsritterliche Geschlecht der Freiherrn von Thüngen*. Würzburg, 1926.

Tocqueville, Alexis de. *Democracy in America*. Ed. J. P. Mayer. Trans. George Lawrence. New York, 1969.

Treß, Werner, "Adolf von Thadden." In *Handbuch des Antisemitismus*, Ed. Wolfgang Benz. Vol. 2/2. Berlin, 2009.

Treue, Wilhelm. "Wirtschafts- und Sozialgeschichte Deutschlands im 19. Jahrhundert." In Bruno Gebhardt, *Handbuch der deutschen Geschichte*, vol. 3. 8th ed., ed. Herbert Grundmann. Stuttgart, 1960.

Ulrich, Albert, *Chronik des Kreises Greifenberg in Hinterpommern*. Dithmarschen, private printing, 1990.

Valentini, Rudolf von. *Kaiser und Kabinettschef. Nach eigenen Aufzeichnungen und dem Briefwechsel des Wirklichen Geheimen Rats Rudolf von Valentini dargestellt*. Ed. Bernhard Schwertfeger. Oldenburg, 1931.

Verhandlungen der evangelischen General-Synode zu Berlin vom 2. Juni bis zum 29. August 1846. Berlin, 1846.

Viktoria Luise, [Duchess]. *Ein Leben als Tochter des Kaisers*. Göttingen and Hanover, 1965.

"Von Thadden." In *Genealogisches Handbuch des Adels*. Vol. 11, *Adlige Häuser*, A II, 401ff.

Wagner, Patrick. *Bauern, Junker und Beamte. Lokale Herrschaft und Partizipation im Ostelbien des 19. Jahrhunderts*. Göttingen, 2005.

Wangemann, Hermann Theodor. *Sieben Bücher preußischer Kirchengeschichte. Eine aktenmäßige Darstellung des Kampfes um die lutherische Kirche im 19. Jahrhundert*. Vol. 3. Berlin, 1860.

Wangerin, Rudolph. *The Family Wangerin*. Private printing, 1975.

Wehler, Hans-Ulrich. *Deutsche Gesellschaftsgeschichte*. Vol. 3, *Von der "Deutschen Doppelrevolution" bis zum Beginn des Ersten Weltkrieges 1849–1914*. Munich, 1995. Vol. 4, *Vom Beginn des Ersten Weltkriegs bis zur Gründung der beiden deutschen Staaten 1914–1949*. Munich, 2003.

Bibliography

Wehrmann, Martin. *Geschichte von Pommern.* 2nd ed. Gotha, 1921, repr. Würzburg, 1982.

Weisbrod, Bernd, ed. *Göttinger Studien zur Generationsforschung.* Vol. 1, *Generation als Erzählung. Neue Perspektiven auf ein kulturelles Deutungsmuster.* Ed. Björn Bohnenkamp, Till Manning, and Eva-Maria Silies. Göttingen, 2009. Vol. 2, *Historische Beiträge zur Generationsforschung.* Ed. Bernd Weisbrod. Göttingen, 2009.

Wellershoff, Maria. *Von Ort zu Ort. Eine Jugend in Pommern.* Cologne, 2010.

Wienfort, Monika. *Patrimonialgerichte in Preußen. Ländliche Gesellschaft und bürgerliches Recht 1770–1848/49.* Göttingen, 2001.

Wietschorke, Jens. "Defensiver Paternalismus. Ostelbischer Landadel im Dialog mit der 'Sozialen Arbeitsgemeinschaft Berlin-Ost' (1918–1922)." In *Historische Anthropologie* 14, no. 2 (2006), 232ff.

Wille, Manfred. "Die Vertriebenen und das politisch-staatliche System der SBZ/DDR." In *Vertriebene in Deutschland,* ed. Dierk Hoffmann, Marita Krauss, and Michael Schwartz. Munich, 2000.

Winkler, Heinrich August. *Der lange Weg nach Westen.* Vol. 2. Munich, 2000.

Wippermann, Karl "Ernst-Ludwig von Gerlach." In *Allgemeine deutsche Biographie* (*ADB*), vol. 9. Leipzig, 1879. [http://www.deutsche-biographie.de/pnd118690787.html]

Witte, Hermann, ed. *Bismarck und die Konservativen. Briefe aus Trieglaff.* In *Deutsche Rundschau* 149 (1911), 334ff.

Witte, Hermann, and Hans Haupt. *Karl Witte. Ein Leben für Dante.* Hamburg, 1971.

Witte, Karl. "Preußen und die italienische Frage," *Die Neue Preußische Zeitung,* February 1859.

Witte, Leopold. "Karl Witte." In *Allgemeine deutsche Biographie* (*ADB*), vol. 43. Leipzig, 1898. [http://www.deutsche-biographie.de/pnd118769596.html]

Index of Persons

Gerlach, Leopold von, 56, 64n101, 91, 120
Gerlach, Otto von, 91, 120
Goethe, Johann Wolfgang, 17, 175
Guesnet, Astrid née von Thadden, 197

Haacke, Georg, 160
Hackbarth, Marie née Wangerin, 99
Hahn, Traugott, 132n78
Himmler, Heinrich, 171n146
Hirsch, Paul, 118
Hitler, Adolf, 21, 142, 144, 147–48, 154, 158,
  160, 163, 180, 187, 210
Hoetzsch, Otto, 142
Holek, Wenzel, 125
Hugenberg, Alfred, 142

Jänicke, Johann, 17

Kant, Immanuel, 175
Kapp, Wolfgang, 121–23
Keller, Countess Mathilde, 97
Keudell, Walter von, 142–43
Kiekhaefer, Carl, 46, 217
Kiekhäfer, Caroline, 72
Kleist, Heinrich von, 17
Kleist-Schmenzin, Ewald, 106
Köhler, Peter, 202n99
Kopelmann, Hermann, 148, 169n77
Köpsel, Henning, 199n26, 199n35, 207
Köpsel, Willi, 151
Kutter, Hermann, 121
Kwasniewski, Aleksander, 208

Lange, Albert, 111, 135, 166n13
Lange, Anna née Ramthun, 88, 92–93, 97,
  110, 136
Lange, Gustav, 91, 123
Lange, Otto (Gruchow), 111, 123
Lange, Otto (Trieglaff), 93–94
Lange, Siegfried, 212n20
Lasker, Eduard, 67–69
Lepsius, Renate, 119
Liebig, Justus, 75
Liebknecht, Karl, 117
Lilje, Hans, 167n32
Luther, Martin, 80
Lüttwitz, Baron Walther von, 121
Luxemburg, Rosa, 117
Lyncker, Moriz von, 110

Mackensen, Stefanie von, 169n88
Mackie, Robert C., 139

Maistre, Joseph de, 17, 44
Mallasch, Eva-Maria, 183–84, 200n44
Maltzahn, Rudolf von, 108
Marwitz, Heinrich von der, 21
Marwitz, Walter von der, 199n15
Marx, Karl, 120
Maury, Pierre, 138
Mellin, Kurt von, 18
Michaelis, Georg, 106, 110–14, 116, 119,
  127, 139, 142–43
Mickiewicz, Adam, 55
Miller, Francis Pickens, 139, 189–90
Momot, Leon, 205
Momot, Magdalena, 205–6, 207
Mott, John R., 139
Müller, Eberhard, 161, 164, 190
Müller, Ludwig, 150, 152

Nagel, Julius, 47–50, 52
Napoleon, 1, 9–11, 16–18, 59, 66, 107, 177,
  208
Natzke, Johann Georg, 26–27, 46
Natzke, Royal, 19, 26, 158, 210, 216–17
Naumann, Friedrich, 112, 115
Niemöller, Martin, 149, 152, 190
Niemöller, Wilhelm, 149
Normann, Käthe von, 181, 199n16
Normann, Philipp von, 181, 199n15

Oertzen, Elisabeth von née von Thadden,
  87–88, 106
Oertzen, Heinrich Victor Sigismund von,
  10, 17–18, 72
Oertzen, Henriette von née von Mellin, 27
Oertzen, Hermann von, 17
Oertzen, Karl von, 88
Oertzen, Viktor von, 18, 27
Ohm, August, 172n169
Otto of Bamberg, 2, 7, 55

Plato, Monika von née von Thadden, 197
Preuß, Hugo, 85–86
Pritzlaff, Johann Karl Wilhelm, 27, 45–46,
  213, 215
Puttkamer, Heinrich von, 39

Rabenhorst, Arthur L., 46
Ramthun, Reinhold, 93–95, 124, 136
Rau, Johannes, 208
Ritschl, Georg Karl Benjamin, 24–25
Ritter, Johannes, 130n33, 130nn36–39,
  130n41

Index of Places